How to Rehearse
When There Is
No Rehearsal

How to Rehearse When There Is No Rehearsal

ACTING AND THE MEDIA

By Alice Spivak

Written in Collaboration with Robert Blumenfeld

LIMELIGHT EDITIONS

AN IMPRINT OF HAL LEONARD CORPORATION

NEW YORK

Published in 2007 by

Limelight Editions (an imprint of Hal Leonard Corporation)

19 West 21st Street, New York, NY 10010

Printed in the United States of America

Book design by Mark Lerner

Library of Congress Cataloging-in-Publication Data is available upon request.

ISBN-10: 0-87910-342-6

ISBN-13: 978-0-87910-342-2

www.limelighteditions.com

Dedicated to my students, past and present,
famous and infamous, and in between

TABLE OF CONTENTS

Thoughts about Stanislavsky and Acting Today

||||||||||||||||||||||||||||||||||||||||||||||||||

Have you heard this one? An old actor with a heavy Yiddish accent goes to an audition for an Off-Broadway play, and announces that he will do "To be or not to be" from *Hamlet*. The director and his cohorts look at each other with great skepticism and some amusement, but they allow him to proceed. After a moment of preparation, he begins the piece and, lo and behold, gone is the accent, and the man seems to become the unhappy Prince of Denmark, delivering the monologue with absolute mastery of the English tongue, and with a spontaneity and realism that astonish his audience, and even move them. It is as if they had never heard the speech before! "How did you do it?" asks the director. "I am just amazed! No accent; and you did it perfectly!" "Nu [Well]," replies the old actor, "dot's ecting."

In New York City in 1965, we were all as excited as we could be. We were about to see real "dot's ecting"—acting from the company founded by the great Constantin Stanislavsky himself, whose methodical System of building a character from the inside out had revolutionized the actor's art. During one of those periodic temporary thaws in the cold war, the celebrated Moscow Art Theatre was coming to New York for the first time since 1922/3, when they had made a triumphant eighteen-month tour of the United States, led by the great actor/director himself. It was that tour that made Stanislavsky virtually a household name in American theatrical circles.

Alice Spivak and I were among those who thronged to City Center on Fifty-sixth Street. But Alice and I didn't know each other at the time. We only met many years later.

The MAT did four plays, including Nikolai Pogodin's Soviet propaganda piece *The Kremlin Tower Clock*, which I did not see. However, I attended the other three: Mikhail Bulgakov's adaptation of Nikolai Gogol's masterpiece, *Dead Souls*, and Chekhov's *The Cherry Orchard* and *Three Sisters*. Knowing no Russian at the time, I brought the English translations of the Chekhov plays with me, and read the upcoming act during the intermissions. I loved the museum reproductions of Stanislavsky's original staging of the Bulgakov and Chekhov classics.

Dead Souls was startling and memorable. The story concerns the con man Chichikov, who buys lists of dead serfs from provincial landowners, hoping to make money by swindling the government and collecting indemnities for the departed as if they were still alive.

The first scene was an extraordinary revelation of what theater can be. It takes place in a restaurant, and there are only three characters: the waiter, Chichikov, and a uniformed State Councilor dining in solitary splendor. Chichikov, seated at a table behind his, keeps his eye on him. We have no idea at that point who Chichikov is or what he wants. In fact, we don't even know yet that his name is Chichikov, unless we have read the program before the play begins. We only know that he, too, is dining alone, and is obviously interested for some reason in his fellow diner, who pays him no attention. The melancholy waiter with the hangdog look serves them in a desultory fashion, and we have a sense of what his entire boring life must be like—the same routine day in and day out. The two customers eat and drink without paying much attention to their food or appearing to enjoy it, but the State Councilor gobbles his food, while Chichikov takes dainty mouthfuls. We are immediately intrigued. Where is all this going to lead us? When the unsuspecting State Councilor finishes his meal, throws his napkin peremptorily on the table, like one used to command, and rises, Chichikov jumps up nimbly and bars his way, accosting him with an obsequious bow, saying as he does so, "Gospodin [Sir]." That was the first word spoken in the entire scene, which was absolutely engrossing and even riveting from beginning to end!

The three Russian actors did everything with complete realism, taking their time in the lugubrious silence called for in the script. I had never seen anything quite like that production of *Dead Souls* before, and I was lost in admiration, although the play itself proved somewhat tedious as it went on. Still, I could have watched them in that restaurant scene for two hours. To me, the actions they performed, the way they performed them, and the atmosphere they created, and the sense of the lives they seemed to be actually living, are typical of the best acting in the Stanislavsky tradition: everything they did appeared completely natural and spontaneous, and "as if" they were doing it for the first time. Nor were they afraid to take all the time necessary to fulfill the demands of the scene.

The acting styles I have seen in several other Russian stage productions of plays and operas and in many Russian films vary from the extremely melodramatic in Serge Eisenstein's epic films *Alexander Nevsky* (1938) and the two-part *Ivan the Terrible* (1943, 1946) to the real, but still poetic Shakespearean style evident in the adaptations of *Hamlet* (1964) and *King Lear* (1970) for the screen; to the most common style: the realistic, seen in the famous cinema adaptation of Chekhov's *Lady with the Dog* (1959), or in Serge Bondarchuk's film version of Chekhov's *Uncle Vanya* (1970). In the brilliantly conceived

2003 television miniseries adaptation of Dostoevsky's *The Id-iot*, every character is uncannily real, individual, and specific, and consequently quite devoid of any clichés associated, for instance, with army officers or aristocratic ladies. And natural, realistic style also prevails in the television series adapted from the Sherlock Holmes stories in the 1980s and '90s—faithful to a fault to the Conan Doyle originals —strange as it may seem for a native English speaker to hear Holmes and Watson conversing in Russian. But the interpretations are very interesting: Watson and Holmes are clearly equals, and Holmes treats Watson with the affection of a friend as well as with the respect due to an intelligent man, who doesn't have Holmes's gifts of ratiocination or his other detective's skills, but is nevertheless a worthy, helpful and esteemed companion. And Watson obviously respects Holmes, but isn't always his fervent admirer.

When I watch these films and television series, I am struck by how completely the actors inhabit their characters, how much they appear to *be* their characters. They bring stories to life seamlessly, and arouse the audience's sympathy and involvement. And they never appear to be "acting." This is exactly what Alice Spivak teaches, and the students in her classes don't appear to be "acting," either. In fact, it is a pleasure to sit in her classes and watch them work.

It was my privilege to meet Alice many years ago, and to study with her. She is the person who really taught me what acting was all about, and she is the sort of teacher who can truly communicate the principles and ideas she espouses. Not only are her insights greatly perceptive, but she imparts them to her students with kindness even when they are negative, as a good teacher should. Each student receives individual attention and understanding, so that he or she feels like learning, and is not devastated by the harsh criticism some teachers use as a way, not of helping students, but of asserting their own superiority. And because she is excited by what she is seeing and by teaching itself, she is exciting and inspirational to be around. She teaches students how to act without being stagy or theatrical or going for some effect, or trying to make the audience laugh or cry. All that can happen naturally if you really act, in the Stanislavskian sense of the word—"as if" you were living in the character's circumstances, from moment to moment, without anticipation, and without having preconceptions about the character that interfere with bringing it to life.

Whatever the working conditions were that allowed the Russian actors and directors to display their art and their artistry—they must have had all the time they needed for rehearsal, all the time in the world—they certainly seldom prevail today in the media or the theater in the United States or anywhere else, as far as I can gather, with rare exceptions. With her vast, decades-long experience not only of teaching, but of actually working extensively as both an actress and a coach in movies and television, Alice Spivak sets forth in this book the conditions that prevail in the media today, and details the methods, techniques, means and ways whereby conditions not propitious to the practice of the actor's art—such as lack of proper rehearsal, or indeed any rehearsal—can be dealt with and surmounted so as to ensure the best possible results. It has been a privilege and a pleasure to collaborate with her on putting this book together from what she has written, as well as from interviews and working sessions with her, and attendance at her classes, where I could observe her in action and take notes on what she did and said. The result of all this work is the book she has wanted to write for a long time. It is replete with wisdom, insight and the practical advice on the art and craft of acting and on coping with conditions in the media that only she could provide.

The Need for This Book

||||||||||||||||||||||||||||||||||||||||||||||||||

Recently, I was working in Los Angeles on the set of a highly acclaimed television series. After finding out I was an acting coach to one of her costars, a lovely young lady came up to me. "I really think I should study acting," she said, "and I was wondering, do you know this guy, Stanley Slavsky? Do you have to audition to get into one of his classes?"

How quickly fashions change, almost as quickly as technology! It wasn't that long ago that I was an acting student. My introduction to Constantin Stanislavsky, the father of modern acting, the founder of the Moscow Art Theatre and the Stanislavsky System, to which all current schools of acting must pay homage, happened around the time I was her age. The major difference is that I was eager to learn the craft so that maybe one day I could become a regular performer in the media. And that young lady was already there, without even having studied acting.

During the 1965 visit of the Moscow Art Theatre, the distinguished Angelina Stepanova, who had worked with Stanislavsky himself, described for a group of assembled acting teachers the three schools of the Moscow Art Theatre: the Moscow Art Theatre School, the Film Institute, and the Children's Theatre School, as they existed back then. The Moscow

Art Theatre taught a two-year course after which the student graduated to a theater in Moscow or to a regional theater, and might work in film as well. The Film Institute taught its students to work on short scenes only, and when they graduated, they were only prepared to work in film. The Children's Theatre required that all students be five feet six inches tall or less. I remember at that time being amused that any school, such as the Film School, would limit its training in any way. Well, unfortunately, that is common practice here nowadays: schools teach limited acting, going so far as to teach commercials only, soap opera only, and so forth. Of course, it is my hope that although these schools may want to focus on one genre, they also advise the serious student to learn acting for acting's sake, so that they can do all genres.

Acting students who love the art and the craft of acting know that they will be spending some—if not most, or even all—of their careers in the media, and not in the theater. To learn the craft and to have a good basis for acting in film and television, one must learn how to create a character for the stage: a three-dimensional human being who will speak the playwright's words and focus a live audience on the play's themes, night after night, remaining fresh for each performance. One must learn what inspires us to step out every night (matinees, too) with confidence and a rush of excitement.

In the early days it was always the great theater actor who became the great movie actor. That changed as the film industry continued to develop and standards were lowered. Tiny pieces of scenes, very often silent, which can be repeated over and over again until the director is satisfied, really require no craft in comparison to the theater. Surprisingly, television acting demanded more craft than film acting, because the "takes" are usually longer on TV, just as they often were in the old days of filmmaking. And in the long-gone days of live TV, in the 1950s and '60s, actors were basically rehearsing and performing a program for the stage, the difference being that they performed it only once. However, as television moved on to tape and film and grew up to be America's pastime, standards dropped again, and the writing and directing became so formulaic that the actors are now required to perform in a "style" that is pseudo-realistic, expressly written for television series from soap opera to nighttime cop shows. Given that these scripts contain no subtext and have almost no basis in reality, it would appear that actors need very little understanding of an acting technique designed to ferret out hidden meanings and develop well-rounded characters. In other words, except for the theater, the study of acting as a craft has become unnecessary, or so it seems. But of course, it is not, as this book will show you.

What is an actor to do, then, in these circumstances? Even in the theater, the director can no longer always be relied on to provide real direction. And when directors do direct, the actor has to know how to interpret their directions, which are frequently given in very general terms or in unfamiliar language. The cliché "louder, faster, funnier" springs to mind. Although it is a well-known joke in the theatrical community, most actors are bound to hear one or another of these words many times in the course of rehearsal!

Asked for her definition of good acting, Maureen Stapleton reportedly answered, "Fast!" "And how would you define great acting?" "Faster!" Naturally, the brilliant American actress—known, among other things, for her emotional portrayals of such Tennessee Williams characters as Serafina in *The Rose Tattoo*, Lady in *Orpheus Descending* (both of which she originated), and Amanda Wingfield in the first Broadway revival of *The Glass Menagerie*—was kidding, but there is a grain of truth in her remark, considering the conditions under which actors work today.

In the media, directors are often, although not always, more concerned with the technical aspects of production than with directing the actors in their performances. They want it done fast, and, if possible, faster. This means that as an actor you have to be self-reliant, and to direct yourself. How you go about doing that, and giving of your best, is what I intend to show you in this book.

—A.S.

ACKNOWLEDGMENTS

First and foremost, I want to thank the late Herbert Berghof, who was my inspiration and who taught me so much. His words and insights are as vivid to me today as they were more than a half-century ago. I owe a great deal of gratitude to his late wife, Uta Hagen, a brilliant teacher, a great actress, and for a long time a great friend. It was she who compelled me to teach, and it was her clear, patient, and thorough approach to teaching that inspires me to this day. I also want to thank the late William Hickey, whose many bon mots I still use. Along with all other teachers of acting, I owe a debt to Constantin Stanislavsky, who, through his infallible System, introduced a process of teaching the art.

I would also like to acknowledge my parents, Pauline and Harry, who lived through terrible times in Russia but were able to make it through the "golden door" into this country, meet and marry, and, with enormous struggle, raise me and my two brothers in Brooklyn, New York.

And I thank my always supportive and wonderful sons, William and Michael Bilowit, who encourage me to go forward. Thanks, too, to my ex-husband, Ira Bilowit, who lifted me out of the darkness and introduced me to the lights of the New York theater scene. When I was eighteen years old, Ira walked me over to the HB Studio to register as a student.

I also want to express my thanks to my friend Sue Harris for her patient support and healthy advice. And I want to thank Jonathan Blumenfeld, oboist with the Philadelphia Orchestra, for information about the rehearsal habits of musicians; and Albert S. Bennett, for helpful editorial suggestions.

And, of course, I thank my collaborator, Robert Blumenfeld, for helping me to make sure that my ideas have been clearly expressed in writing, and for the many delightful discussions we have had which stimulated me to recollect so many pertinent experiences.

And lastly, I want to express my gratitude to my publisher, John Cerullo, for taking on this project; to my always-helpful editors, Carol Flannery and Jessica Burr; to my invaluable copy editor, Sarah Gallogly; and to the graphic designer of this book, Mark Lerner, who has done such a beautiful job.

How to Rehearse
When There Is
No Rehearsal

PART 1

Acting and Current Working Conditions

CHAPTER 1

The Stanislavsky System Explored

|||||||||||||||||||||||||||||||||||||||||||||||||||||||

"You can't have aesthetics without ethics!" Herbert would shout at us, paraphrasing Stanislavsky. "The word *ethics* actually appears in the word *aesthetics!*" You have to juggle with the English words a bit to see what he meant by that last remark, but he was right—and not only in English, but also in his native German: *Ästhetik; Ethik*. And Constantin Stanislavsky himself had talked about what he thought of as the actor's "ethic": the moral obligation to use all one's talents, art, and skills in the service of the play and the audience.

Herbert Berghof's humanitarian principles enlightened me then as a young and ignorant student, and they have inspired me ever since, as an actor and most certainly as a teacher. Herbert was my first real acting teacher. I had dabbled in acting when I was sixteen years old, at a school that basically taught us little more than "line readings"—how to sound happy or excited or sad. In other words, it taught us next to nothing, because line readings mean nothing without the actor understanding the reasons for the character's emotions. Those reasons are not preconceived and calculated, but spring organically from an inner source.

It was my great good fortune to stumble into Herbert Berg-hof's classroom when I was just seventeen, and to learn about Stanislavsky from him. In 1949, Herbert founded the HB Studio, where he was later joined by his wife, Uta Hagen. It became one of the most well known of the many acting schools that dot the theatrical landscape in New York City, and it is still going strong even though Uta and Herbert are no longer with us.

When she started teaching at HB, Uta was already an acclaimed actress, having played the title role in Shaw's *Saint Joan*, starred as Desdemona opposite Paul Robeson in *Othello* on Broadway, and replaced Jessica Tandy as Blanche Du Bois in the original production of *A Streetcar Named Desire*. Herbert was a refugee from Hitler's Germany, and had been a handsome, brilliant star in Max Reinhardt's theater company. After he arrived in New York, he worked and studied with Irwin Piscator, who had fled Nazi Germany earlier and had started a school in New York called the Dramatic Workshop, which was devoted to Stanislavsky's teachings.

Herbert embarked on learning English, and embraced his new language with a passion. Because of that, when he later established his own school, his students were blessed not only with his great knowledge of the theater, but also with the added benefit of his love for English words and their definitions. To Herbert, Webster's Dictionary was the premier acting book! With his prompting, I quickly got into the habit of looking up words not only for what they meant in a complex line of dialogue, but also for the inspiration they might give me in defining the subtext of a script. He pointed out that even subtle differences in the given meanings of any word could be earth-shattering in their implications.

One example from the 1950s that stands out is the phrase "the Method," attributed to Lee Strasberg, which had just become the popularly accepted term for the Stanislavsky technique. To Herbert, this was a gross distortion of Stanislavsky's original word, *sistema* (simply "system" in English); it was a bad interpretation, rather than a direct translation from the Russian. If you look up the two words in Webster's, you can see why Herbert was against the use of the word "method":

Method: a means of manner of procedure, a regular or systematic way of accomplishing anything.

System: a group of interactive, interrelated or interdependent elements forming a collective entity.

For Herbert, Stanislavsky had not come up with a sacrosanct, unalterable method of working, but rather with a set of principles and guidelines—a system, in other words. Herbert further stated his frustration by pointing out that there may be a "cooking method," and there is a "solar system," but there is no "solar method." According to him, Stanislavsky was not devising a *how-to* method for building the character, but instead a system of searching for the *why* of a character. Why does the character behave as he or she does? Why does a character laugh or cry? What causes certain things to happen in a scene?

Stanislavsky's System was all about determining the causes of events in a scene and in a play as a whole. If we were only learning a "method," as opposed to a "system," we would be able to manufacture results by just mixing together the right ingredients. When a character is supposed to cry, for instance, tears can come from thinking about something sad. But the larger work consists of digging into the character as written and learning what makes the character sad—what he or she failed at or lost, and why it meant so much. Now, if an actor is stuck and finding it difficult to arouse the required emotion, there is nothing wrong with "thinking about something sad"—but *only* when the actor is stuck, or is given no time to truly learn the role. It is much more fun to become a detective and to get at the root of the character's actions and words.

In the early days of the Method, actors and actresses were so excited by the results of some of the exercises they had learned in the classroom that they came to rely on these tools and lost sight of the play itself. Their own emotions and their experience of playing them out on stage became more important than the playwright's words. Hence the Method was born, and the System was lost.

The influence of Constantin Stanislavsky (1863–1938), who spent nearly his entire life acting, directing, and teaching in Moscow, was felt throughout the theatrical world. His theories and ideas on the craft and art of acting were set out in several books that were widely translated and read by those who had never seen him or the celebrated Moscow Art Theatre that he founded in 1897 with Vladimir Nemirovich-Danchenko, but were eager to learn. What he had to say was interpreted and reinterpreted by generations of actors and their teachers, and there was much conflict over what he meant. To confuse us even more, his ideas changed with experience over the course of his lifetime.

The world-famous Moscow Art Theatre was devoted to productions that embodied an innovative and realistic concept of acting. What remained a constant in Stanislavsky's work was the idea that acting is an art form instrumental in educating the masses, and in uplifting and inspiring them. I was fortunate to learn this principle early on from Herbert Berghof, and I teach my students that believing in it can help any actor to create something valuable even from a mundane or mediocre script. It helps the actor survive in film and television today, with its literally never-ending soap operas, regurgitated sitcoms and dramas, and is even useful in television commercials. In other words, whenever you are called upon to exercise your craft, you want not only to do your best, but also to see if you can create something positive, enlightening, and uplifting for the audience, if only by telling the truth.

Stanislavsky's technique is still the basis of contemporary teaching. Whatever the approach of the various schools, their aim is to help the actor to *experience* the events of the play and *become* the character. In the last century, actors who were trained to do this would have a much greater emotional effect on their audiences than actors performing in the old-fashioned, nineteenth-century style in which they illustrated the character outwardly, using masks and makeup and/or "theatrical" gesturing and articulating—that is, talking in a way that people never do in real life—and giving line readings, with calculated, often unreal intonation. While the old, rather melodramatic styles of acting might amaze the audience with the actor's physical and vocal skills, the new subtler, realistic style mesmerized them into believing that what they were watching was actually happening right in front of them. And when the actors are good, it is!

During Stanislavsky's formative years, there was an ongoing, now legendary competition between the French matinee idol and star Sarah Bernhardt, and the great Italian actress Eleonora Duse. Bernhardt's acting, with its grand gestures, declamatory style, and flashing eyes, appears in some ways stilted and unreal, but her own originality and genius must have been major factors in her sensational success. Still, it is difficult at this remove in time for us to understand quite what all the fuss was about, although apparently she moved her audiences to tears. On the other hand, George Bernard Shaw said of Duse that "she immeasurably dwarfs the poor little octave and a half on which Sarah Bernhardt plays such pretty canzonets and stirring marches"; and that "with a tremor of the lip, which you feel rather than see, and which lasts half an instant, she touches you straight on the very heart." Duse rejected the old-fashioned style, and preferred to be *real*: "I do not use paint," she said, "I make myself up morally."

As a young actress, I came across another quotation of hers, which I still use. She was criticized by certain Italian critics for being the same in many of her roles. She countered with, "I am sorry, but when I am on stage, the only thing I have to give is *my* soul."

Stanislavsky was a great admirer of Duse, and thought Bernhardt brilliant, but believed she valued fame over art. He was the innovator, but not the inventor, of realistic character playing. It would be simplistic to suppose that actors before

Stanislavsky did not want to be real in their acting, and to create the illusion of reality for their audiences. In fact, Stanislavsky was inspired to come up with his System by having observed and admired, in his youth, great performers who stood out from those who did sing only for the sake of singing beautifully, or dance just to show off their agility, or declaim in artificial voices, or raise their right arm and stalk offstage, nose in the air, in what was pretty much the standard, conventional way of ending a scene. These exceptional performers who had seemed to really embody their characters fascinated him, and he wanted to know how they did what they did. According to Nikolai Gorchakov in his classic book *Stanislavsky Directs* (Limelight reprint, 1991), even later in life, Stanislavsky said admiringly to some of the young actors in his studio after a performance he particularly liked, "How do you do it?"

Actors today sometimes perform in nineteenth-century style by accident. They think they are being real or "natural," but they are only imitating other actors. I once had a student who was a professional stripper. In a modern-day equivalent of the nineteenth-century exit gesture, every time she exited a scene in class, she did it with a little kick, one leg up. At one point, I finally said, "You know, Marlene, I don't think you should do the kick." And it turned out she didn't even know she was doing it! It just came naturally to her after doing it so many times at the end of her act: You exit, you kick.

Players have performed naturalistically for generations, but before Stanislavsky they were in the minority. Many twentieth-century acting teachers have pointed to Hamlet's speech to the Players in act 3, scene 2 as proof that realistic acting existed even in Elizabethan days: "suit the action to the word, the word to the action... and, hold, as 'twere, the mirror up to nature; to show virtue her own feature, scorn her own image..."

When I was first studying with Herbert, I was taught two words: "representational" and "presentational." Modern acting based on Stanislavsky's System is presentational: I "present" the character; I "am" the character. Nineteenth-century and earlier forms of acting were representational: I illustrate the character; but I am not the character.

Today's audiences can observe an old style of acting at its most extreme and stylized, with ritual gestures, movements, masks, costumes, and makeup, in the fabulous, four-hundred-year-old kabuki theater of Japan. Whenever I get the opportunity to see kabuki performed, I am moved, carried away with its beauty. Its choreographed direction and music tell a story in shorthand, so to speak, requiring athleticism from its all-male cast that is studied and learned from childhood on.

In many silent films, the old style of acting is modified so as to give an idea of realism that strikes us today as most unnatural. Certain actors, such as Greta Garbo, are wonderfully real, while others are laughably shallow.

And at times you can see what seems like nineteenth-century acting in opera, where some singers unfortunately make almost no attempt to act. It is worth noting that Stanislavsky himself directed opera, and tried to get the singers to study acting in depth and to apply their learning in their performances. He must have achieved some wonderful results, judging by a tradition that still prevails in Russian opera houses, where the acting is often brilliant.

Stanislavsky himself was well known as an actor, and created such major roles as Astrov in *Uncle Vanya* and Vershinin in *Three Sisters*, both of which were first produced at the Moscow Art Theatre. Stanislavsky proposed to write up a version of the System he had come up with after much searching and analysis, but he never completed it; others did, based on his notes. His first book, which he did finish and see published, was *My Life in Art* (Little, Brown, 1924), which is the story of his career as an actor and director, and of how he discovered his System. *An Actor Prepares* (Theatre Arts Books, 1936) is the title of his second book; and his System would be further explained in two more volumes, *Building a Character* (Theatre Arts Books, 1949) and *Creating a Role* (Theatre Arts Books, 1961).

Stanislavsky's books, while fascinating, are more like novels than anything else, and you have to extract the information from them. This makes it difficult to learn what he has to teach. Also, he deals with conditions in the early twentieth century, and things have changed radically since his day. So by all means read his books, but realize that they are in many ways historical, and not necessarily practical.

So much has been written by and about the legacy of Constantin Stanislavsky and his revolutionary influence on all of the world's stages that it does not warrant any in-depth analysis here. Suffice it to say that realism in acting is the standard popular style of our day. Except for such "museum" theaters as Japanese noh and kabuki, the Comédie Française, or the Piccolo Teatro di Milano, which does commedia dell'arte plays, other styles are considered anomalies or oddities—interesting experiments to be seen occasionally, but unacceptable as regular fare.

This would not necessarily have been the case if the art of filmmaking had not evolved around the same time as Stanislavsky was developing his System. Movies, especially after the addition of synchronized sound in the late 1920s, required a toned-down, simpler, and less theatrical approach to acting, due partly to the size of the actor's image on the big screen, and partly to the fact that actors no longer needed to project their voices and performances to a live audience. Close-ups demanded a relaxed and stiller physiognomy: if they were too busy and expressive, the actors would appear inappropriately grotesque. And in some silent films, they do! "Acting out"— that is, projecting a performance—quickly became undesirable, and much too "theatrical." Internalized acting, which meant keeping the emotional life of the character inside, as well as being thoughtful and consumed with feeling, became necessary. The actors' eyes, seen close up, could reveal everything, without a word being uttered. The audience could be deeply moved by such acting, which is why silent film was popular even before the invention of the talkies ruined the careers of so many silent film actors, some of whom couldn't speak a line convincingly. But in film, as opposed to theater, the camera angle and the final editing, not the actor, primarily tell the story.

It is also interesting to note that realism in playwriting arose shortly before Stanislavsky devised his System. Before Chekhov, Henrik Ibsen (1828–1906) was the foremost playwright of realistic drama, with such iconoclastic plays as *A Doll's House* (1879), in which he dared to expose the hypocrisies in the institution of marriage, which involved the denigration and subservience of women; and to treat the subject realistically in a contemporary setting for the first time in theatrical history. He had put "real" characters on stage who spoke in common, everyday language, precursive of the dialogue in twentieth-century plays. This was no Molière farce winking and laughing at marital infidelity, or at the conflicts between parents and children, or at an older man's doomed infatuation with a younger woman, but a slice of life as his shocked audiences might have lived it. Like other outspoken progressive thinkers, Ibsen was revered by some and reviled by others.

As Stanislavsky's System spread to other countries, it was added to, subtracted from, re-interpreted, and re-formed, depending, as you might expect, on the cultural context in which it was adopted. In the United States, where a more practical approach was needed than that of the Russian school, because time and money are of the essence and productions have to be seen by the public in a matter of weeks, three main branches sprang from the original tree. They are still influential today: the Actors Studio, which opened in 1947, and whose guiding light from 1949 on was Lee Strasberg; the Neighborhood Playhouse, which Sanford Meisner took over in 1935; and the Stella Adler Conservatory, started by her in 1949. All of them wrote books, the titles of which you will find in the bibliography; there are some things of value in each book.

Each chose to approach the System from a different vantage point. Lee Strasberg emphasized the psyche of the character, using more Freudian ideas than I believe Stanislavsky would have agreed with, although he was very fond of the Russian scientist Ivan Pavlov's psychological ideas on reflexes and reactions. It was Strasberg's teaching that became synonymous with the Method. He emphasized classroom exercises in emotional and sense memory. Sanford Meisner, breaking away from Strasberg and the Actors Studio, emphasized relating through talking and listening, as opposed to delving into one's own past experiences. And Stella Adler, disagreeing with both of them, insisted on a classical approach to the playwright, emphasizing the importance of script interpretation.

As far as I am concerned, all of those approaches stressed a part of the Stanislavsky System while neglecting the rest. Also, I think it is unfortunate that the Strasberg and Meisner approaches, in contrast to Adler's, seemed to promote exploring the character's emotional life as a first step in building a character, something that Stanislavsky warned against. Discussing what could be considered the revolutionary idea that actors should truly feel and experience what the character feels and experiences, he had come to the conclusion that emotional events were results—ends, and not the means for arriving at a performance. Trying to find emotions before you had really explored circumstances, relationships, and objectives was putting the cart before the horse.

The three schools of acting cause a lot of confusion among today's American acting students, who tend to believe almost religiously in one school or another. Many Meisner and Strasberg students mistake the classroom exercises for performance, and show the audience the exercises they use for arriving at the performance, instead of acting the performance. I choose to take a more holistic approach to Stanislavsky, who would probably have been dismayed by the various interpretations of his System. By "holistic" I mean that the actor should not approach the role emphasizing any one piece of the puzzle above the rest—such as a character's emotions or relationships as lived moment to moment—but should explore the role in logical steps, in order to achieve the full embodiment of the character. Relationships are to be explored, objectives defined, the physical place mapped out, activities decided upon, and, in a later step, character traits revealed and chosen. Layered in this way, no one element takes precedence, but rather each becomes part of the whole.

Over the years, I have observed acting companies that were devoted to one school of teaching or another. I have found their rehearsal procedures to be lopsided, making for an unnecessarily bumpy road to the actor's discovery of the character. For instance, the cast would focus all its energy on bouncing lines off each other, or off the walls, and opening night would come along with many of the play's secrets still unexplored. In other cases, the cast would be encouraged to bring in all sorts of personal and emotional exercises, which they would then be hard put to insert into the written material, so that the events in the play became secondary to the actors' own private inner lives.

More commonly, I have coached hundreds of individuals who, after years of Strasberg or Meisner training, didn't have a clue as to how to analyze and break down a script. I do not fault the theories behind these approaches, but rather the single-minded overemphasis on one or another approach, to the point of blinding the students to what the play and playing are really about.

What separated Stanislavsky's techniques from the other artists of his day was his insistence that the actor's concentration be focused on what was happening inside the character and on what surrounds the character on stage, thereby establishing a *fourth wall* between himself and the audience. Privacy, relaxation, and concentration, leading to physical and emotional freedom, were the key elements. Creating a character required intense study and practice. There were questions to be formed and answered, but none were to concern the outer effect: a character was to be built from the inside out. All theater conventions, such as grand entrances and exits, over-sized expressions and poses, were discarded. The actor no longer practiced with a mirror, attempting to perfect a show of sadness, happiness, and so forth. In Stanislavsky's school, actors learned not to watch themselves, and not to listen to the sound of their own voices. This was certainly revolutionary in his day. It permitted the most sensitive rather than the most flamboyant actors to become the great performers of the twentieth century.

In my training, I support the idea that freedom and relaxation come from occupation with the character's objectives and activities. And the equally necessary privacy comes from involvement with doing, and is the outcome of examining the character's circumstances. Unlike "Method" teachers, I do not advocate separating privacy, relaxation, and freedom from the analysis and exploration of the situations in the play, just as I do not believe in working separately on emotional results. This is what I was originally taught by Herbert Berghof and Uta Hagen—and what they taught has been corroborated for me over and over in my years of teaching and coaching.

Herbert would use his love of language to bring this point home: if you listen to the expressions we use when we talk about emotions, he would say, you would know that they aren't "something we wish for in life, nor should the character the actor is portraying." He pointed out that even laughter is painful and undesirable to us; after all, we often say, "I could have died laughing!" It is going against nature to "ask for" emotions. They will come about if the actor examines, breaks down and personalizes all the elements in the play. So I train my students to look at the whole picture.

It is clear that Stanislavsky's observations and teachings were based on what he saw as the universals of human behavior. These include the ideas that we all want something, and that we all struggle in some way to get what we want and to overcome the obstacles in our path. Also, time, place, and myriad other physical and emotional circumstances all awaken some response in us, and will condition how we cope with circumstances.

When we read a play, we are looking for what is universal in it. It is true that all the universals exist and have existed for us in our own past experience, but by jumping to that past experience first, using affective memory and so forth, before we really know where we are, we risk jumping to conclusions.

What we as actors should look for in a play is the logical, simple, and human response to the situations given by the author. Once we examine the subtext for the character's motivations, relationships, background, education, value system, and so forth, the character's reactions and dialogue become natural responses to events and are therefore *personalized*—that is, endowed or imbued with the actor's personal understanding of them, due to his or her experience of all the elements. We have personalized what was fiction, and made it real for ourselves.

Learning all this at the HB Studio, I felt unburdened of the responsibility of portraying a character who was interesting and dramatic for the audience, but instead was free to *live* the experience, finding the character in myself. This revelation brought me renewed excitement, since I was reminded that my original desire in becoming an actor was to feel what it is like to *be somebody else*. I was relieved to find out that my childhood fantasy of being in someone else's skin was also an art form!

In bookstores, I see titles like *Stop Acting* and *No Acting Please*, as if acting had a bad name. These titles seem to reflect the kind of acting, or rather non-acting, that is required in front of the camera. Many acting students have been made to believe that acting in film and television has to be "small." I disagree. And I'm hoping this book dispels that idea. It is the script that is "small." The actor is only doing what is appropriate to the material, giving to it the required energy. And the fact that the actor need not project the voice should not be construed as meaning that he or she has to act "smaller."

Any action, whether it is in a Shakespearean tragedy or in an episode of a nighttime television series, should be played fully. I am reminded of Norma Desmond, the faded movie star played so memorably by Gloria Swanson in *Sunset Boulevard* (1950). Joe Gillis (William Holden) says to her, "You're Norma Desmond. You used to be in silent pictures. You used to be big." And she replies, "I *am* big. It's the pictures that got small." She may, of course, have been referring to the "talkies," where it was no longer necessary to gesture extravagantly with the hands and to make faces in order to get your point across.

In 1961, when I was still in my early twenties, Uta Hagen asked me to monitor two of her classes for three weeks while she was away. I was overwhelmed but quickly said yes. She knew how hard I had worked on her exercises and how much I had concentrated on her ways of teaching acting technique and interpretation.

It so happened that the students were pleased with me as a substitute teacher. This led to an invitation in 1962 to join HB Studio's faculty. Before my own classes were to begin, however, I substituted for other teachers, which built up my confidence a bit more.

Stephen Strimpell, another new teacher; William (Bill) Hickey, who had been teaching for a few years by then; and I got together to formulate a technique program. In the process of deciding on a week-to-week series of exercises and improvisations, so that we could substitute for each other if needed, we arrived at the final exercise of Acting Technique I, which was choosing a scene from a play and improvising on it. Based on Constantin Stanislavsky's procedures for improvising a scene, we ended up with eleven steps. It was these eleven steps that became for me the foundation of all rehearsal:

1. Read the play and discuss it with your partner.
2. Read the scene aloud and discuss it.
3. Close the books and stand up to plan and lay out the *place*.

4. Choose the *circumstances*, past, present, and future: where you have come from, what time it is, and where you are going.
5. Choose the *physical activities* and the *objects* (props) you will use.
6. Decide on your character's overall objective in the scene: the *primary objective*.
7. Decide on and/or improvise the *prior relationship*, i.e., the first meeting.
8. Improvise the scene itself.
9. Sit down, open the books, and read the scene again.
10. Discuss any revisions you feel are needed in the discoveries you are making.
11. Improvise the scene again. Keep any lines that "stick" from the dialogue. Otherwise, do not feel obligated to remember the exact words. If working well, the improvised scene should play out longer than the scene itself.

The following week, students would do the scenes, memorized. If, as was true in many cases, it was their first scene, it was always a shock for them to discover that despite the weeks of freedom and growing sensitivity and emotional vulnerability that they were experiencing in the improvisations and exercises, they suddenly regressed into frightened, clumsy puppies. They had come smack up against a written scene, and realized there was more technique to study. "There!" I would say, "You have to take Technique II." Aside from expanding their knowledge of the necessary tools for character building in the advanced technique courses, I recommended that the students take Scene Study at the same time in order to continue using the tools in a practical way.

Over the fifteen years I was on the faculty of the HB Studio, I perfected my Technique I, II, and III courses, and taught Scene Study as well. The HB Studio is still the school I recommend to actors who want to learn a solid foundation for acting, inspired by Herbert Berghof's principles and Uta Hagen's methodology.

And since that time, my experience as a freelance acting teacher, actress, and coach has taken me far and wide, working on various film and television projects in many of the fifty United States and as far away as India. All of this has necessarily demanded experimentation with what I still regard as the gospel of Stanislavsky, in order to conform to working conditions that the master himself could not have foreseen. This book is meant to remind us that his basis for character exploration does not change while searching for practical ways to meet the obligations for professionalism in the media.

CHAPTER 2

Why Rehearse?

IIIIIIIIIIIIIIIIIIIIIIIIIIIIIIIIIIIIIIIIIIIIIIIIIIIIII

Commitment and Practicing Alone

The definition of *rehearse* is: (1) to practice in preparation for a public showing; (2) to perfect or cause to perfect by repetition. In French, the word for rehearsal is *répétition*, meaning, of course, "repetition."

Herbert Berghof, with his love of words and their origins, would have enjoyed the following fascinating bit of trivia: the second syllable of the word *rehearse* derives from Old English *herce*, meaning a harrow, which is a kind of rake—a farm implement, used to break up and even off plowed ground. The prefix "re-" is from the Latin, meaning "again": a field was harrowed and then harrowed again—re-herced. The word took on the more general meaning of "repeat"; by extension, this became "rehearse," in its modern connotation.

"Herce" derives from the Latin word *hirsutus* (hairy; shaggy; bristly), which describes the harrow's spiky teeth, and explains why "harrow" also came to mean "terrify"—the hair on your neck stands up when you are afraid. And *herce* is also the root of *hearse*, a vehicle carrying the dead to burial. Before it meant a kind of rake, *herce* meant "a framework over a coffin"! With its ornamentation, the framework resembled braided hair, and was possibly sometimes made of hair. Although probably nobody would use the word in this way, *re-hearse* can mean "to put the coffin in the hearse again." This is not something you want to do when you rehearse a play—you don't want take it away to bury it; you want to bring it to life!

Why rehearse? Why go through the harrowing process of raking things up over and over again? Why not just get up and perform? Don't you already know how to do your dance steps, or sing, or play your instrument, or recite your lines, once you have memorized them? To a professional performing artist these would seem like very odd questions, indeed, if not downright ludicrous ones. Don't even ask them of singers, dancers or instrumentalists!

Musicians are in the habit of practicing many hours every day for their concerts. Some piano and violin soloists practice eight hours a day for days on end, and orchestra musicians often practice four or five hours, in addition to their teaching engagements, or the orchestra's rehearsal hours and concerts. My teacher, Uta Hagen—whose mother and stepmother were musicians, and who was herself an operatic soprano when she was a young woman—used to tell an anecdote about an oboist she knew, who was among the world's greatest players. One day, he felt tired, put down his instrument, and did not practice for his normal eight hours—incredibly demanding hours for an oboist, by the way. According to Uta, he never picked up the oboe again! It was his contention that his playing would be less than perfect if he resumed it, so he felt compelled to give it up forever. Uta herself loved playing the piano, but refused to play for anyone else to hear, because she had stopped practicing long ago. I remember how impressed I was with her story about the oboist. In fact, it helped me to reach maturity as an actress, as I developed my craft and art.

At first her story frightened me. I thought about how superficial and shallow I was. I didn't think I could devote so much time and intensity to studying as that oboist had put into his instrument. I began to wonder if I had the necessary commitment to become an actress. This preyed on my mind for a long time. After a while, however, I began to trust myself, because when I had an assignment to do in class or a role to learn in the theater or in a movie or television show, I worked extremely hard and always met my obligations. Uta's story taught me that complete devotion to the artistic task at hand is a necessity for the artist. Without that wholehearted commitment, you will never achieve your goal of giving as good a performance as you are capable of.

There was an occasional conflict with my husband and two sons, who sometimes felt neglected or left out. And I struggled with guilt feelings over that, because of my total concentration on whatever assignment I had before me. I owe a great deal to a professor of psychology at NYU whom I knew in those early days of my career. He helped me to alleviate my guilt about not giving enough attention to my home life whenever I was studying for a role or coaching a student by explaining to me the difference between quality and quantity: to give your full attention to what is before you for whatever limited time you have is equal to and better than giving to it a greater quantity of time, but without your complete concentration.

In my eagerness and wholehearted desire to act, I became aware that I was observing events and people around me as material to be used later on. At first, I felt guilty about that, too, but I later forgave myself because I came to realize that it was an "occupational hazard," as Herbert Berghof once described it. He told a story that shocked me at the time. When he was a young actor, a colleague of his had died tragically. He remembered thinking at the funeral, even in the midst of his grief, about how he could use this event and his response to it in a role he was working on.

I find that being an actor sensitizes a person; one can no longer be an ordinary citizen. We actors look at things a bit differently from most non-actors, empathizing with other people's lives in our imaginations, and putting ourselves in their place.

All these realizations gave me a sense of security and the feeling that I was committed to acting, that I was on the right path, and that I was preparing myself correctly for a life in the theater, just as I would be preparing myself correctly for a performance by rehearsing.

To return to the question that opens this chapter, why rehearse? The simple and obvious answer is: because if you don't rehearse, if you don't prepare yourself correctly, you will be completely lost, and you will have not the slightest idea of what you are doing. You will not be able to "become" the character and to live through the circumstances of the character's life from moment to moment, as if you were living them for the first time, as if they were actually happening and unfolding as events do in real life. You will not succeed in creating the illusion of reality for your audience, or of involving them in what they are seeing. In other words, you will not be doing your job, and your performance will be unconvincing. And how can you possibly know what you are doing if you haven't understood it, and gone through the process of bringing the character to life—a process of discovery, since you can't know everything about a character immediately, any more than you can completely know someone you have just met for the first time? Hence this book: what to do when there is no time to rehearse, as is the case in the media.

As a young acting student, I recall vividly how my classmates and I would groan about the fact that there was no way we could practice acting on a daily basis, unlike the dancer and the singer, or even the writer and the painter, both of whom often sketch out the material they are working on before putting pen to paper—or finger to computer keyboard, nowadays—or brush to canvas.

Acting is an interpretative art form. It is also a collaborative form: it requires a script written by someone (the actor might write his or her own script) and more than one person to practice with. And even in a solo performance you need a director, or someone else who functions as a "third eye."

Acting is the only performing art that cannot be measured by musical notes, breathing, high kicks, turns, leaps, flexibility, fingering, bowing, blowing, and so forth. The actor has only himself and how he internalizes a scene and projects feelings, and he must never stand outside himself to observe the outcome. The instrumentalist can hear the music and pick out his mistakes, but if the actor should listen to how he sounds, he will forfeit his subjectivity and no longer be acting. So, unless you are in school, there is no daily practice.

When I meet an ambitious young acting student who is concerned that he or she has no way to practice the craft between classes or between rehearsals for class, I suggest reading books, especially poetry and theatrical and historical biographies, listening to classical music, taking hikes and enjoying nature, or watching an old film masterpiece on television, or on tape or DVD, as a daily exercise. From biographies and autobiographies, the student learns about characters, their personalities, backgrounds, and other cultural and social information, all of which can be used as references for future roles. Great works of art, music, theatre, and movies help to sensitize and inspire the acting student. It might seem obvious, but in the twenty-first century young people have so much to choose from in the way of superficial entertainment—hundreds of television channels to choose from, MP3 players, and cell phones equipped with cameras and minuscule televisions—that it requires an effort to look for what would truly be nourishing.

It is also obvious that the more experience the actor has in life, the more material he or she has to draw on. When I was forced to stop taking classes in order to have a baby, I had a revelatory experience. I continued to attend class until it was no longer possible to walk up the three flights of steps to the HB Studio, which, in those days, was on the third floor of a small factory building in Chelsea. After having my son, I waited until he was seven months old before returning to Uta Hagen's advanced acting class. I had a great deal of trepidation, believing that I must have fallen far behind the other students, and that she might demote me to a beginner's class. To my surprise and delight, I had not fallen behind at all; instead, my acting had improved! This was a revelation to me: at twenty-one years old, I had discovered that life itself can be a class in acting.

Others in my class never considered marrying or raising children until much later in life, wanting to get their careers in gear first. Looking back, I have found that many of them now feel they may have missed out on the other things they wanted in their lives, whether they are making a living in acting or not—sadly, more often not. I am neither advocating nor opposing early marriage—I certainly don't remember planning to marry young and to start a family as early as I did—but now, as a teacher, I encourage my students to continue in fields they may have been interested in besides acting. And if they have a relationship with a partner and/or are planning to have children, I tell them not to give that up for their acting career. Rather, I tell them that it is best to juggle their commitments, as difficult as that may be on occasion, and not to put things off for acting. After all, there are no guarantees in the acting business, as everyone who enters it should know. More importantly, living and experiencing one's own life is a basic requirement for acting. I had to grow up substantially to fulfill the responsibilities of taking care of a baby, and this life experience definitely showed in my exercises in class.

To fully interpret and encompass a role, one needs to find parallels with one's own life in order to understand the character more deeply and to personalize the material—that is, actors build a role by drawing from their relevant personal experience. Therefore, I think that choosing to live a life with a single focus—one's career—as some ambitious acting students do, may actually hinder one's growth as an actor. I also think it is a good idea for acting majors in colleges and universities to take as many courses as possible in the humanities—especially in language, literature, history, psychology, and the other social sciences, as well as in the natural sciences. How can they bring a character to life if they have no knowledge and no life experience, and if all they know is acting technique and show business?

When I coach children, I naturally am very limited as to what I can teach them. Their still unformed and uninformed brains can only encompass so much, and they have so little life experience for me to use to fill out the character for them, as compared to adults. I play with them, in order to keep them relaxed and free to experiment, and I avoid making "puppets" out of them, as some coaches and stage parents are wont to do. On the other hand, when I work with young adults, I challenge them to read and observe more and learn.

In his day, Stanislavsky took many months rehearsing a production for his theater. Almost nobody does that today. The great English theater and film director Peter Brook worked for six months on his world-renowned production of Peter Weiss's *The Persecution and Assassination of Jean-Paul Marat as Performed by the Inmates of the Asylum of Charenton under the Direction of the Marquis de Sade* (or *Marat/Sade*) for the Royal Shakespeare Company. I recall laughing in wonderment when, after *Marat/Sade* was a hit on Broadway in 1964, the play, with that incredibly long title, was listed on the schedule of various summer stock theaters around the United States. Summer stock productions traditionally rehearse for a mere six to nine days! My experiences in those summer theaters taught me to expect to finalize my performance only in the very last show of the one- or two-weeks run. When a summer stock company put on *Marat/Sade*, it would have to have been similar to an amateur children's production. Without enough rehearsal before opening night, the shows themselves become the actors' rehearsals. But unfortunately such "rehearsals" take place under the pressures of a public performance, and are therefore not very edifying.

I'm sure there are theater directors nowadays who rehearse plays at length, and longer than the minimum required three weeks, but, more often than not, in countries other than the United States. Sadly, it bears mentioning again that in America, "time is money," and no producer is willing to pay for more rehearsals than is required by the actors' unions. As a matter of fact, Actors' Equity and the Screen Actors Guild "protect" their members by limiting rehearsals depending on the theater or film contract, and demand payment for any extra day the film actor is required to be present. I certainly support the unions' rules, but the truth is that they sometimes unintentionally hurt the actors more than they help them, since producers in general, now more than ever before, want to keep a tight budget when it comes to the actors. Actors are then forced to work on their own, at home, alone, compromising their performances, which should be worked out in rehearsal with their fellow cast members. Also, accustomed to having little or no rehearsal time, many American directors today would not know what to do anyway with the three weeks allotted to rehearsal in the theater, or with the week or two so rarely allowed for it on a movie shoot.

In my experience as an acting coach on feature films, TV pilots, movies, and miniseries I have been asked to conduct rehearsals, on more than one occasion, while the director was away scouting locations. Rehearsals during pre-production on a film are not as intense as they are in the theater, because, for one thing, the cast of actors will never need to learn all the lines or even the blocking. For another, scripts continue to change during production anyway, and the scenes are generally shot out of sequence. Locations that have not yet been visited will be a determining factor in the final physical life of the characters. And research, wardrobe, makeup, and hair will certainly take up a good portion of the film's rehearsal period. Rehearsals can and do proceed at a leisurely pace, allowing for more discussion than would be advisable even for the theater. Also, there will be day players whom the principal actors will not even meet until the day of the scene in which they appear, which means that all the relationships cannot be explored before the actual shooting.

It is a sad fact that today's American film directors, in general, have no knowledge about the actor's process, unless they started out as actors, as did, for example, Robert Redford, and my favorite, Sidney Lumet, whose films include *12 Angry Men* (1957), *Dog Day Afternoon* (1975), *Network* (1976), *Garbo Talks* (1984), and so many more memorable films. He began as a child actor, and later became a successful director of theater and live television as well. And he is one of the few directors working today who absolutely loves actors. He is in no way terrified of them, as many of the newer directors are, and he speaks to a star or a day player with equal respect. And Sidney Lumet likes to rehearse! In fact, he insists on it.

Today more than ever—and such things never happened in the old days of the Hollywood studio system—movies big and small are being filmed by first-time directors who may have come right from film school, or from doing short subjects, or from screenwriting or even from doing film criticism. It will come as no surprise to the experienced film actor that inexperienced, insecure first-time directors tend to be demanding, even combative, with their actors. I taught for years in workshops and university graduate film schools, and continue to coach privately technicians, animators, writers, and documentary filmmakers who want to make the leap into feature films. What sadly prevails among them is their fear of actors, whom they tend to treat like the enemy, as opposed to members of a company that it is their job to guide and nurture. They are afraid of the actor's ego, and would rather fool around with the props, the set, and the lighting, which never talk back. Needless to say, all this makes for a difficult atmosphere in which to work.

For the majority of movies made in the U.S., there is absolutely no scheduled rehearsal. During a film workshop I taught at the Young Filmmakers Foundation in the 1980s, I invited the famous director Robert Wise to lecture to the group of mainly documentary filmmakers and aspiring screenwriters who were attending. He said that with all the movies he had directed—forty-one in all, including *West Side Story* (1961) and *The Sound of Music* (1965)—he had asked for, and had been given, only one week's rehearsal for just one of his movies, *Audrey Rose*, in 1977. The reason he wanted the extra week from the studio was that he felt intimidated by its star, Anthony Hopkins. He rightly assumed that Hopkins would be expecting rehearsals, which he was used to having in England. Also, Wise felt he needed to establish a mutually respectful working relationship with the brilliant Hopkins. Things worked out quite well, so they must have had an excellent collaboration.

Rehearsing Scenes for Class

After I left the HB Studio and struck out on my own, I eventually stopped teaching technique per se because of my coaching schedule and taught only scene study. And after a few years of teaching advanced scene study classes, I made a wise decision: I decided to build on the series of steps Bill Hickey, Stephen Strimpell, and I had devised years before. I created a rehearsal guide for doing scenes for class, and began to hand it out to my students. The need for this became clear to me after I found that even my advanced and experienced students often gave vague, convoluted answers to my questions about how they were working on the assigned scenes between classes. And sometimes, when they read to me from the notes they had taken during my opening-day lectures, it sounded as if those notes had come from the mind of someone in a mental institution.

Eventually, following the guide when rehearsing for my class became as important as the class itself, so much so that I now consider that I am giving classes in how to rehearse. First of all, I knew from experience that students learned a great deal more, and in less time, when they really did the work, and brought in "finished" assignments. The rehearsal guide acted as a "stage manager," organizing each meeting and its goals. I wanted fully prepared scenes for class and not scenes that were put together hastily and without planning.

What I devised and edited over the years was a step-by-step process of rehearsal, requiring that the students meet for at least five one-hour rehearsals with their partners over a two-week period. Influenced by Uta Hagen, I believed two weeks were necessary for practical reasons, and arranged my class schedule accordingly. Living in New York City and attempting to put aside an hour five times in one week is impossible for the students who work in day or night jobs as well as act in showcases and audition for commercials, soaps, films, and so forth. I added private work, too—that is, homework students could do on their own between rehearsals with their partners.

Ironically, at the same time as I was developing this teaching approach, which committed students to bringing a completely rehearsed scene into class, other schools were springing up all around the city that were devoted to non-rehearsed "cold readings." It was the stated purpose of these schools to prepare the students for "the way the business works." Since movies and television did not include rehearsal, they believed it would be a good idea for the acting student to learn how to get along without it. This way of thinking became and remains prevalent today, with classes in "instant characterization" and "rules for camera acting" proliferating. To my mind, this is very unfortunate and has been a great disservice to new, up-and-coming talent in this country, as compared to the kind of training actors receive in the United Kingdom, for example.

What is missing when there is no rehearsal is enormous. Instant acting is just like instant coffee: it lacks body, color, and flavor; it resembles the real thing, but without the rich, deep taste. Instant acting always relies on clichés, and on carbon copies of what has been done before. Unfortunately, it fits in perfectly with regurgitated screen and television writing and the lack of direction so prevalent today, particularly

in television series and soap opera, so much so that there
doesn't appear to be anything missing. To make a comparison
to other art forms, instant acting is like painting by numbers,
or composing music with a synthesizer.

I do believe that, as Americans, we are losing the game. The
British actors are taking over in the American media. Since
they are trained in the classics, they certainly appreciate and
know what to do with rehearsals. They can take a dull piece
of writing and imbue it with universality. And they can play
American roles convincingly, with perfect, specific American
accents—which many foreign actors in previous generations
could not do. The old-time studio moguls did not require
Ingrid Bergman, Deborah Kerr, Charles Boyer, Ricardo Mon-
talban, or George Sanders to speak "American," but instead
roles were created for them, or their accents were completely
unexplained, and for fans like myself it didn't matter. Today,
for a viewing audience that is inundated with choices in movies and television, film and television producers require fine
actors like Ralph Fiennes, Russell Crowe, Jude Law, Nicole
Kidman, Kate Winslet, Cate Blanchett, Clive Owen, Eric Bana,
and others to compete. They learn to perfect all sorts of American regional accents. (Recently, I've joked with my students
that there is a special American dialects coaching room next
door to customs in all the major international airports.) For
the past few years, it is quite evident that they have been replacing American actors, and in my scene study classes, I am
trying to keep up with them.

CHAPTER 3

Film and Television:
The End of Rehearsal

||||||||||||||||||||||||||||||||||||||||||||||||||

In 1987, I was doing an episode of the series *The Equalizer* in which I was playing an acting teacher; the leading actress in the episode was a "student" in my class. The writer telephoned me late at night the day before the shoot, and confided in me that the scene was too short. It needed a few extra minutes, and he wanted to know if I could suggest something, maybe a monologue from Shakespeare, for instance, because he wanted something that was in the public domain. "Well," I said, "I don't think Shakespeare's such a good idea. She might be a little frightened of doing a classical monologue, because she has only done soap opera until now." So he called her, and then called me back: I was right; she really didn't want to do Shakespeare.

I thought a moment, and then I suggested Sonya's brief monologue from act 2 of Chekhov's *Uncle Vanya*.

"Who's Chekhov?" he asked.

I was a bit shocked, but I patiently explained who Chekhov was.

"Is he in the public domain?"

"Well, yes, he is." The writer thought that was fine, so over the phone I dictated an adapted version of the speech—to avoid copyright problems with the translations. Sonya is talking to herself just after Astrov, who does not requite her love, has left the room. His indifference has revived her memory of a hurtful incident: she had overheard two women talking about her as they were coming out of church, and one of them had said, "What a pity she's so plain," which is the last line of the speech.

The next day I was in the makeup trailer, when I was called urgently to the set. The director came running up, and said, "Thank you! We loved it, but we decided to change one word. The actress is so young and beautiful that calling her plain really makes no sense, so we changed the line to 'What a pity she's so pretty.' "

I was flabbergasted, and I didn't want to let them use the speech, because they had made such complete nonsense of it. But the actress herself intervened: she really wanted to do it, and persuaded them to use the original version. When we rehearsed for camera, I watched her playing it with the kind of pseudo-reality so typical of soap opera acting on television, so that when she got to the last line, it really wouldn't have made any sense to the viewing audience. I grew concerned, but she was open to my giving her advice, and I told her to remember that she was playing an acting student. "You sound too 'real,' polished and professional. Try to be more awkward with the piece, and don't do it as if it were a finished scene, because, remember, you are doing it for class. So try searching for the words more." She did as I suggested, and the scene turned out to be believable, much to my relief.

But the entire incident really made me think about the sometimes astounding ignorance and lack of judgment of some television writers and directors. This is what we are up against in television—and, believe me, in the twenty years since I did that episode of *The Equalizer*, things have not improved. In fact, they have gotten worse! Television directors, sadly even those who once directed theater and/or film, are not interested in really working with actors, or so it appears. And I know for a fact that some of them wouldn't know how to work with actors or to rehearse even if they wanted to, or if they had the time.

Unlike television, films, by necessity, allow for at least some rehearsal time, because throughout the work day the crew takes many hours setting up for the camera and lighting, so the actors can use their down time to review, and to prepare for the upcoming scene. And even when the actor is on his mark in front of the camera, he usually has a few extra minutes while the camera and lights are being adjusted further. It is at that time that the actor can ground himself in the surroundings, relax and prepare for the take. And, of course, some directors have the power to petition the studio and receive pre-production rehearsals. The director Sidney Lumet usually gets two weeks of rehearsal beforehand, which he knows how to use well. He was among the early television directors and was used to working on the live television dramas of the 1950s and early '60s. An hour-long drama would be rehearsed for two complete weeks, and then it would be broadcast live, and without interruption. Nowadays in taped or filmed television, there is no time to rehearse anything, even if the director knows what he's doing. And nothing *is* rehearsed. All they do is get ready to shoot.

Television, in general, is under severe time constraints, while film is often under budgetary constraints. The television show must be done to fit into a certain time frame, and each scene has its own time limitation: it has to finish in time for the commercial breaks, which can interrupt the show for five or six minutes at a stretch. The same kinds of time restrictions do not apply, of course, to public service or non-commercial, pay-television channels like HBO or Showtime, where the programs, on occasion, even exceed the scheduled time limit. But they absolutely do apply to all commercial network television programs.

You might think that working conditions in television mov-

ies would be different from the run-of-the-mill, episodic series. In my on-set coaching career, I worked primarily with
feature films at first, as well as on occasional television pilots
and specials. I then moved on to television movies, or MOWs
(Movies of the Week), as they are called by people in the business. In fact, MOWs constituted ninety percent of my coaching work in the 1980s and '90s. (There are far fewer produced
today because of the success and popularity of reality shows.)
For the most part, their four-week shooting schedule for ap-
proximately one and a half hours of dramatic programming
(leaving space for the commercial breaks in the two hours of
broadcast time) introduced me to the rush-rush of what television was becoming. An independent feature of that length
would normally take at least twice that long to shoot.

At the beginning of my experience with MOWs, I recall
working with actors on a script we were exploring, and suggesting changes—an ordinary occurrence that I had gotten
used to in feature films. Soon this type of freedom proved
to be impossible, as the machinery became more and more
oiled, and the process of making the MOW became set in its
ways. It was finally made clear to me one day that not a single
word could be changed without the network's approval.

Two or else three cameras were used at all times to accommodate what I felt was the inhuman speed at which the
MOWs were made. A multi-camera shot provided no "wiggle"
room in which to finesse lighting and blocking for the frame,
let alone the possibility of enriching the performances before
reaching the important close-ups, which are too numerous
and indiscriminate, in order to accommodate the small screen.
The directors don't feel they have to rehearse the scenes, except to have the actors run through them for the benefit of
the camera, and the two or three cameras going simultaneously save time by providing all the "cuts" in one take. The
first time an actor I had been working with on movies up until
then came smack up against this fact, he cried, "I feel as if I've
gone to war!"

Recently, I had a shock while working on the television series *Law & Order: Criminal Intent.* When the star of the show, Vincent D'Onofrio, asked for a reading of the scene before we shot it, I realized that it was the first time in my experience that one of its stars ever read an entire scene with a guest player before shooting it! Sad to say, more time and care go into preparing a thirty-second commercial than a full-length television drama!

Television Commercials

It's ironic that television commercials are among the best-produced pieces of television these days. An entire day is devoted to those thirty seconds, and sometimes more. As somebody once said, "During daytime and prime time the commercials are better than the shows, and only late at night are the shows better than the commercials." I thought this was a very astute comment.

In the last three decades or more, the production of television commercials is where new film editing, photographic and animation techniques are discovered, helped by the vast sums of money industry will pay for them. The irony is that, in this way, American industry sponsors our artists. Perhaps that's as it should be, since the United States never had a tradition of culture, like older countries, where the government supports and funds the arts; and since we are a prosperous country, it is only fair that those who have prospered the most—the industrialists—pick up the tab for innovations in filmmaking and actors' survival.

Major directors such as Alex Proyas, Spike Lee, the late John Schlesinger, and many others have directed commercials, and great cinematographers like Academy Award winner Philippe Rousselot work on them, because, for one thing, they pay so well. And commercials are actually rehearsed! As an actor, you have plenty of time during the setups to work on your little scene—a great deal more time to develop whatever it is you have to do than you are given in film or television programs. It is true that there isn't just one director: the sponsors and the advertising agency all oversee the results; and yet actors can create the best performances you see on television because much more specificity—humorous or serious—is demanded of them.

I used to say only half jokingly that if Shakespeare were alive today, he would want to work in films, because his language is so visual. Here, for example, are the first four lines of the Prologue to *Henry the Fifth*:

Oh, for a muse of fire, that would ascend
The brightest heaven of invention!
A kingdom for a stage, princes to act,
And monarchs to behold the swelling scene!

And later in the same speech:

Think when we talk of horses, that you see them
Printing their proud hoofs i' the receiving earth;

What a shooting script that would be! In fact, what a shooting script it became in the two films made from Shakespeare's play, the first by Olivier, and the second by Kenneth Branagh. It is obvious to me that the great Bard of Avon was practically crying out for electricity ("a muse of fire"), which would lead to photography, which would lead to the movies! And perhaps he would want to work in television *commercials* even more so than in feature films, because he would have greater resources to find the best visual way of telling a story. He probably wouldn't want to work in soap opera.

Soap Opera and Nighttime Television Drama

In a way, soap opera is closer to theater than other kinds of television programs, because, for one thing, there are so many lines to memorize. The contract players have to spend their weekends studying all the scenes to be shot the following week. During the taping day, the actor spends some of the morning in wardrobe and makeup, and then in blocking scenes for the camera. There is no rehearsal per se in soap opera. The taping is done in the afternoons, after lunch. In general, each taped sequence includes so much more text than is done in films or nighttime television that in the beginning, when soaps were broadcast live, the soap opera actor got used to reading from cue cards. Even up to the recent past, the joke among actors was whenever they saw an actor looking anywhere else other than at the character to whom the lines are addressed, he or she is reading from cards.

Also, in soap opera the actor plays a character that has no beginning—other than the minimal background given in the audition scenes, and that is subject to change at any moment—and no end. There is no final scene or resolution that is known to the actor during what may turn out to be years of performing the role, until, at the last moment, one is thrust upon him or her. There is only a middle; only the center of the story exists, and with each new plot twist, of which there are many, it is told and retold day by day. In such circumstances, it is very difficult for the actor to develop a full-blooded character, since there is essentially no story to tell, or at any rate, two-thirds of it is missing, and the character has no arc of development, any more than the story does. This must be the reason why all of the characters on soaps seem so overwrought.

When a character is going to be written out, for whatever reason, there is finally some closure to his or her story—frequently a rather abrupt and unsatisfactory closure, but an ending nonetheless. Of course, the actor is not informed of this until the writers come up with it in the final weeks. Even if the character is being dropped because the performer wants out of his or her contract, the actor still won't know until the end how the character is going to be put to rest.

And there is very little physical life in soap operas. There are few props, because the directors cannot take the time to include any activities or work with them. Usually, in fact, there are none. The actors are simply talking heads. These talking heads are directed to move, and very often the moves are difficult to justify, because they are there only for the camera, not for any organic reason the actor might have. The talking heads will move to the door, or go sit on the couch. And, if you watch carefully, you will see that many times the talking heads are not talking to each other, because the director would like to be able to videotape both faces at the same time. This means that one actor is forced to look at nothing—in the direction of the camera—and the other actor is looking at the back of his or her head.

The process of taping a soap opera can be quite a harrowing experience for the actor, until he or she gets used to the conditions of having to memorize all the lines without rehearsing them, and of then being blocked and having to perform for the camera on cue. Directors usually do only one take, possibly two; if they have to do more than two takes for any reason, they start to get very annoyed. Yet the soap contract players over time get very used to the system, including the exposition and repetition in the writing. The danger for them as actors is that, in order to survive these conditions, their emotions become "mechanical" or "manufactured." The actors in such a situation can lose all sense of how one works to build a character.

In fact, the television medium on the whole has done more to harm actors and the creative process of developing characters than any other influence. It may not have destroyed acting altogether, but it has certainly reduced it from an art form, one of the oldest known to humankind, to being merely a craft, and, at times, a rather uninteresting one at that. There is no doubt that television in the United States has now become the major source of employment for actors. This is one reason why actors from other countries, where there is less television and less time pressure, and who continue to work in the theater, can do better performances than many American actors do nowadays. They do better work on their own television programs, as well, where there is usually some time set aside for rehearsal, and in the case of the United Kingdom, the writing is exceptional compared to ours.

In nighttime television drama as well, an actor playing a principal role week after week can easily become very soft and lazy. An example: When I was still a new teacher at HB Studio, I remember Herbert Berghof helping his friend E. G. Marshall to "recuperate" from the five years (1961-65) that he had spent as the star of the series *The Defenders*. He badly needed to get back to the theater, which was, of course, his first love. Based on an early experience of his, Herbert knew exactly what to do for him: first, he selected a one-person play for E. G. to perform, and, as experienced as the veteran actor was, he was nevertheless petrified when he saw how many lines he had to learn. Since he had relied on cue cards for the last three seasons of his show, he hadn't had to learn any lines at all for a very long time. Nevertheless, E. G. agreed to do it.

When it came time to perform the play, Herbert equipped him with a listening device, to be placed in his ear, and the stage manager in the booth would read the lines to him, which E. G. repeated, quite brilliantly—all this in front of the audience. Apparently, Herbert's "cure" was very effective. E. G. Marshall regained his lost confidence and went on to continue his very distinguished career as one of America's great actors.

Recently, I was surfing channels on my TV set, in order to point out the different kinds of acting performances required for the various genres to one of my private students, and I had a small epiphany. I was struck by the contrast between the acting in soap opera acting and in the popular nighttime show *Law & Order*—a contrast forced on the actors by the very dissimilar writing and directing used in each. Of course, I found both less than satisfying in many ways. But I suddenly recognized the addictive power each type of performance holds over its audience. All the emotions portrayed in the soap opera are very elemental—passion, hurt, anger, fear—and this can be a catharsis for the viewers, although the absurd story lines are about murders, bigamy, kidnappings (which used to be a favorite), and incest, all taking place at the same time, and none of which could possibly be normal occurrences in the viewers' lives. The characters, and therefore the actors, carry on, argue, cry, and make speeches, confessing, pleading, and fighting for their lives. Generally, they are compelled to act out one extremely emotional scene after another. This could be construed as a great exercise for actors, if only they had something to base all this emotion on! They have had to learn how to manufacture emotions out of thin air, and, if they began at a young age, which many have, they have never learned how to dig into a good script with substance and subtext. But there were certainly variations in the performances on the soap opera episode I watched, and the more seasoned actors were indeed impressive. But I couldn't help thinking, "What a waste of feeling, given the writing!" I have sadly observed over the years that most if not all of the actors who have cut their teeth on soap opera remain confined to daytime drama.

By contrast, the *Law & Order* episode I watched was just as unreal, but here the actors were underplaying what would in real life constitute major events. The scripts for nighttime drama are just as unrealistic as those for soap opera; the dialogue, though there is much less of it, is just as one-dimensional. Another difference is that nighttime series try to stay within the boundaries of what could be plausible events, even though everything is rushed through to a conclusion. The plots of daytime shows stretch out over weeks and months; nighttime shows must, in an hour, reach a conclusion that would take many weeks to get to in real life. Watching *Law & Order*, I began to think that, in the end, the downplaying these actors are asked to do may be the more frustrating experience, since the actors rarely get a chance to flex their muscles or, in other words, experience a catharsis. But these crime shows, too, are very popular, because their viewers love the fast-moving, dramatic stories, with all those abrupt cuts. In any case, with the unnatural behavior required by both sorts of programs, which are continually being churned out by the barrelful, I fear that the art of real acting in America is disappearing, pretty much like fast food replacing haute cuisine or even just good old-fashioned home cooking.

There are a few exceptions to the rule in television, and they are usually to be found on premium subscription channels such as HBO. *The Sopranos*, for example, established and maintained an actual artistic point of view with some honest, fully developed characters and good comic scripts.

A few years back, I was one of the players on Sydney Lumet's nighttime series *100 Centre Street*, and I had the pleasure of watching him direct the first three episodes, which he rehearsed and shot like a good movie, although he used television's standard three cameras. The skillful and sensitive way he used the high-definition cameras provided all of the actors in a single scene with a flow of action such as you might experience on stage. We were all playing out huge chunks of the script without a break, and we were completely able to work off each other. But Mr. Lumet did not have time to continue directing all the episodes in the series, and on the fourth episode, he and his producers were obliged to bring in another director, who proceeded immediately to set up the three cameras facing one way, obscuring our view of each other. In other words, he "directed" the episode the way television is normally done, with as many shots against one wall of the set as possible. The valuable experience in the earlier episodes with Lumet allowed the regular performers to adapt. I personally felt let down, but the results were not bad for the small screen, as it turned out. Nevertheless, the fun we all had working together as a cast was squelched.

The Situation Comedy (Sitcom)

The half-hour sitcom, like the soap opera, is a little closer to the theater than nighttime television and film, because, once again, the actor has to learn all the lines, the scenes are done in relatively long takes, and most are played out in front of live audiences. Also, there are rehearsals, if one can call them that—they are devoted mostly to rewriting and blocking for the camera—for several days, and then the shows are taped before audiences at the end of the work week, usually on Friday.

The so-called rehearsals are attended every day by the writers, the producers, and even the casting directors. The network executives are brought in at prescribed times as well—and this is where it gets scary. Changes in script and direction are continually made throughout the week before the show is ready to be taped, and this is often catastrophic for the actors, one or another of whom may be cut down, removed, or replaced during this time. Once, to my horror, the entire show I was hired to work on was canceled before the taping!

What passes for rehearsal, including searching for the funniest line readings, is done by teamwork. All the people watching rehearsals have their say, and the actor has to try out each line reading until there is a consensus of opinion. It is only when the actor is the star *and* the producer that he or she has the final word.

The majority of sitcom directors are more like traffic cops than directors. They must answer to the writers, the producers, or writer/producers, and ultimately to the network executives; the way any particular scene turns out must meet with the approval of all of these. Hence the blocking for the actors rarely derives from the logic of any particular character or situation, and usually an actor will have to move around the set for no particular reason and with no real motivation, only in order to accommodate the three cameras. In such cases, the actors themselves have to look for reasons for making the required moves.

During the day of the taping, the studio audience watching the performers from bleacher seats usually can't see them very well, because there is a lot of equipment in their way.

The actors have to work very hard to get laughs. Traditionally, there is a stand-up comic placed in the audience who encourages them to laugh even more. Unlike the warm-up comedian who tells jokes in order to get the audience in a good mood before a talk show, such as the David Letterman or Jay Leno shows, the comic at a sitcom taping has to be there throughout—often for many hours—because the sitcoms are just not very funny, especially after repeated takes and hearing the gags more than once. Canned laughter will eventually be spliced into the final broadcast, mixed with the real laughter from the audience. At times, the audience will be seeing what are called "remote" scenes—that is, scenes that have been shot elsewhere on location, and that are shown on television monitors to the audience while the actors on the set are preparing for the next scene. As you can imagine, the audience's laughter is similarly remote and will have to be embellished.

Actors doing sitcoms are often convinced that they have learned how to play comedy. Likewise, comedians are convinced that they have learned to act. But over the years of playing sitcoms, they can unlearn what acting in a comedy really is, or where it comes from. In fact, many seem to revert to the nineteenth-century Delsarte system of gestures and of vocal indicating.

Don't get me wrong: the actors in sitcoms may be wonderful actors, but what they have to work with is usually pretty slim. I was once driving around Hollywood with a couple of well-known performers, one of whom was visiting from New York. He gazed around and said, "Just look at all this wealth, all going toward creating mediocrity."

"Oh, no, my friend," said the other man, a transplanted New Yorker who had chosen to live in Hollywood, "all this wealth is going toward *re-creating* mediocrity."

This is true. Hollywood, which started out as a film capital, has gradually become a television city over the past four decades. It is no longer really renowned for filmmaking, as it was in the days of the studio system and its stables of contract players that provided so much work for so many gifted people. And now most of the writing in television and films has become hackneyed and only revisits what was done previously, which might have been mediocre to begin with.

The writers don't seem to be able to write a true "situation" comedy at all nowadays, and have resorted to a series of punch lines. How different from the early years of live television, when such brilliant comedy writers as Neil Simon, Mel Brooks, and Woody Allen were perfecting their craft writing for the hilarious *Your Show of Shows*, starring Sid Caesar, Imogene Coca, Howie Morris, and Carl Reiner, and for other early classic shows. And Sid Caesar's show was live every week, back in the 1950s. Today, *Saturday Night Live* is the only constant live broadcast, and its sketch comedy is written and rewritten throughout the week. The show is played twice on Saturday night before a live audience, with changes made in between the two shows. And for all the great talent that passes through SNL, the sketches are at best hit or miss. However, what are the odds for turning out excellent shows, especially if you are running for over two decades?

The early filmed and/or taped sitcoms were written by such greats as Nat Hiken, Phil Silvers, and Bob Carroll, Jr., who wrote *I Love Lucy*. Each weekly episode had a hilarious premise and was written especially for the unique talents of performers who generally came out of vaudeville, such as Jackie Gleason, Art Carney, and Larry Storch. And the shows weren't expected to run for so many years that its original inspiration would inevitably dry up.

In the late 1960s, I did a tour of a revival of William Marchant's comedy *Desk Set* (a play that had been made into a film in 1957 with Katherine Hepburn and Spencer Tracy). We opened at the famous Elitch's Gardens Theater in Denver, Colorado— the oldest existing summer theater in the United States, where Sarah Bernhardt and Eleonora Duse had performed. The star of our production was the brilliant award-winning actress and comedienne Shirley Booth, known, among other things, for her performance as Hazel the maid in the highly successful television sitcom of the same name. As far as I and many others were concerned, she was a genius at comedy. She hardly needed to study Stanislavsky's System (I am sure she didn't), because she did it naturally anyway. And her comic timing was perfect, because it always came from her infallible sense of truth and her essential understanding of her character.

At the curtain's rise, I was on the telephone deep in a conversation. After our dress rehearsal, Shirley called me into her dressing room. "Would you mind very much if I gave you a note?" she asked. "No, not at all! I would be very appreciative," I answered. "Well…" she said, "you know, in that opening speech, you should go 'down' on the last word of the last line, because you're missing a laugh." I was getting laughs during the telephone conversation, and this would have been one more. "Yes," I said, immediately translating her note into a new attitude toward the "person" I was speaking to, "thank you so much!" I turned to leave her dressing room. She stopped me and said, "But, Alice, remember, in order to get the laugh, you can't let the audience know that's the reason why you're going 'down' on that word!"

Because of Ms. Booth's instinctual approach to acting, she innately understood about building a character from the inside. She may never have technically reasoned that a single line of dialogue is actually a psychological action, but, because of her inherent ability and sense of comic timing, she automatically spoke her lines as the results of real thoughts. She worried that I would follow her advice, but at the same time just do a line reading, which of course would not get the laugh, so she added that parting bit of advice.

Timing is different for the actor than it is for the comic, who has a direct relationship with his crowd and can work the joke to make sure he gets the punch line in at exactly the right moment. However, if punch lines are in a script, as they are, for example, in Neil Simon plays, the actor must personalize what is going on between the characters, and find exactly the right objective that makes logical sense and allows him or her to earn the laughs.

An example of Neil Simon's brand of humor, even in what might be considered one of his more serious plays, *The Gingerbread Lady*: Evy's daughter, Polly, is appealing to her recovering alcoholic mother to let her move in with her.

EVY: Mother, heh? Some mother…. When am I here? I'm out all day doing absolutely nothing, and I still manage to come home late. I saw you more when you didn't live with me.
POLLY: I'm not complaining.
EVY: Well, complain, damn it! What are you so forgiving for? I was a slob last night. A pig and a slob.
POLLY: It only happened once.
EVY: Wait, it's early, the new schedule didn't come out yet.
  [LAUGH]

In that exchange, the love each character has for the other must be real, the guilt Evy feels must be real—her purpose is "to test her daughter's decision"—and then the joke works. It is "set up," as the phrase is. Unfortunately, in a half-hour sitcom nowadays, which is built less on "situation" and more on a series of generic funny lines vaguely wrapped around a single premise, the writers would feel the above dialogue takes too long to set up one joke, so they would take the same situation and, instead of one belly laugh, like the above, put in three weak gags:

EVY

Mother, heh? Some mother… When am I here? [Polly grimaces; LAUGH] I'm out all day doing absolutely nothing. [Polly interjects something like "Nothing is better than something in your case!" LAUGH] I saw you more when you didn't live with me. [Polly responds with "Good! Then it'll mean I can be on my own a lot more." To which Evy takes a pause to react, and says in a warning tone, "Oh no you don't, young lady!" LAUGH]

And on and on, watering down the original conflict until it is far less emotional, less realistic, and less clever. Today's sitcom humor is all made up of wisecracks and putdowns.

One word of warning: There are some people, and they are very rare, who seem to have been born without a sense of humor. And those people really shouldn't touch comedy. They don't or cannot see what is funny about a situation and often don't get the joke.

On one sitcom once, the producer asked me if I had any well-known students who might be suitable guest stars. I suggested one who had been a famous supermodel and was now an aspiring actress. "Can she do comedy?" she asked.

"Well, she's pretty good," I replied. "She is still a student, but I could be there on the set to coach her through the scenes."

"Oh? You coach comedy?"

I stopped and thought a moment, then I said, "Well, yes. I have coached actors in works by the great comedy writers like Molière and Shakespeare and Oscar Wilde and Noel Coward, and even Neil Simon, Bruce Jay Friedman, and Elaine May."

The producer looked at me quizzically, not knowing quite what I was talking about. "Oh!" I said, as if the light had suddenly dawned. "You mean *sitcom*! Yes, I've coached that, too."

PART 2

Rehearsing on Your Own

INTRODUCTION

Developing the Process

||||||||||||||||||||||||||||||||||||||||||||||||||

In what may be an apocryphal anecdote, the great American actress Helen Hayes was once asked by the brilliant director Joshua Logan, who believed in the Stanislavsky System, to do homework. She drew herself up to her full short height and said indignantly, "Homework? I should do homework?" She was one of the very few who perhaps did not need to do homework on a role, but most of us need to do a lot of homework, as much as time permits! And there must be very few actors who do not enjoy doing homework in any case.

What do you do when you get hired for a film or television role, and find that there is no real rehearsal? How do you build a character with integrity in such circumstances? The main purpose of this book is to answer that question, and to show you how to achieve the satisfying performance you want. Part 2 describes the ideal rehearsal period, which includes a reasonable amount of time for the actor to develop and build a character, and part 3 offers advice on condensing the process for work in today's media.

In this section of the book I suggest steps to develop and build a character in the most organic order; one flows naturally into the other, and they all work together. These eleven steps are the ideal way to develop a character, in ideal circumstances. And for film and television, when you have only a little time in which to work on them—on your own, with no official rehearsal—they can be condensed in time and gone through more quickly.

The order of the steps evolved out of my work with students in the fifteen years I taught technique classes. I assigned improvisations, which were exercises in a graduated sequence leading up to scene study. Everything in the improvisation was to be planned except for the dialogue and the events; in other words, place, circumstances, objectives (conflict), and relationship were all agreed upon by the students in advance. It was not my aim to teach improvisation by itself, but instead to use the form to solve problems in written scenes.

Alone at first, the student performed a familiar task in a familiar place, with a full set of circumstances (where he or she came from, the time and day, and where he or she was headed). The goal was to create privacy by knowing where you were and by having an objective, in this case a physical one. You had to know why you were doing whatever you were doing at this particular time. Then I added a partner to the space with his or her own physical task and an agreed-upon factual relationship. The acting partners could be brothers, brother and sister, friends, lovers, husband and wife, roommates, sisters, or strangers, but with no further qualifying judgmental facts about the relationship, such as that it was friendly, loving, or hateful. The goal here was for them to work together in the same place and time, and experience their relationship by simply being in each other's presence, without preconceived judgments. The reason for this is that all relationships in a play or screenplay should be given the opportunity to grow into the friendships or enmities that may be indicated in the material. In other words, you have to know who your fellow actors are before you feel free to kiss them or slap them.

Up until this point, the exercises were silent for the most part. Although speech was not restricted, the emphasis in the exercise was on the physical life, and little would have to be spoken. In the following weeks, I added the conflict, which required words, of course. At first, one of the acting partners was to need something from the other; and I followed that up with both partners needing something from each other, and each partner unwilling to accede. In other words, the conflict was set up so that each individual had an objective while simultaneously being an "obstacle" to the other. Their physical tasks at this time became secondary to the main conflict.

To these planned exercises, over the next few weeks, I added (1) *inner objects*, which are people or events not present but in one's mind; (2) room conditions, such as light, dark, smells, or being quiet; and (3) physical conditions, such as being in a hurry, or having aches and pains. At this point we worked on what Uta Hagen called "muscular memory."

As a brilliant alternative to the original Stanislavsky exercises for using sense memory, Uta believed that what you do muscularly to alleviate a physical condition causes the desired sensations. At the same time, this is controlled by the actor, and will prevent the physical condition from taking over the scene. To use "muscular memory," you should, while alone and undistracted: (1) think of a time when you had the physical condition that is required in the scene; (2) pinpoint where you were most affected (if you had a headache, for example, was it hurting most on top of your head, on either temple, or elsewhere?); (3) describe as best you can what it felt like (pounding, shooting pains, throbbing), and (4) ask yourself what you did to relieve it.

The last step is "muscular," such as internally "pulling away from the pain," or "pushing up against it" or "staying over or under it" in your imagination: I am sick to my stomach, and it feels like something is rumbling in there: if I push up against it, that act alleviates the rumbling. How often have we seen an actor "playing drunk," rather than trying to sober up? But if, when drunk, you are feeling sleepy and your eyelids are heavy, you can re-create the sensation by pushing up against your "drooping" lids, and you can try to walk steadily and carefully. If you are hot, as you would be in any Tennessee Williams play, you can tell yourself "I feel hot and I can feel my clothing sticking to me. I can pull away from my clothes, and that will help alleviate the unpleasant sensations."

When you are preparing for an entrance, review the steps you take to create and then to alleviate the suffering caused by a specific condition, which should cause the sensations you want without your having to be continually conscious of them—and without the condition becoming what the scene is about.

After physical conditions, I asked the students to add emotional states, such as being joyous or depressed. Since all of the inner objects, physical conditions, and emotional states had to be justified through added circumstances, for emotional states I suggested imagining an event or circumstances that have nothing to do with the conflict, but that could create an emotional state of being, such as winning the lottery (joy) or hearing about the death of a near one (grief). Just as with physical conditions, emotional conditions (or states of being) cannot and should not take over the scene. They are conditioning forces only and will affect behavior accordingly, fluctuating in intensity just as sensations do in life. Scenes are never about "how I feel" but rather about "what am I doing." Near the end of the term, I had the students add the use of *endowments* and, finally, *substitutions*—thinking of people and events from their personal lives, which served to deepen the relationship and create a particular or characteristic behavior pattern.

In the final two weeks of Technique I, I would assign a written scene from a play, to be performed at first as an improvisation and then as a fully learned scene. What I wanted the students to understand was that the written dialogue was the result of all the elements they had been studying—place, circumstances, relationship, conditions, and conflict. And they also learned that although dialogue or stage directions give information, the actor should never jump to conclusions based on that information until after having explored what was beneath the dialogue, in the subtext. The students also had a choice of scenes so that they could do what interested them, although they generally left the choice up to me.

Fifteen years of teaching this program to my beginning technique students evolved into this book's logical, step-by-step approach, practically and philosophically based in the Stanislavsky System, to analyzing and breaking down any script with the aim of building a character. Nowadays, in my advanced scene study classes, I give my students a way to re-hearse their scenes, in the form of a printed Rehearsal Guide, which I go over with them in class. The following process of rehearsal mirrors the longer process of a full-length play, but is condensed in time. The students are asked to prepare five-minute scenes, which they rehearse for five one-hour sessions after having read the play first. The students do not direct each other, ever—any more than actors in professional pro-ductions that are under the supervision of a director are sup-posed to direct each other (but some do anyway, often to the great discomfort and annoyance of their acting partners).

1. In the first rehearsal, the student actors discuss the play and talk about its story and its themes. They then label the scene by where it occurs in the story: this is the scene where he proposes marriage; this is the scene where they decide to get divorced. Simply put, the scene can be labeled a meet-ing scene, a parting scene, a love scene, a fight scene, and so forth. The idea is for them to agree to be "on the same page."

After discussing the play and labeling the scene, the stu-dents then read the scene aloud to each other, sitting at a comfortable distance so that they will talk in a normal tone of voice, and not whisper or mumble. They begin to build a re-lationship to each other by looking up from the page at each other as much as possible. They simply tell their lines to each other and listen to the lines told to them, with no obligation to "act them out." Rather, they should treat the lines as "information" to be passed on to each other. I suggest to my students that all personal pronouns (I, me, my, you, your, yours) are to be taken personally. In other words, I mean *myself* and *yourself* when I say these words. This is called a *first reading*, and they can do as many "first readings" as they wish, using exactly the technique just described; but, of course, because of a growing familiarity with the text each time, it will be easier for them to look up at each other and to communicate with more than just the words each time they do it.

The dynamic of the first reading is always the basis from which to read dialogue from the printed page to your acting partner, or, in the case of auditions, to the reader (see page 85). The main goal ought to be the simple communication of the sensitive information that is in the given lines. With each reading, the references beneath the dialogue (inner objects, your own instincts as to the character's objective, etc.) grow richer and the meanings of the exchanges become more personal. I have been to hundreds of first readings where, if I shut my eyes, I could see the entire scene, just as if I had been listening to a radio play, except that the actors were not "acting," but instead focusing their attention on building a relationship with the person or persons with whom they were reading.

In a non-directed scene for class, the students begin to work on the relationship without yet making choices as to subtext. The students do as many readings of the scene as time permits in the first half of the one-hour session. From the beginning, they are aware of the inner objects that may exist in the text (see step 3). Also as part of this first scene rehearsal, the first attempt at the objectives for each character will be defined (see step 4). In the second half-hour, further decisions will begin to be made as well regarding the place, the circumstances of time (past, present, and future), the prior relationship of the two characters, and the activities (see steps 5, 6, and 7).

After this first rehearsal session and before the second one, the student is asked to make a simple character background chart (see step 8).

2. In the second rehearsal session, which most students find to be the most difficult one, the students set up the physical place and bring in the "props" so they can try to do the activities previously decided on. They continue to work on the relationship and the inner objects as they move physically through the scene. Blocking is not an issue, nor is picking up cues. The students may lose their way and stop and start. I tell the class that this step in the process mimics that very awkward time during early rehearsals for a play, when the actors, still holding their books and not yet familiar with the physical place, are directed to move around, handling props, if they have them, while still trying to keep in touch with the other actors and listen for their cues. It is an unavoidable hurdle. The session concludes with another first reading, as described above.

3. In the third rehearsal session, the scene is divided into three equal parts (a minute and a half to two minutes). While continuing to work on the relationship, the inner objects, and the activities, the students rehearse the first part until they feel comfortable enough with it, and can add the second and then the third parts. They then rehearse the entire scene. During the whole of the process so far, the students have not memorized their lines and are still holding their books, even while doing activities. Some lines may actually begin to stick in their memories by now. But there is no necessity for cold memorization or cramming lines, and the layering of the scene in three parts, building up to its climax, should help the students learn the lines as responses to their partners, and is also at the basis of the scoring process (see page 117). The procedure of layering described is to be used for the third and fourth rehearsals and can be done in each session more than once. After having worked through the entire scene twice,

the students can start with the first part again, and continue building the scene this way for as long as time allows.

4. In the fourth session, the students use the same procedure as in the third. But in this rehearsal, I ask them to put the books down somewhere on the "set," and only refer to them if and when they do not remember the lines. Blocking will have begun to form spontaneously, but the student is not obliged to set it; it may be allowed to change in a spontaneous way. And the activity, which is the secondary, physical life, will fluctuate—that is, the activity may or may not be completely done each time. The student may stop or start the activity based on his or her impulses during the moment-to-moment conflict. The activity is secondary, and it may or may not get done, but the student is *always* occupied with the ever-deepening primary objective.

As part of their homework after the second, third, and fourth rehearsals, the students look over their chosen objective and determine if it is changing or has changed because of deeper understanding of the conflict in the relationship (see step 4).

5. In the fifth and final session before the scene is presented in class, the students have a "dress rehearsal," rehearsing the scene as many times as possible. Any questions about choices will be saved for class.

These five one-hour rehearsals for a five- or six-minute scene for class can be likened to three weeks of rehearsal for a complete play. In the media, you have much less time than that at your disposal. In television, you have to make quick decisions because of various limitations not only in time but also in what is required of you in the way of instant and stereotypically written characterizations. Nevertheless, you will want to work on the script using an orderly procedure, as described in depth in the steps presented below in part 2. In part 3 we'll look at how you can use those steps to create a character when your rehearsal period is short, or even non-existent.

First, however, we'll examine some concepts you'll use during the process of preparation: impulses, instincts, concentration, relaxation, substitution, and endowment.

Impulses and Instincts

When you build, first the situation and then the character—which is the process the following steps take you through—you are relying to begin with on your instincts and impulses. All your choices should be based on those very instincts and impulses, which are then refined, defined, and noted down.

Actors are often afraid of "being in their heads" and learning too much about the craft of acting, which is a misconception. Without understanding and definition, inspiration vanishes. In fact, if you choose to know nothing and to do no work on the character, once you start performing, whether it is on stage or in front of a camera, you are inevitably going to be in your head a lot, since you will have to fill in the blanks while you are under the pressure of being observed, and not in the privacy and safety of your own living room or the rehearsal studio.

Moreover, when you make correct decisions at the proper time, what you have decided will be "forgotten" and woven into your performance. But if you have never made choices, you will be trying to make them while you are performing, in front of the audience or the camera, and it will be too late. It may seem like a paradox, but rehearsing thoroughly, analyzing the script, and making all the necessary decisions actually creates spontaneity and leaves ample room for inspiration. Herbert Berghof used to say, "You choose your objectives, one, two, and three, so that number four will be inspired!" It is only the untrained actors, the amateurs, who fear that making decisions about their performances would be too "intellectual." The only thing to beware of when making decisions is not to make them too early in the process, before your instincts are awakened out of your growing familiarity with the material.

Even the mere act of jotting down what you intuit is the cause, or the hidden objective, for what happens in the scene can actually get *more* of your creative juices flowing. There are those actors who feel they don't really have much imagination or impulses or instincts, until they discover that the process of making choices helps to enliven all three.

But what is an instinct? What are impulses? An instinct comes from your deepening sense of the character you are playing, of what the character might or might not be inclined to do. These instincts about the character and about yourself as the character arise from your growing understanding as you explore the script. You will have an instinct, for instance, regarding facts about the character's background, if they are not supplied by the author. You will be using your instincts when defining your character's traits. You have instincts about the character's objectives. All sorts of instincts about the character will occur during each step, related to what makes the character tick and what motivates him or her.

An impulse, on the other hand, is the spontaneous feeling that arises and makes you want to do something—to move someplace, to sit or stand up—at a specific moment during rehearsal. It is a momentary sense—a whim, if you will, or an urge—that something has to happen at a certain moment in the situation you are in, and it is usually based in logic. Something is telling you to get closer or farther away from the other person.

I agree with Uta Hagen, who believed that sometimes, if the script dictates a particular action and you find you have no impulse to do it, you should go on and do it anyway. You can't just stand around waiting for the proper inspiration when you are in rehearsal. The feeling and the understanding may just come along with the doing.

In the theater, even on evenings or at matinees when you

don't feel like doing a performance, as soon as you get out there on stage, you will be on "automatic pilot." The performance that you have thoroughly prepared in rehearsal has become part of you and it takes over. This doesn't mean that you are not there every moment, navigating, and focusing all your energy on the other characters and physical activities. But just by hearing or otherwise sensing your cue, you should automatically have the will to do the action that you have rehearsed and, at the same time, to allow it to be filled with the emotion, as well. Your performance has become "reflexive," à la Pavlov, if you will. And if there is some sort of interruption in your concentration, such as a piece of scenery falling down or a light that doesn't come on, or a cell phone ringing or someone coughing in the audience, you will be able to "recover." (See "Concentration and Relaxation," which follows.)

I often point out to my students the title of a play by John Van Druten, *I Am a Camera* (upon which the musical and movie *Cabaret* are based) as an apt description of the actor's ultimate experience on stage. When you make a film, you are in front of the camera, but when you are on stage you are indeed the camera: whatever you are focused on, you want the audience to be focused on as well. In other words, your intention should be to draw the audience's attention not to your own person so much as to the objects you are concentrating on. In this way, you are indirectly directing the audience, and they are with you every step of the way.

Working in *front* of the camera, needing to rehearse all alone, the actor requires sharp instincts and an immediate sense of what is between the lines and what the scene objective might be, because he or she will be given no time to experiment or to reach the point where the performance is on automatic pilot. Moves and physical positions will for the most part be dictated by the mechanical requirements of the camera, the set, and the shooting script. Here, the actor cannot move on a whim. The actor works in short spurts, "accumulating" his or her performance (see page 215). Yet, as in the theater, the actor must be committed to living moment to moment, and to making a full and personal interpretation of the character.

Concentration and Relaxation

I was never taught to separate concentration or relaxation from the work on the text and the character, and I do not advocate doing so. Concentration on stage requires knowing all the given circumstances, and personally and logically choosing the rest. Only if the actor has purpose and reasons behind his actions is she or he able to concentrate on the task at hand. If you do something only for the sake of doing it, by rote, or just to obey the direction given you, it will be very hard to sustain your concentration more than a few times through the scene. And without concentration the actor's work is non-specific, general, and vague; it hardly reaches beyond the footlights.

Concentration can only be attained and maintained if you are involved in the actions, both physical and psychological; and the actor's involvement requires purpose and reasoning behind the actions. The same thing holds true for lines learned by rote: I've observed many times how lines that are memorized without the sort of work I am describing here quickly disappear from the actor's mind.

If concentration fails you on stage due to an unanticipated event, which can (and will) happen, such as a disturbance in the audience, or some technical failure, such as a light not going on when it is supposed to, or a bell going off on the wrong cue, you have to find a way to "recover." If you panic, it will only prolong the lapse of concentration, and make it more difficult to get back on track.

There is an old theater legend attributed to Josephine Hull, the veteran character actress: She and the ingénue were on stage when the telephone rang by mistake, because the stage manager had inadvertently placed his elbow on the buzzer. The actors froze on the spot, and, after a long and agonizing moment, Ms. Hull jauntily walked over to the telephone, picked up the receiver, listened for a moment, and announced to the petrified ingénue, "It's for you, dear!"

For lapses in concentration, I teach a modified version of a Michael Chekhov exercise, "the circle of concentration." When an interruption occurs and it becomes necessary to bring yourself back into the place and the moment of the play, Chekhov talks about imagining yourself as the center of an ever-diminishing circle that at first is large enough to include the entire theater and gradually shrinks in size until you are the only thing in the circle. At that point, the actor should have all his concentration on the situation he is living in the play. This seemed to me something that would require many, many hours of practice beforehand. Looking for something more practical, I experimented with another exercise: I guided my students to focus instead on what was directly in front of them, in their line of vision, and to speculate about it, bringing their full attention for the moment to it.

When my students' concentration fails due to a disturbance or a missed line—a common occurrence in the classroom—but they do not want to stop the scene, I tell them to look at their partner, or, if they are involved in a physical activity, to look at the object they are handling or at a piece of furniture, and to begin to speculate about its properties. They might wonder about its age, its strength or weakness, how much it is worth, and so forth and so on. If they are looking at the other actor, I would say, "Count her eyelashes." It is the only time on stage where you may consciously indulge in thinking, and in just a matter of seconds, you are back in the play! And you will probably have remembered your next line.

Of course, if interference occurs during a camera take, the director will call, "Cut," and recovery for the actor is not a challenge here. I have been on sets, however, when the actor, usually an inexperienced one, will cut the take himself because of a fumble or a failure in concentration. This can be extremely irritating to the director and/or the other actors.

I suggest instead that you attempt to "recover" through conscious speculation, and simply continue with the take.

Relaxation is another very important part of the actor's craft that I do not advocate separating from the performance. It is a product of full concentration on whatever is occupying the character. As I have mentioned earlier, the actor is completely relaxed when he is fully occupied and involved in whatever he is doing. Even if you are supposed to be sleeping in a scene in a play or a movie, you must be actively involved. You must find a way to occupy the mind so as to allow the body to be inert for the time being. I suggest "dreaming" a simple scene—not a story, but perhaps a place from your memory. And then, on cue, think about a part of your body (probably the most uncomfortable part will come to mind), and then wake up. You will feel as though you had really been asleep.

Too often, I have witnessed student actors doing relaxation exercises (some of them very noisy) prior to a scene or an entrance, or even before an audition while in the waiting area. Then they arrive at the moment of beginning, and tense up! You will not be relaxed on stage or in front of the camera if you are not concentrated on the task in hand.

Of course, you certainly want to be relaxed before beginning a performance, and you want to be able to concentrate on what your preparation is, whether it's thinking about the previous circumstances of your character while getting into your makeup and wardrobe, or lying down. Sadly, I have felt victimized on occasion by noisy, sociable cast members in the dressing room. No doubt they mean well, but in such a situation, relaxation is hard to achieve. On a movie set, as well, the actor is continually bombarded by the hustle and bustle going on around him, and is constantly being approached by one or another of the department people from makeup or costumes or props. In such cases, you have to cordon off territory that is yours, and take your time to just sit quietly and think. You may need only moments, or at times you may want hours.

Classroom relaxation exercises, though, should remain in the classroom. In any case, I prefer another kind of preparation prior to a scene or exercise (see page 135). I recall teaching a class at the HB Studio, waiting with the class for a new student to appear from behind the curtains to do his exercise. After an inordinate amount of time, I sent a student to check on him, and the poor fellow had fainted in the middle of some sort of relaxation technique he had been taught!

Substitution and Endowment

One of the most important tools at your disposal is *substitution*, a replacement by the actor of people, places or things from the actor's own life that are analogous in some way to those in the script. You don't need to look for substitutions in the relationships immediately, although this is commonly and erroneously taught in some "method" classes. Only when the other character you are dealing with is a family member, should you use a substitution right away, and the choice should be someone from your own family. Since the dynamics that constitute interfamilial relationships are universal, your personal relationships with your own family will work for you whether you are working on *Death of a Salesman*, *Long Day's Journey into Night*, or *The Glass Menagerie*. The point here is the unique power of what my father used to call "blood relatives" to penetrate deeply into your psyche, to make you especially vulnerable, easily hurt, fiercely protective, or overly proud. The love/hate relationships found in all plays about parents and children, or siblings, require an immediate substitution so as to make the actor feel he or she has a more personal stake in the lines from the start. In plays of this sort, there is a familiarity the characters must have with each other, to the point of being able to predict almost what they will say or do next. Such substitutions will give you permission to react to the other characters in the many complex ways that families do. It is also true that the familial relationships you choose don't have to parallel directly the

ones in the play. Those actors who are only children can substitute one of their parents (perhaps from a period in their
younger life) for a sibling; or one can substitute a sibling for
an absent parent.

However, in other types of onstage relationships, you don't
need to look for substitutions immediately. Many times substitutions will come about naturally or be "chosen" unconsciously (see page 68). It is better to save substitution for near
the end of the rehearsal process, when you know what you
want to feel more of: love, hate, bitterness, anger or joy; or
when you want to feel freer with some behavior: making up
after a quarrel, fighting, loving, and so forth.

The technique of substituting consists of the following
steps:

1. Choose the person, place, or thing from your past that you want
   to use.
2. Imagine that the other character, place, or object is the one from
   your past experience, and begin to behave accordingly. Replace
   the person you are relating to in the script with someone you
   are vulnerable to. As a substitution for place, you might imagine
   yourself in your old bedroom. To replace the given situation with
   one from another time, you might relive the traumatic day your
   family moved when you were a child.
3. Be surprised how "changed" or "different" the character, place, or
   object you are substituting has become. This is to insure that you
   are not trying to "see" the past object but are committed to relating to the one before you right now. If you have substituted your
   brother for the other character, for example, marvel at the way
   he is relating to you as if he were the other character who, in the
   play, is your roommate, and older, and a woman, who wants you
   to do this or that!
4. Once a substitution has been chosen, and you have rehearsed
   with it and feel that it works, it will be "forgotten," and the person,
   place, or situation in the play should now be invested with the
   desired emotional value.

Substitutions also can be chosen from the actor's imagination, rather than her or his past, or they might be drawn from the actor's memory of a film or novel or short story, or from politics or public figures. For instance, if you have to hate the other character—a particularly powerful emotion—you might use some hated political demagogue who arouses your anger every time he or she appears on television. To use Herbert Berghof's words, if any choice is "hot and cooking," it will be integrated into the fabric of your performance and will always be there for you, even after you no longer recall what it was.

When you *endow* a person, place, or thing, you view and treat the person, place, or thing "as if" it possessed an additional quality or qualities that are not actually there, but that exist only in your imagination: my partner is bald, or naked, or is dressed in a clown suit, or is a member of the Nazi party. The room is filled with insects, or newly painted, or reeks of garlic. These "additions" are there to inspire certain behavior on the part of your character.

Objects very often require endowments on stage: tea that is supposed to be whiskey, a cup of soup that is supposed to be hot, or an actual fire in the fireplace, or heat coming from the stove. How many times have you seen an actor pick up what is supposed to be a packed suitcase, and you just know there is nothing in it, because he has not endowed it with the weight it should have? As a matter of fact, all of acting is endowment, because all of acting is "as if": as if this place were my place; as if this story were my story; as if I were in a certain place at a certain time; as if I were living through the character's life moment by moment; as if each moment were happening for the first time; and as if I were the character.

Remember: Whether you use endowments, which are partial imaginary investments of qualities in an object, or substitutions, which are complete replacements of objects, these choices do not change anything in the objects themselves. But they make *you* more vulnerable, and are used solely to free your behavior in a particular way. For instance, you may have to fall in love or in hate with the other actor, or dissolve into tears at the sight of someone or something. The choice of an endowment or a substitution is a way to bring this about.

By the way, how often have you heard a wife in a sitcom or film (or maybe your next-door neighbor) screaming at her husband, "I am not your mother"? We tend in life to project feelings that we have toward our parents or siblings or other people from our past experience onto current relationships. This is something that is usually unconscious, and that we would actually rather not do. In acting, however, we choose to do so, in order to achieve the feeling we are looking for.

Impulses and instincts, concentration and relaxation, substitutions and endowments are the fundamental requirements for the art of acting in our time, but they in themselves do not lead you to becoming the character, your ultimate destination. The following eleven steps are the building blocks.

CHAPTER 4

Step 1: How to Read the Script

IIIIIIIIIIIIIIIIIIIIIIIIIIIIIIIIIIIIIIIIIIIIIIIIIIIIIIIII

When you read any play, screenplay, or television script for the first time, read it from beginning to end just for the story. You need to know how your character fits in as a cog in the wheel and a mover of the plot. You also have to understand the network of relationships among all the characters, as well as the nature of those relationships. And you need to know the beginning and end in order to know what you are doing in the middle. (This is why soap opera is a kind of non-acting situation: you are always in the middle; there is no beginning and no end.) If you don't know the story's conclusion, how would you ever know what a character really wants, which may be different from what he or she seems to want at the beginning?

When beginning your work on a script, the first thing you have to know is whether it is a comedy, a drama, a melodrama, a tragedy, or an abstract absurdist piece, like the plays of Samuel Beckett or Ionesco. Sometimes I will see a scene in class, and realize that the students did not know what kind of play they were doing. "I didn't know this was a serious drama!" I will say. "I thought Neil Simon wrote comedies. Isn't this by Neil Simon? You don't get the gags. You have to develop the skill to see the jokes, and to know what a punch line is, besides being able to read between the lines."

Even comedians can't always read a comedy. I inevitably get into squabbles with standup comics while coaching them for sitcom pilots. They often refuse to see the humor in somebody else's writing. I say to them, "I understand your point of view. I know you're funnier, but this is the comedy that the producers want to tape."

You also must know if the play is contemporary or from another period, and if it is written in a style that you will eventually have to explore. Is the play from the realist or naturalist school of drama, or is it a romance or a fantasy set in some mythical place, like James M. Barrie's *Peter Pan?* The kind of play and the school of writing and period it comes from will make a difference in how you begin to interpret it and end up performing it. All material requires you to make a commitment to its style—embodied in your character's behavior—and the musicality of its language, which will become organic as you do the work necessary to personalize the material.

While classical plays are rich in style and language, and have no subtext—what is underneath the words that gives them intention and personal meaning—because the poetry says it all, modern plays, from Ibsen on, contain subtext, which is psychological and is more or less hidden between the lines. Sometimes modern plays are written with individual language and style, such as those of Clifford Odets, David Mamet, Tennessee Williams, or Harold Pinter. Movie and television scripts, on the other hand, are devoid of both most of the time. The actor has to search hard and long to find subtext in them, and their style is formulaic. Their language, which may be minimal, is ephemeral and subject to constant change anyway while in production.

For movie and television auditions, actors are often given only "sides," or pages excerpted from the script that contain only the scene(s) they will be reading for the casting director and/or the producers and director. In some cases, if you're lucky, you will be given the whole script. With sides, you have to do a lot of guesswork about what has happened before the scene and what will happen afterwards. You will therefore always be at a disadvantage in this situation. But you will want, if possible, to be able to make good educated guesses.

If you have done a lot of plays, or worked on many scenes in class, you will have achieved a background and you will have references to rely on. One very good reason for taking classes, and for reading a lot of plays, is to develop such frames of reference, and to be able to take those educated guesses. I always enjoy the amazement in my students' faces when I "guess" what the rest of the play or screenplay is about from a scene or two. But then, as somebody said—nobody knows who—there are only seven plots under the sun. Nowadays, in the era of genres—action-adventure, science fiction, horror, romantic comedy, crime—there may be even fewer.

I don't agree with the multitude of schools that believe that acting can be taught with dull or mediocre pieces of writing. What the acting student needs instead are the inspiration and the revelations that can only be found in good and great plays, old and new. I am vehemently opposed to the classes today that assign movie scenes and television episodes for the students to prepare. As Herbert Berghof shouted at us many years ago, "Just because there are gangsters out there doesn't mean I have to teach you how to rob a bank!" Since there is no substance or subtext in most film or virtually any television material, the student will need the references he can gather from great plays when he is lucky enough to get an audition for a job on television, and is handed the minimally written script. And, if he is lucky enough to land the job, he will also need the practice and training, or else he will arrive on a set that is always pressured for time and, without any rehearsal or substantive direction, will merely "act" his role, which he is often required to do in exactly the same way he did it at the audition. For many actors, this can be very unfulfilling, to say the least.

Those classes in "instant acting" where actors are given

only two or three pages to work on at home, or even asked to step out of class for a few minutes and then come back in, do a real disservice to actors. The real lesson of such misguided teaching is the wrong one: the actor really doesn't have to know what went before or what will come after. All he or she has to know is how to interpret the give and take that is right there on those pages, and to do them "naturally." This is of no help to actors who want to create characters—in other words, to actors who want to act.

If, in one of those "instant acting" classes, the students are given a simply written scene, with no scene leading up to it or any scene following it, what happens in the scene's subtext is left to guesswork. For instance, in an ordinary date scene, two people who are strangers meet in a restaurant on a first date. The conversation is polite and friendly, with bits and pieces of their past history as exposition. There is nothing in the script that reveals how they feel about each other or about how the date is going. Typical! Just as in life, a first date can be filled with nervousness and stress arising from the desire to impress the other person, and from worrying about whether you are failing or succeeding. And this is all mixed in with your negative or positive impressions of the other person. The subtext consists of intense speculation, of an interior monologue that each person is going through.

But if you had the entire screenplay or play, then you would know how the meeting was arranged in the first place, or if it is a chance encounter. You would even know where the relationship ends up—and all of this information would help you create a meaningful subtext for the scene. For instance, if there were high hopes and excitement in the arrangement for the meeting scene, this could lead to a subtext of letdown and disappointment. Or, if there was a great deal of anxiety or even paranoia about the date beforehand, these facts could inspire a subtext of surprise and relief. Of course, things can turn out as expected, but it is more common for things to be different than anticipated—and this is more interesting for actors to play.

If you know that the couple eventually marries, then that knowledge will intensify your positive speculations about each other, and lead both of you to feel the electricity between the characters during the date scene. But if the date scene turns out to be the first and last time these people see each other, that might mean that during the date one or both characters are indifferent, bored, or just turned off. In other words, knowing how the characters begin and how they end dictates what to play in the moment.

There may be many variations to play when you are analyzing or interpreting any one scene, but they had better add up to the resolution of the play as a whole.

In a play or screenplay, the seeds for the success or disaster of a relationship can be found in the first meeting of any two people. I only wish this were as easy to determine in life itself.

In William Gibson's two-character play, *Two for the Seesaw*, Jerry and Gittel are alien beings to one another. He comes from Nebraska: "That's out in California, isn't it?" asks Gittel on their first date. She was born and bred in the Bronx, New York. They barely understand each other's language, but Jerry is needy and homeless at this point in his life, having left his wife and career, and Gittel is the all-around nurturing type—what used to be referred to as the Jewish girl with the chicken soup. What a great match, and, at the same time, what seeds for disaster! Yet each actor must play out the first meeting scene with increasing interest and attraction to the other, and with high hopes coming from a void that they each feel in their lives. Then they must struggle mightily throughout the play to overcome the obstacles that were painfully apparent in the beginning, until the ultimate failure at the end. It is a play with a great many laughs that ends in tears.

I played Gittel once, and I remember feeling stuck at the beginning of rehearsals, because I couldn't get it out of my head that my character was going to let herself get badly hurt by letting Jerry into her life. I wanted to warn her, and I thought, how can I be so foolish? I remember vividly calling my good friend Bill Hickey to ask for his advice. "Where are you?" he asked. "Baltimore," I replied. "What are you doing about your kids and your classes?" he went on. I then told him about my complicated arrangements: my mother and mother-in-law were going to take turns babysitting the children when their father was working, and I had rescheduled my classes at HB Studio so that, once I began playing, I could commute between the theater and home, and also make up the classes I would have missed. "Isn't that going to be difficult for you?" he asked, "Why are you going to all that trouble?" I was taken aback. "Bill," I replied, "how can you ask that? I want to act!" There was a pause, and then I heard him say, "Well, Gittel wants Jerry!" I hung up the phone knowing I couldn't have gotten a better note.

To make my point more clearly: actors will arrive at a deeper and more emotional performance if they question their characters' motives, *only* after having read the whole play!

Sometimes, the actors may receive only sides even after they have been cast. Woody Allen, for instance, is famous for not revealing the entire plot of his films to most of the actors in them. But he knows what he wants, and he knows how to get it. And he will take care of a great deal in the editing process later on. He has also been known to rewrite, recast and re-shoot after the initial production is done. Still, how can the actors know what their characters really want, if they haven't been able to read the script?

I had parts in a few of Mr. Allen's movies. For *Another Woman* (1988), I recall how a group of well-known actors and myself had received pages of a scene that were mostly blank. Each page might have had a line or two in the middle and maybe a line at the end. We were on location in New Jersey, and in our dressing area the half-dozen of us who were playing party guests in this particular scene went around the room trying to coordinate the pages and to guess who was responding to whom. It was amusing, but harrowing at the same time. There was no way at all to prepare our little gabfests. We simply had to rely on Woody to put us in position, and then explain to us the relationships he wanted.

All films are, in part, improvisations; the director and/or writer and sometimes the actors themselves rewrite from day to day. Screenplays go through three major transformations:

1. In *pre-production*, numerous drafts are written and revised until the final shooting script is settled on.
2. During *production*, due to many different circumstances, including unforeseen ones, such as weather and location changes, there are quite a few rewrites.
3. In *post-production*, during the editing process, the scenes can be changed around or cut out; further shooting may be required to bring together the final cut.

This list shows you the very nature of the art of filmmaking—and this is another reason I don't feel screenplays are good material for scene study classes, except perhaps for the works of such master writer/directors as Billy Wilder, Ingmar Bergman, or Joseph L. Mankiewicz, whose writing could almost be transferred to the stage.

There is a skill to reading a play, because everything—story, themes, and characters—is all in the form of dialogue. There is no narrative, as there is in a short story or a novel, to describe for you what is happening or how someone is feeling, and to clarify what might otherwise be obscure. A novelist can describe a character's thoughts or motivations, but in a script you have to deduce them. Nobody is simply leading you through the plot; you have to take yourself through the labyrinth of the story. You have to envision what is not being described, and it is up to you to imagine what actions are taking place. In short, you have to get used to a literary form in which you will eventually have to do a lot of detective work in order to figure out your character's motives.

Finding the Themes

So you have to read a play for the plot, well and good; and you have to be aware of the period and the style of language in it. But you also have to read it for the themes. In other words, what is the author saying? Why has he or she written this play? When you read a script, you must look beyond and beneath the plot to see what the author is saying about the characters, and what themes they embody. There may be more than one thing that inspired the play, but the first theme you want to find is the main, overall message.

I got into many an argument about "messages" on some movies I coached, and especially movies made for television, as you can imagine. The producers and the network would often have the attitude, "If you want to send a message, use Western Union!" But it is my firm belief that all plays and movies send a message, and in the commercial world we live in, it is usually the wrong one: Make money!

Before play rehearsals begin, it is much too early to make hard and fast decisions about your performance. But searching for the theme can provide inspiration for all the hard work that follows. For instance, you might conclude that the theme of Shakespeare's *Hamlet* is "crime does not pay," nor does a compulsion to avenge the crime. This can help set you on the tragic path to self-destruction that Hamlet takes as he brings all the other characters down with him. In Arthur Miller's *Death of a Salesman*, the dominant theme is that the American dream of success can elude a man, and that an obsession with this dream will lead not only to painful rifts in the hero's family but also to suicide. Knowing this theme will help the actors to be aware of the cloud of failure that hangs over every scene. In Ibsen's *A Doll's House*, the theme of inequality between the sexes, which in this case destroys a marriage and breaks up a family, has inspired every generation of stage and film actresses since the play was first produced to want to tell the story.

It is true that most produced screenplays today often lack any kind of depth where important issues are concerned. And, although television scripts have more dialogue than screenplays, they usually have even less to say, since television programming must avoid controversy in order to appeal to the widest audience. In any case, the themes of a script, if you can discern them, will tell you a great deal about the character you are playing, and how and where you fit into the story. And they can even help you make the choices you need to play the part.

It is also true—and this is a common experience for most of the successful actors I come across—that when you get to work on plays that have substance and depth and are thematically interesting, you will be experiencing a rare privilege in today's mass-media-dominated world. Recently, a television program was devoted to the one hundred most inspiring movies ever made. During interviews with the directors and particularly with the surviving cast members you could feel their joy at having had the opportunity to be a part of such stories as *It's a Wonderful Life*, *To Kill a Mockingbird*, and *Casablanca*.

Even though you will follow the same steps outlined here when you work in movies and television, the experience is generally less rewarding—except perhaps to your bank account. But if you have had the experience of working on great material, you will be that much further ahead when you work on lesser scripts. You will find it easier to speculate on the character's past life, priorities, motives, and relationships, because you will have a wealth of material to draw on.

Finding the Playwright's Music

Very importantly, you must also read a script with the idea of attuning yourself to the playwright's music, to the cadences, rhythms, and melodies of the playwright's language. And you can begin to do this right at the start.

Shakespeare, of course, is known for the musicality of his writing, for the relative ease of speaking in iambic pentameter, for his brilliant rhythms and original metaphors, and for coining English words as well. But all great and good authors write with an innate musical sense of their own, and in their own styles, with their own heightened, sometimes poetic prose—with their own *theater language*. Without understanding the music of a play, without having a feeling for it, it is very difficult for the actor to get into its subtext, or into what the character is doing and what relationships are being presented in the play, or even to understand what the theme of the play is.

I have found that American acting students, unlike their British counterparts who cut their teeth on Shakespeare, can have a tin ear when it comes to the music in contemporary plays: the lilting Irish-American melodies in Eugene O'Neill, the beat of the New York streets in Clifford Odets, the immigrant Jewish tunes in Neil Simon, the staccato Chicago rhythms of David Mamet, the gospel sounds of James Baldwin and August Wilson, and so forth. Not all American playwrights, but certainly the great ones, write with a musicality, as distinctly as Stephen Sondheim, Aaron Copland, and Leonard Bernstein compose music. Add to this list the music of nineteenth- and twentieth-century English and Irish writers, such as George Bernard Shaw, Oscar Wilde, Noel Coward, Harold Pinter, Tom Stoppard, Brian Friel, Martin McDonough, et al.

And Chekhov's music is second only to Shakespeare's, if the translator can only capture his tone and melody. Chekhov's musical language illuminates the pre-revolutionary Russian scene just as powerfully as do the compositions of Tchaikovsky; or as the compositions of Stravinsky and Rachmaninoff do the revolution's aftermath.

When current acting students overlook, ignore, or simply cannot hear the music in the language, the results are very unfortunate—wooden, stilted productions and awkward speaking of the lines, among other things. Part of this ignorance is due to developments in the 1950s, when American actors, under the influence of the Actors Studio, began to base their performances so heavily on their characters' psyches that often the playwright's intentions (as opposed to the actors'), and with them the playwright's "music," were obscured. Actors even developed an awful habit—still prevalent today—of paraphrasing the dialogue, or of adding words here and there! A familiar example: you often hear actors muttering the words "see," "look," or "listen," or the phrase "I mean," before every line; and, even worse, "yeah" and "dude."

Moreover, in the 1950s, a popular method of writing for some playwrights—for example, Michael Gazzo, Lanford Wilson, and, in England, Shelagh Delaney—was to bring tape recorders to rehearsals in order to capture what the actors said during improvisations, so as not to "put words in their mouths." Exploring these plays today is especially problematic for the acting student who is trying to define the character, because the dialogue is so peculiarly suited to the original actors in the original production! The actors in these cases created more or less a cacophony of voices, making the play an obstacle course for other actors who later on are trying to find a simple objective for the scene.

The playwright's music is served best with ensemble playing—all the actors raising their voices to create harmony and illuminate the theme—just as with an orchestral piece. Except for some regional theater companies, most American theater consist of casts of actors from diverse backgrounds, experience and training, very unlike the national theaters of older countries. As a result, audiences here are used to having to wend their way through actors' individual and uneven performances to find the play. And in the film world, it is rare these days that a director has his own company of actors, such as the great European filmmakers Ingmar Bergman and Federico Fellini had.

Sadly, the number of American actors with tin ears increases with each new generation. Much of this is due to the influence of television. The blunt and tuneless speech of the television series has so insinuated itself into our consciousness that actors are embarrassed to speak well, let alone listen to and enjoy speaking in an author's own heightened theater language. This is not necessarily true of British actors, many of whom enjoy language, and are well spoken and well trained in vocal arts.

A while back, I began a series of invitational scene readings with my advanced acting students. I devoted each of the evenings to a particular playwright—Shaw, Simon, Pinter, and Chekhov—or to a theme such as an evening of 1950s dramatists, melodrama, or American comedy writers from George S. Kaufman to the TV sitcom. During the brief rehearsals, I found myself forced into becoming a taskmaster of "line readings," and almost took to using a metronome, as some directors do, just to bring about the correct music inherent in the selected scenes. Because I was pounding away at them in this way, the students quickly developed precision, and a more energetic speech that delivered the playwrights' intentions. And, I might add, this sped up their progress in general.

Often, when I see a fine film performance by British actors, I am struck with how they cast a shadow over their American counterparts. The British actor takes account of the playwright's music, even if it is only movie dialogue, and can round out the character, often adding the missing dimension, and appears to be enjoying the process. We should do the same!

CHAPTER 5

Step 2: Developing the Relationships

||||||||||||||||||||||||||||||||||||||||||||||||||||

According to the Stanislavsky System, a character is built on the basic question, "Who am I?" But we cannot know the answer to that question until much later in the process. In fact, I think we must begin by asking another question, "Who are *they*?" Who are the other characters, and what is my relationship to them?

These are existential questions—that is, they are questions that have to do with the nature of our existence. In fact, the twenty-first-century actor, breaking away from the old concept of theatrical illustration, and intent on inhabiting the character instead, could benefit enormously from considering the uses of the philosophy called "existentialism."

In Herbert Berghof's favorite book, the dictionary, we are told that existentialism "holds that man exists as an individual in a purposeless universe, and that he must oppose his hostile environment through exercise of his free will." Man must give life meaning that it does not intrinsically have. And he must be "engaged"— committed to a course of action—and involved in his choices in life. He must live them. To be sure, this is a simplification of a complicated point of view, but as a place to begin, it holds a germ of truth that is useful to the actor.

Existentialism had several founders in a number of European countries, but for Americans it is most closely associated with its popularization in France by Jean-Paul Sartre (the author of *No Exit* and other plays) in the middle of the twentieth century, following the devastation and slaughter of the First and Second World Wars, when people were trying to understand how such horrors could have happened, and to find some sense of security, as well as some meaning in life.

Like humankind in the world, the actor starts out all alone in the universe of the play, until he first approaches the "who" and the "what" of everything that surrounds him. We are who we are, and we behave as we do because of outside stimuli, which we are compelled to respond to. As in life, who we are depends in part on the person whom we are with. You act one way with your mother, another way with your father, another with your friend, and so forth. To build a character in a play and breathe life into it, we must therefore begin with relationships.

If an actor has a preconception of a character—that is, a character image, an idea of the character's mentality or psychology, a mental concept of the way the character walks, talks, and sounds, before he has acknowledged the relationships—this preconception will only result in playing a one-dimensional stereotype, and not a three-dimensional person.

Although today's media pressures actors unmercifully into playing a preconceived character—a cliché—the actor must try to do whatever he can to avoid it! Nor should he be influenced by the character description given in the beginning of the play or screenplay, which is written for the reader only, and not for the actor about to begin his or her work.

But aren't plays written to be performed? What playwright envisions a reader as he or she writes? None other than George Bernard Shaw, who wrote long prefaces about his plays' settings and characters, and a multitude of stage directions that would drive any performer trying to follow them crazy. Shaw admitted that he was writing a "novel" for the reading public, and that his lengthy descriptions were not intended for theater artists. If you ever do a piece by Shaw, take him at his word. Enjoy the novel, but ignore it as stage directions.

On the other side of the Atlantic Ocean, Tennessee Williams described some of his characters in poetic prose. Blanche in *A Streetcar Named Desire*: ". . . something about her uncertain manner suggests a moth"; the young Alma in *Summer and Smoke*: "She has a habit of holding her hands, one cupped under the other in a way similar to that of receiving the wafer at Holy Communion"; Lady in *Orpheus Descending*: "She could be any age between thirty-five and forty-five . . . a woman met with emotional disaster in her girlhood; verges on hysteria under strain. . . ." These descriptions are beautifully written. But, aside from the fact that you cannot know what they mean without having examined the play, it is obviously impossible to try to embody them, nor can you achieve a character that fits them without understanding the character's relationship to his or her situation and to all the other characters. Character breakdowns given in audition material, especially for film and television, often consist only of a short synopsis of the characters' actions in the scene. These are of no help at all; if you replaced them with the words "blah blah blah," you would be just as far ahead in your understanding of the character. They are often badly written and laughably illogical: "Jane comes from a dirt-poor background, but she behaves as though she deserves everything." Does the author mean to say that because she is from a poor background, she deserves nothing? Or take this one: "Joey feels he is so far ahead of the cops and is by turns arrogant, self-pitying, defensive, stubborn and childlike." Obviously the description consists only of directions the producer wants you to follow, and is not really about Joey's character.

Any actor does himself the most good by ignoring such descriptions when beginning to work on a character. When you are well into your work, you can look back at them for further clues, and perhaps for corroboration, or they may mean nothing. Training and practice using a wide variety of good plays help the actor to research everything he or she needs to know, which is derived from the dialogue and the events of the script. And the actor's instincts will be sharpened, the imagination wide-ranging, and emotions readily available.

Your relationship to the other characters in the play is the first step in the search for your character. For instance, how do I really feel about my parents, siblings, spouse, or children? What is my relationship with them like? At first, the factual answers will be supplied in the script, and the personal nature of the relationships will grow in an organic way through the give and take with the other actors. Uta Hagen called this process *particularization*.

While you are using the other actors per se, and probably making unconscious substitutions, or have actually made a conscious substitution (see page 66), the relationship will grow with each rehearsal. The initial shyness or even coolness you may have felt in a relationship with a lover, for instance, will fade away, and you will one day find your heart beating when you look at him or her. This is not an uncommon experience, and the occupational hazard in this kind of case is obvious. In fact, you can read about it in the tabloids and hear about it on gossipy talk shows.

You must "surrender," which means giving yourself over to what you have found and chosen throughout rehearsal in order to eventually surrender emotionally. I had a strange experience once. I was playing the wife of an actor who was much older than I, and very cranky. All through rehearsals he was difficult to work with, and he even complained about me to the director. By the time the first preview came around, I believed that I actually hated him, which was not the appropriate feeling for my character. The play began with a scene with my daughter, and his entrance cue came up. Thank goodness the door was upstage, which meant that I had to turn my back to the audience, because I was sure that my resentment towards him would show on my face. The old man walked in, and I remember thinking such vile thoughts that a sudden surge of pity for him rose up in me. How could I hate him? He was actually a nice old man and a good actor. With this thought, which happened in a matter of seconds, I was able to run up to him and give him a kiss, as I had been directed to do, but with a very genuine feeling of compassion, if not love. If I had not permitted myself to feel the anger, I would never have found the affection.

First Readings

Building the relationships between you and your fellow actors begins with the first readings of the script aloud. You have to give your full attention to the sounds of the other actors' voices and to the expressions on their faces. And you must remember, too, that all dialogue is a response to stimuli. Regard all your lines of dialogue as simple responses to the other person's dialogue, and not as something isolated from them. Your own lines are there to evoke a response from the other actor, as well.

When, during coaching sessions, I sometimes marvel at a student's confusing "line readings," it is always because they did not really pay attention or listen to what their lines were in response to, but rather said them in a way that was in accord with their preconception of how the line should sound.

The first readings and all the subsequent uses of the dialogue are technically called the *give and take*—talking and listening, sending and receiving. You are never talking *at* the other actors but rather *to* them. William Hickey once said, "Never talk to the other actor's ears, but to his mind!" And I often say to my students, "You know, only one person—the playwright—wrote this. The playwright is both characters. He split his mind in two to write this give-and-take dialogue, and you as actors have to reunite his mind."

Authors will often put punctuation, such as an exclamation mark, at the end of a sentence, to indicate strong emotion; or they will italicize a word to indicate that it should be stressed. And there may be parenthetical stage directions, too, that are supposed to tell you in what manner to deliver a line. Eventually, you will get back to all these things and see why the author put them there, and then you can decide whether to ignore them or not. But it is wise to ignore them at first until you do know what they mean, from a personal and not an intellectual point of view.

Until that point, such indicators can be a trap, because they only provide you with empty attitudes. They can lead you to jump too soon into playing "out" a moment before you really know why, while at the same time distracting you from developing the relationships with the other characters.

You begin to develop these relationships in the first readings by looking up from the script as much as possible. At first, actors are fearful of doing this, worried about losing their place. Since no one is standing guard over you to pick up cues during those first readings, you can keep your head up and not in your book, looking at and talking directly to the other characters and watching as well as listening to their responses.

To my dismay, I have often seen a roundtable reading of a play or movie on the first day of rehearsal totally wasted by actors with their heads in their books. It seems as if they are reading only to hear the sounds of their own voices, or as if they are "saving their performances" (a fallacy) by mumbling. The absurd idea of "saving" one's performance is prevalent today. It is a companion piece to the belief that rehearsing is not essential. How far we have come from premeditated "acting" and showing off as performers! Ask any other performing artist to practice only partway while preparing for a performance and he or she will look at you amazed! By not relating to the other actors at all, an actor loses a valuable opportunity to begin to build a role. Right from the start, using the dialogue as a "bridge" to the relationships—responding and evoking responses—will help you make important decisions later on.

The give and take of responses to get responses continues throughout the rehearsals, as well as the performances. This ensures that you will always be fresh and spontaneous, and that you will avoid being repetitive, or anticipating the next moment. Anticipation, like lack of concentration, dissipates your energy.

As a young student, I recall becoming very discouraged when Herbert Berghof criticized me for not "receiving." I would know all my cues and be letter perfect with my lines, but, according to my teacher, I did not *receive* what was being said to me—that is, it was having no effect on me, although I thought I had listened to the words. I was completely in the dark at that time as to what to do. I felt dull and insensitive, without any vulnerability.

It was a long and painful struggle, until I finally learned from Uta Hagen's clear and patient explanation that receiving depends entirely on sending! When every one of my lines was delivered—or, to use her word, "landed"—followed by a *speculation* as to what the response would be, I became open and alert to all that was happening between myself and the other character, and emotionally involved. I don't want to mislead you into thinking that you have to plot your thinking. Just open your mind to speculations, which can and will vary in every rehearsal, as well as in every performance. Just as you cannot humanly repeat a moment in acting, where everything happens "for the first time," in the same way you cannot repeat a speculation.

Whenever I've heard a casting director or director praise an actor for being "a good listener," this simply means that the actor is concentrated on the effect he or she is having on the other person. The following simple exchange gives you examples of speculation (in parentheses) that could be attached to a line of dialogue in order for it to "land" on the other person, to have an effect, and to cause you to listen to the response:

SHE: Hi! (*Are you still mad at me?*)
HE: Where were you? (*Were you outside the door the whole time?*)
SHE: Waiting for you. (*I can see you are still mad.*)
HE: Well, are you coming? (*I know you want to.*)
SHE: I'll get ready. (*I want you to have more respect for me.*)

A more generic speculation for any line would be: *Did you get it? Did you get what I just said?* I am not suggesting that you write down your speculations in your script, but rather allow them to happen spontaneously. Without speculation, it is hard to sustain listening to words you have obviously heard before. And without listening you risk playing a predetermined "line reading," or using a false attitude:

SHE: (*Worried*) Hi!
HE: (*Suspiciously*) Where were you?
SHE: (*Feigned innocence*) Waiting for you.
HE: (*Brusquely*) Well, are you coming?
SHE: (*Downtrodden*) I'll get ready. (*Slinks out of the room*)

You will find attitudes in the form of stage directions, like the above, written into many scripts. Following such directions will only lead away from truly relating to your partner and down the garden path of illustration.

I like Uta Hagen's term, "landing," for making sure that you observe whether or not your words are really being heard by the other character, because of its physical connotations: You feel like you are really getting somewhere. When you are landing an action, which means you are sending each line of dialogue each and every moment in order to have an effect, you are pursuing your character's scene objective (see step 4), and you are fueling the motor that drives the play. It is important, too, to look at any speech, no matter how long, as a series of moments. As in life, you don't want to anticipate that you are going to speak without interruption.

It is a very common mistake for an actor to regard a speech of more than two or three lines as a "monologue," which it certainly is not. When you are talking to another person, it is always a give-and-take situation. A monologue is spoken only when you are alone on stage, either to yourself or to the audience, or on the telephone, or to an imaginary creature. In recent years, "monologue books," which consist mostly of speeches from scenes, and not of true monologues, have played their part in perpetuating this misconception. The fact is that you must view any speech as intended for and meant to have an effect on the listener, in order to avoid the trap of framing the speech in the way an opera singer sings an aria! So as not to deliver the speech in a declamatory way, it is necessary to understand that your character is talking that much only because the other person is silent and unresponsive. Every line of the speech has to arrive at its destination, and to drive the objective, which may or may not succeed in the end.

The point can be illustrated by the following Yiddish theater joke: An actor received a round of applause each night after delivering a long and dramatic speech to another character in the play who had no lines. One night as he and his colleague exited the stage to the usual thunderous applause, he whispered to him, "Wasn't my scene wonderful tonight?" His fellow actor was surprised, and responded with, "What do you mean *your* scene?" The first actor replied, "Of course it's my scene." Well, the next night, during the long speech, the other actor chose not to listen to a single word. Needless to say, the scene died and there was no applause. As they exited, the first actor cried out to his colleague in desperation, "All right! All right! *Our* scene!"

In every scene, characters fall into one of two categories: leaders or followers. The leader in any scene is the character without whom the scene would not exist, and not necessarily the one with the most dialogue. He or she could even be a silent partner. It is one character's need that brings the scene

about, and usually that character remains dominant throughout the scene. This knowledge can assist in determining your
objective and increasing your understanding of how and why
the events in the scene unfold as they do.

For instance, suppose you are alone, and someone unexpected arrives: no doubt, the one who arrives causes the scene
to occur. In *A Streetcar Named Desire*, in the first scene as well
as in the rest of the play, Blanche du Bois' presence is what
causes the events of the play to happen. She is the leader, and
her sister Stella, who arrives to welcome her, is the follower.
In this case, the leader/follower relationship is one that has
also prevailed for their whole lives. Yet each scene must be
examined to discover who the leader is, and who the follower.
When Stanley Kowalski arrives home to find his wife pow-
dering her nose instead of making his dinner, it is clear that
Stanley causes the conflict, and is therefore the leader of this
scene, and of the following one with Blanche.

Unquestionably, in David Mamet's *Speed the Plow*, it is
Charlie Fox's urgent need to make a movie that produces
the excitement and humor in the first and third scenes of the
play. However, in the scene in the middle of the play between
Bob Gould and the girl, it could be a toss-up as to whose
objective is the leading cause of the scene: both he and the
girl seem to have an agenda. Yet without Gould's invitation
the girl would not be present; therefore, technically, Bob is
the leader of the scene, although by the conclusion, it is the
girl "leading him around by the nose." Another example: in
the classic brothers' scene between Happy and Biff Loman
in *Death of a Salesman*, Happy's need to encourage Biff to stay
home, though never spoken, causes the scene. At the beginning of the scene, Happy's subtle action of lighting a cigarette prevents Biff from falling asleep, and is the catalyst for
their conversation.

American actors are generally insecure if a script contains
too many words or florid language. They have a hard time
with Oscar Wilde's plays, for example. Wilde's dialogue is ver-

bose, even though it is witty, and beautifully crafted speeches full of verbal action often take the place of physical action. The typical American actor would rather resort to an expletive and/or a gesture, but British actors relish language.

In the following short exchange from a scene in act 2 of *The Importance of Being Earnest*—arguably the greatest comedy written in English—the American actor might want to bring its language to life by resorting to physical moves, such as shoving, or poking a finger in the other character's face. Such physicality can be suppressed and placed in the subtext as a desire that will not be acted out physically. Being aware of the subtextual, silent speculation—questions, challenges, and so forth—delivered with each line, the American actor can begin to "own" Wilde's language, just as English actors do, although at first it may feel foreign.

Again, my suggestions for the characters' possible speculations appear in parentheses. Technically, they could be construed as moment-to-moment actions, not to be written in cement, but spontaneous. This sort of work can help the actor develop an appetite for the stylish language:

Jack and Algernon retire into the house with scornful looks.

JACK: This ghastly state of things is what you call Bunburying I suppose? (*Admit it, you bastard!*)

ALGERNON: Yes, and a perfectly wonderful Bunbury it is. (*Take that!*) The most wonderful Bunbury I have ever had in my life. (*How do you like THAT?*)

JACK: Well, you have no right whatsoever to Bunbury here. (*Pummel, pummel!*)

ALGERNON: That is absurd. (*You're a jackass!*) One has a right to Bunbury wherever one chooses. (*Haven't you heard?*) Every serious Bunburyist knows that. (*The subject is closed!*)

Of course, it is wonderful when, through study and practice, American actors begin to develop a desire for stylish language, not just in British plays and the classics, but also in the plays of great American writers such as Clifford Odets or Tennessee Williams or Eugene O'Neill.

Make a habit of "sending in order to receive," even when you are forced to work on the script in silence, by yourself— for example, when you are studying your lines for the next day's shoot, or when you are preparing them for an audition. Do not make the mistake of focusing your attention on your lines only, without regard for what is going on between you and the other characters. In fact, the true meaning of your own lines can only be fully understood when you see and hear the effect they are having on the others, even if only in your imagination. Keeping this in mind also makes it easier to learn them.

Revealing the Subtext

During the first readings, the actor who has been concentrated on building the relationships with give-and-take will begin to feel the stirrings of what's going on beneath the lines. In contemporary plays and in the media, as well, it is the subtext that conveys the drama to the public. Certainly, in the cinema, audiences don't listen to the words with as much attention as they do in the theater, since in a film there is much more stimulation for the eye than the ear, except maybe when the loud background music overwhelms you. In fact, some aficionados still decry the arrival of the talking pictures that replaced the silent film. These serious film historians say that the great art of making moving pictures was and still is in silent movies.

In the theater, silence can carry a significance as great as or greater than the words themselves, when the actor has filled the silence and occupied it, so to speak. I remember sitting in the top row of the balcony, and yet seeing "close up" the tiniest gesture Jason Robards, Jr. made in the original production of *Long Day's Journey into Night*. He could light up the darkened theater with his whole character's being and state of mind, and without a word of dialogue. He was so intensely alive that I felt I could read his mind even from that distance. And in that same production, I can recall actually seeing Fredric March's eyebrow lift ever so slightly, as he eyed a glowing light bulb, before he stood on his chair to unscrew it! Or, in *The Gin Game*, I remember hearing Hume Cronyn's soft whisper reach my high perch, as clearly as if he were speaking right into my ear. As a matter of fact, the most indelible impressions made on me by great performances were in my youth, when I was seated in the back row of a theater balcony.

As the subtext emerges, the first thing to do is to search for the primary objective. Your choice of the primary scene objective, the "what I want to do," begins after the first readings, and is hopefully chosen not from an intellectual perspective, but from a personal, emotional, and revelatory one. As the relationship with your partner(s) begins to take shape, your instincts are awakened and your emotions come to the surface, making it easier to choose the primary objective. This is the cause of the events and the source for the dialogue in the scene, and is hidden between the lines. We do not want to look for the objective in the words themselves, but rather to use the words as "clues" to the character's psychology.

The objective can be elusive. We begin with one choice for the objective; then, during rehearsals, we dig deeper and deeper, redefining it, until we find the true one, which almost immediately disappears into the fabric of our performance and becomes reflexive, a "cue" to behave in a certain way, inspired by the sight of the other character or the words being said. The important thing to remember is that you must avoid jumping to results, even at those times when you do not have the luxury of rehearsing with the other actors and gradually building the relationships. In film and television, time for study is compressed, but you can still choose to work from the inside out, in order to achieve the most personal and organic results.

One of the great tragedies of the age we live in is the negative effect technology has had on relationships in general.

At first, the darkened movie houses isolated us from each other—unlike theater, which is always in partial light, and is a communal experience—and then television took us away from the public place altogether and plunked us down in the privacy of our own home. Now, it seems, technology also requires us to rehearse alone, as if relating to the other actors is secondary and unimportant, when in reality it is the ensemble of players that creates the art! Once again, I want to stress that it is the experience of practicing rehearsed scenes for class, at least, and working in theater, that gives the serious actor the needed skills to overcome the problems the media besets us with. The ability to find personal clues in a movie or television scene comes from working before a live audience.

CHAPTER 6

Step 3: Paying Attention to the Inner Objects

ıllıllıllıllıllıllıllıllıllıllıllıllıllıllıllıllıllıllı

What is an object? The basic definition is "a physical thing existing in the world"—a book, a stone, a tree, an animal, a person; objects can be animate or inanimate. Aside from existing in its own reality outside the mind, a physical object exists also as our mental representation or image of it. All objects therefore have both an inner and an outer aspect. And they have the importance or unimportance for us that we give to them.

Uta Hagen believed that the difference between a good actor and a great one is how he or she relates to objects, which, for acting a role, falls into two basic categories: outer objects and inner objects. "Outer objects" are the other characters and the physical objects onstage—furniture, stage properties (called "props"), and so forth. The necessary use of physical objects inspired Uta to create her well-known Object Exercises, which are detailed in *Respect for Acting*. But inner objects are equally important.

The use of the term *inner objects* refers to those objects that are not actually present in the scene or the play, and never were or will be—that is, they exist solely in the memory of the character. They often appear in the form of written exposition and have been chosen purposefully by the author. In other words, they are words, phrases, and speeches in the character's dialogue that describe background, or offstage, information. The only thing that exists for the actor is the mental representation of the object, and never the object itself. Inner objects are people, places, things, or events that are from the character's past, or from a present that we never see—like Protopopov, the character with whom Natasha is having an offstage affair in Chekhov's *Three Sisters*. We hear his name, but we never see him. Inner objects are the products of the actor's imagination, and they will always have to be chosen as substitutions from our own past experience, imagination, or a mixture of both.

While you are still in training, it is essential to form a habit of seeing the inner objects in a script in your mind's eye at the moment you mention them—starting with your first reading. When an inner object, a bit of past information, is mentioned in your dialogue, a flag should go up for you, and you should start to create a mental image for it from the very beginning. In doing this, you are attempting to fill in details of the character's background. Such inner objects are a window into the character's past.

The inner objects are the first things you personalize in building your character in a play. If in your dialogue you mention someone, something, an event or a place that is not and never will be on stage, you must try to "see" spontaneously who or what you mean, creating a reference. The actor is never obliged to choose inner objects for what other characters speak about, even if they are talking about you. In other words, whatever impression they make on you, you may believe them or not. The first thing you "see" spontaneously may not be the object you end up with, but you have begun the search!

When you begin working, you are always using yourself, and you should pay attention to what your instincts may tell you. Therefore, whatever or whomever comes to mind will suffice. If you are talking about "mother" or "father," you can simply see your own mother or father. The same is true for "brother" or "sister," if you have one. If a former lover is mentioned, your instinct may be to use one from your past, but you can also use someone imaginary, such as a movie star you might have been infatuated with. The same holds true for places and events: you can remember an actual one or create a new one.

It is always clear to me when actors know what they are talking about and when they haven't got a clue, no matter how skillfully they may use the words or display the emotions. Once they have personalized the inner objects, and are thinking about what they are saying, the writing suddenly comes alive, and the emotions they thought they had already achieved become so much deeper, more original and surprising. In other words, without references, the actor is an empty shell and is unintentionally telling lies; see the anecdote on page 251.

The search for the inner objects is an organic process. When I was a young student, I was told to choose my inner objects even before rehearsals began. Over time, I came to disagree with this; the search for the right inner object should be continual and spontaneous, and it is more often revealed during rehearsals rather than between them. But if instead you skip over references to inner objects as if they were just words in the speeches, or replace them with superficial attitudes, you run the risk of leaving an empty space in your performance.

At the opening of Chekhov's *Uncle Vanya*, Dr. Astrov suddenly recalls an incident in which he was called late at night to the scene of a railway accident, and a patient whose life he was trying to save died. The exhausted doctor was, of course, deeply upset. Where did the accident take place? How long did it take to get there, and what was the ride like? What did the scene of the accident look like? What was the weather? Was it cold? Who was the patient, and what did he look like? What was the makeshift operating table like? These are all objects that have psychological, emotional attachments to them, and must be made particular through the actor's imagination,

If you find something analogous in your own life and experience that might have some emotional validity in the play's circumstances, you will substitute the situation or person you know for the event in the play. Although you may not be a doctor whose patient died during an operation, you have probably had some other terrible experience that would allow you to understand Astrov's feelings. And since the railway accident took place at night in bad weather, the memory of gloomy, rainy nights in your own life will serve you. Until the actor sees these particulars, he will only be pretending to have an attitude about what happened—for instance, "I am sad."

"Playing" an attitude is vastly different from "having" an attitude. A real event or object that is conjured up in your memory carries its own "attitude." Without chosen inner objects, the actor automatically cuts himself off from a multitude of other feelings that may also be possible and just as true—and just as much what the author had in mind.

In your personal life, think of "mother," or "father," or "home," and then attempt to pinpoint just one single feeling regarding them. You will find it impossible to do so. Our feelings are always complicated, and always ambivalent. It is not realistic to plant just one feeling on a memory, i.e., "sad." The actor who does this is playing a general quality, or a "mood," rather than the conflicting emotions that we all experience with regard to any relationship or event.

The word "ambivalence" means the simultaneous existence of seemingly contradictory or mutually exclusive feelings, such as love and hate, or anger and desire. Ambivalence is the most common and human of all feelings about our past and our present: what we grieve about may also make us laugh or become angry, depending on the context. So when you are faced with a fictitious character's fictitious past, you want to build, from the start, three-dimensional references that include ambivalence, just as they do in real life.

During the first readings, the actor must remain alert to any inner objects in his dialogue. If the actor skips over the inner objects in the first reading, and either assumes or presumes some attitude, he often forgets to go back to them. And beginning actors will not even know they are missing them. As a coach, I have spent a large part of my sessions with actors training them to think about *what* they are saying when they speak lines regarding the past from the beginning, even while reading cold.

In nighttime television drama, for instance, there is always the "interview" scene with the cops or the lawyer. The tendency is to worry about the attitudes the character has, which are usually written into the scene, and not specifically about who the "victim" is that they are being questioned about, or about the events surrounding the crime. By "seeing" these things in all their details during his responses, the actor can find an original way of being the character, rich in ambiguity, and much more interesting than what is on the pages. Also, the actor who may have assumed an attitude for the inner objects in the beginning, and has never gone back to re-examine the objects for personal substitution choices, will be in for a shock when under the pressure of the first performance before an audience or on camera. At that time, the "hole" he has left in his performance is suddenly apparent to him, and it's too late to do anything about it.

Let's take a simple example: "I met her in Paris on a rainy night and we didn't hit it off at first." Some former girlfriend may spontaneously come to mind for who "she" is, or perhaps a fantasy of a movie star; a sight in Paris (the Eiffel Tower) can be the setting (or another city); and any number of possibilities might occur to you for the rain and for what was occurring between you. I remind actors to keep up the search through as many rehearsals as necessary, although it is also possible that the "right" choice may be made immediately, and will stick. How will you know the "right" choice from an intellectual one when it reveals itself? It can only be described as a quickening of the pulse, a blush, a smile, or tears in your eyes. It happens to you. You can't make it happen. You simply have to be open to it and allow it to happen. The thing to avoid is choosing substitutions intellectually, rather than instinctually.

Allow the thoughts to come to you spontaneously. Then, as you become more familiar with the material, let other choices occur that might belong to your evolving character even more specifically. These are the choices that are eventually "forgotten" in your performance, and take on emotional reality for you. On the other hand, of course, if you are all alone with your sides for tomorrow's shoot and no rehearsal is scheduled, a list of possible choices may be just the thing you need!

In Arthur Miller's *All My Sons*, the character of Larry Keller is missing in the war and presumed dead before the play begins. Although he never appears, he influences the outcome of the play as a major character would, and is as meaningful to the others as if he were there. He is an inner object for his girlfriend, Ann; his brother, Chris; his father, Joe; and his mother, Kate. Of course, each actor will see his own Larry as an object of love or guilt. This offstage character is more than mere exposition; the subject is emotionally explosive, and dictates the events unfolding in the play.

The difference between too much exposition of the wrong kind and exposition that is logical and flawlessly written is found in soap opera. In a typical speech written for a soap opera episode, the writer(s) are compelled to explain much more than would be explained in normal conversation, for the purposes of keeping the viewing audience up to date. A wife is talking to her husband. She mentions their child's name, also when he was born, what has happened since his birth, and when the inevitable kidnapping occurred, as if the husband and father of the child didn't know any of this. All this information is qualified with lots of anguish, of course, to make it "real." And of course the husband's dialogue never includes such responses as "But darling, why go through all this again?" because she will be saying the same things all over again in the next episode, and perhaps in the next few weeks as well.

On the other hand, there may be a great deal of exposition in the best writing, too. Chekhov and Williams are prime examples, but all of their exposition—another term is "back story"—is woven into the dialogue in a skillful, poetic, and perfectly plausible way.

To return to the opening of *Uncle Vanya*, Dr. Astrov is waiting for the arrival of people he soon tells us he has galloped miles to see. They have gone out for a long walk, and there is no knowing when they will return. He is standing about in the yard with the old Nurse, with whom he has nothing in common, and to whom he really has nothing to say, but he feels constrained nevertheless to make conversation. What else is there to do? The idea of the distance he has traveled and the time it took him leads him to think of time and how it is wasted. "Nurse," he says in the first line of the play, "how long have we known each other?" "Oh, let me see . . ." she says; and she then reminisces in a perfectly logical way suitable to the circumstances, while also giving the audience intriguing introductory information that is a bit mysterious, but that later events will prove to be crucial to our understanding of the story. "Vera Petrovna was alive then... Sonya's mother," she continues, explaining who Vera was in case Astrov had forgotten, at which the actor playing Astrov might smile, because she has just told him something that common sense should have made her realize he remembers perfectly well. Vera Petrovna, who has died, is an inner object for both the Nurse and Astrov.

Blanche du Bois' famous speech about her dead young husband in act 2, scene 2 of *A Streetcar Named Desire* reads like an aria, and can become any actress's downfall if she does not continually remind herself that she is telling it to Mitch for the first time—this is the first time she has told this to anyone—in order to achieve her objective, which is "to win him over." And yet she must visualize the entire story in all of its wealth of personal detail. The same is true of Nina's vivid description of her travails as an actress in act 4 of *The Seagull*. In this scene, she is telling the story to Constantin, in order to achieve her more self-involved objective, which is "to regain her courage to go on."

It is the rare play that contains no exposition, since all characters live in the past to some extent—and since the audience needs to be informed. In Samuel Beckett's iconic *Waiting for Godot*, widely considered the icon of the twentieth-century Theater of the Absurd, the author makes the existential point that the two main characters have no past that they recall and no future that they can understand. They are just "waiting." I find that in a play like Beckett's, or those of other absurdist dramatists, such as Eugene Ionesco or Tom Stoppard—*Rosencrantz and Guildenstern Are Dead* is a good example—the actor can have a glorious time by treating each line of dialogue purely as a response in the present moment and nothing else, with no reference to anything in the past. Other than waiting, there isn't even a primary objective in *Waiting for Godot*. Moment-to-moment playing in cases like these, or if you have the rare opportunity to play an amnesiac, will surely put you in a weird and wonderful place, experientially.

Things, people, and events that are talked of but do not "live" in the play create references for the actor to be used just as significantly as the actor uses his relationships, as he journeys through the play to its resolution. Exploring these inner objects is part of the great pleasure of acting a role.

CHAPTER 7

Step 4: Finding the Objective

||||||||||||||||||||||||||||||||||||||||||||||||||||

Herbert Berghof's definition of acting was "to do things truthfully for a purpose." He went on to say that all human beings have a purpose or an objective during all their waking hours, and even when they are asleep. There is only one exception to this rule: when the human being is an actor on stage who has never chosen an objective or doesn't know what one is!

The character's will to achieve his or her objective is entwined with the actor's will to act. If there is one thing an acting school cannot give you, it is the desire to do it at all. Years ago, I had an unforgettable conversation with Uta Hagen about *talent* and its definition: Does having talent mean having sensitivity, imagination, and creativity—and is it something you are born with? We came to the conclusion that one can be taught to be more sensitive, imaginative, and creative, but no one can be taught the compulsion to act!

In my technique classes at HB Studio, I had a student who was always eager to get up every session to do his exercise, but was strangely inactive in his work and appeared lazy and vague. Each time, I asked him what his objective was, and each time after he answered I had to tell him it was not working—until one day, after frustrating months of trying, he sailed through, glowing with determination. I said, "Frank, that's it! You now have an objective!" He turned to me and said, "That's it? But that was so easy!" He had discovered that what he wanted as the character was entwined with what he wanted to do as an actor, which was to succeed!

When you have read the play and begun to develop the relationships, and to deal with the inner objects, all of which reveals the subtext, your next step is to look for the character's objective, which is the motivation, the raison d'être, the justification, the aim, the goal, and the answer to Stanislavsky's question, "What do I want?" The objective is the heart or core of the piece, and what drives it forward.

You must always begin by looking for your character's objective in each scene—this is called the *scene objective*, or the primary objective. Discovering your character's objective for each scene is what enables you to discover your character's *play objective*. The objective—even the smallest one, the *beat objective*—is never found in the text, but is hidden in the subtext. If the lines absolutely state something such as "I want to find out what you are up to," or "How are you?" the chosen objective cannot be what is in the statement. Rather, it may be "to impress you" or "to prepare you" for something.

When I teach students how to choose the objective, I advise them to read the scene aloud to each other a number of times. Only then will they begin to perceive what is between the lines—that is, what is causing the scene to happen. They can then define and discuss their possible objectives. This is better than trying to choose an objective intellectually, in advance, by simply reading the text and having an idea—even if it's a very good idea—as to what they think the author intended. I also tell my students to discuss their objectives with each other in the first meeting, only so they can "set the stage" before further exploration. After that, any changes in their choice of objectives—due to a deepening understanding of their characters—they should keep as a secret to themselves so as not to dissipate the objective's power for them.

The word I like to use most often for the scene objective

is "throughline": each actor has a throughline for the scene. I like this word because it creates a visual picture in the student's mind of an actual, physical line that runs through the scene. It suggests a tension wire on which the text bounces along, leading to the character's ultimate destination. A better word than tension is "immediacy." The immediacy of the scene objective must be considered. What you want in any particular situation and *why now?* Why not before? Or, can it wait until later? A simple examination of the past, present, and future circumstances provides the answer. Without the throughline pulled taut throughout the scene, the life on stage grows lax; it feels slow and can become just a boring conversation instead of a conflict.

Very often, when I ask actors what they think the primary objective is, they will come up with a long, confusing paragraph ("Well, first I come in, and then . . ."), paraphrasing the events of the scene. But listing the events is not something that will propel you through the scene. It will not infuse you with the energy to take the scene to its conclusion. A throughline commits you to sticking to the unalterable law in Stanislavsky's System that there is only one primary objective in every scene; that objective should be expressed succinctly, in one simple sentence or phrase. The word "spine" is sometimes used in this context, but I prefer to reserve that word for the character's life drive (see step 10).

Also, people often use the word "action" where I use "objective," but an action is best defined as a "something done in the moment," whereas an objective is what you want to do overall. The actions—the moment-to-moment doings—are what help you to achieve the objective, whether you succeed or fail in attaining it. So if Errol Flynn and Basil Rathbone are dueling as Robin Hood and the Sheriff of Nottingham, the sword fight consists of the actions of thrusting, parrying, and ducking, while the objective is to defeat the other person.

An objective must always be defined as a positive statement; it is never what I *don't* want to do. Although in a great many scenes it is easier to determine what the character is avoiding or refusing to do, the actor has to turn something negative into something positive: "I don't want to tell you" becomes "I want to keep it secret," and "I don't want to go" should be instead "I want to stay."

You want to develop the habit of determining the scene objective at first by listening to the give-and-take dialogue not just once but a few times. This habit can also be of help when you are breaking down and analyzing a script by yourself for the media, when you have to make choices mentally. Depending on the complexity of the material and the breadth of your experience, you may want to read the scene(s) through with a coach or another actor; or you may be able to "hear" the dialogue in your own mind. It is the *theory* behind the correct and organic way to work that you want to learn so that you can put it to use in the lonely conditions of preparing for television or film acting.

One of the easy ways to find the scene objective is to look at the beginning of the scene—your entrance—and then at the very end, which may be your exit. What does the character say or do at the very beginning, and what happens at the end? You then ask yourself "Did I fail or did I succeed?" The "choice" of whether the objective failed or succeeded is easier to determine than it is to determine the right objective. The character is let down at the end of the scene, or has slammed the door on the way out, or in some way suggests he has given up. At this point, if the actor looks back at the very beginning (his entrance) to determine what he actually came in to do, essentially skipping over all the twists and turns of the dialogue that follows, he has opened the door to finding the correct objective. The same can be said of the success of any objective. The important thing is to have a workable choice to begin with, and one that is not stated in the text. Try it! You may change your mind about the objective and its success or failure after further experimentation, but at least you are starting on the right foot. Remember, there is only one primary objective in each scene, and it should be defined as simply as possible.

In a typical screenplay, the scenes vary in length. Sometimes they have very little dialogue; and some scenes have no words at all and only describe action. But each scene should have a throughline for the character. By the time there is a shooting script, the scenes are numbered as well. After reading through the entire scene, I would reread the first line of dialogue or of description of action, whichever came first, and then read the last line, and ask the actor, "What is your instinct? Do you feel as though you have succeeded or failed in getting whatever it is you entered this scene to achieve?" Surfing through the entire screenplay in this way, you follow the character's journey to the end, selecting an objective, or throughline, for each scene. The objectives for the numbered scenes become a "map" for the actor to follow no matter when in the shooting schedule a particular scene will be filmed. The actor, looking back at the initial choice of objective, is reminded of all the previous scenes; and this pinpoints where he or she should be at that moment, emotionally and psychologically.

Another rule of thumb in looking for the scene objective is to note that in comedy, objectives almost always fail, whereas the character may succeed in the overall play objective. I suppose this truism dates back to slapstick comedy, where the hero slips on a banana peel but gets up and brushes himself off. In drama, especially tragedy, objectives more often succeed. This may stem from the early Greek tragedies, when the destiny ordained for the characters by the gods was always fulfilled.

Beginning actors are commonly caught up in the words. They almost always ask, "How do I say this?" But as you gain experience, you realize that the words are only the result and not the driving force in a contemporary scene. They are "the ends of thoughts." In the classics, especially in those plays that are written in poetry, there is no subtext to uncover. The objective is clearly in the words themselves. It would be very difficult to look beneath Shakespeare's words to analyze what he meant, aside from what he was stating so eloquently. Here the actor's job is to shine light on the antiquated language, which contains all of the character's psyche and emotion.

Also, in contemporary writing, understand that you, the actor, will know more about the character than the character knows about her or himself. Most characters do not always know what they want on a conscious level. A character doesn't go around saying, "This is my objective," just as you don't in real life. Be assured that by the time you are ready to perform, you as the actor will not be conscious of the objective, either. The wonderful, mysterious element in acting is how choices—the right choices—are absorbed and "forgotten" in the process.

Bear in mind, too, that with rehearsal, the objective you came up with at first will necessarily change later on as you grow more and more familiar and comfortable with the physical and psychological life of the character. Even for a scene in a film or television show, you may find that on the day you are going to shoot the scene, you can reconsider and change the scene objective you originally chose. And in a movie scene you will be playing pieces of the scene in various cuts, which will also have an effect on what your original purpose was, changing it to some extent each time you approach the situation. See page 231 for more about this aspect of doing camera takes.

For example, in a scene between lovers or between a husband and wife who are at the breaking point, if your first choice of an objective in the scene is "to find out if the other person still loves me," by the time you are on your feet and off book, you might discover that the true objective has changed. Rather, it has become "to test myself and see if I still love him or her!" Then in the next rehearsals you might discover that the real objective is "to break off the relationship without guilt." How you define and describe what is happening between you changes, because you are naturally growing more familiar with your feelings as you rehearse, and the nature of the objective deepens. When you are satisfied that you have really found the right objective for you, then you have arrived at the point in rehearsal where your objective is fully integrated with your emotional, psychological, and physical life, and can be absorbed. You are now ready to play!

Here are some examples of deeply hidden scene objectives. The actor has to get below the surface of the words and the events, and define the character's true purpose.

In the second act of *Orpheus Descending*, by Tennessee Williams, Lady yells at the younger Val, calling him a thief, when all along she wants him to take her in his arms—a desire she represses. Val prefers to keep the relationship on a platonic level, fearing what might happen otherwise. Yet in the end they do make love, and both have failed in their true objectives: hers, because she didn't want to have to beg him to stay; and his, because he felt too much empathy to turn away from her. And the play ends tragically.

In the last act of Lillian Hellman's play *The Children's Hour*, Karen and her fiancé, Joe Cardin, both want to end the relationship, but he is not as conscious of his desire as she is of hers. Although Joe pleads with Karen to continue their relationship, his true but unconscious objective is "to be let off the hook," while hers is "to wipe the slate clean."

All through Michael Weller's *Loose Ends*, Paul and Susan are struggling to keep a commitment to each other that is thwarted by Paul's character objective, which is "to be free and single." Although on the surface he is fighting to keep the relationship between them "honest," in the subtext he is tempting her to break it off.

Because of the lack of rehearsal in the media, you don't have a chance to experiment with the objective. So you have to come up with something that gives you a burst of energy and the inspiration to play almost immediately. The more familiar you are with dramatic literature and with the rehearsal process, the easier it will be to find the most personal and pertinent objective, without rehearsing. In film and television, the director, who is often of limited help, will probably never use the word "objective," but will provide hints, or in some cases make demands, about your performance that you must then know how to translate into objectives.

Remember that the objective always has to be put into a succinct phrase that includes a verb infinitive, because acting is active; acting is doing. You are essentially asking yourself "What do I want *to do*?" If you ask for a glass of water in the scene, the objective is not simply to get the glass of water; it involves a statement such as "I want to quench my thirst," or "I want that person to serve me," or some other equally active phrase that would describe it. Perhaps, in fact, your objective is to get something from the other person—not necessarily something material; you may want something emotional or psychological, like "I want you to prove to me that you are faithful."

Another subtle reality for actors to explore is when the scene objective is qualified by the use of an adverb or a phrase that influences what you want to do: "I want to leave *without guilt*," or "I want to let you down *gently*." The qualifying word or phrase in these cases gives the actor a logical reason why the scene continues even after the objective apparently has succeeded, or when your character speaks of leaving in the first few moments but stays on. In act 3 of George Bernard Shaw's *Mrs. Warren's Profession*, Vivie wants to show her mother the door at the beginning of the scene, but engages in an emotional and philosophical battle of wits with her. To perform this scene with logic, the actress who plays Vivie would have to qualify her objective: "to send her off without feeling guilty about it," or "to get rid of her with the complete understanding that there is no turning back!" And in act 3 of Ketti Frings's *Look Homeward Angel*, Eugene Gant has packed and is ready to leave. But he is stopped from doing so at first because the woman he wants to go off with has already left. Eugene then proceeds to fight with his overbearing mother for five minutes before finally making his exit with the line, "I'm already gone." His throughline in this complicated scene could be "to find the courage to leave."

As another aide to uncovering the scene objective, I distinguish three separate categories of objectives:

1. The *relationship objective*, the most common one if scenes have more than one character in them, particularly in those scenes with two characters; they are usually made up of people wanting things of each other or wanting to do something to one another.
2. The *situational objective*, which deals with the situation in a scene, such as "I want to relax" or "I want to work," in which case you are either alone, or the relationship to the other character(s) takes second place.
3. The *character objective*, which signifies a constant need, based on behavior the character exhibits throughout the play.

If you are outdoors and you want to get a suntan, or you are indoors and you want to get ready to leave, your objective is *situational*. You want what you want from the situation, place, and circumstances, and not necessarily from the other character or characters who may be present in the scene. Rather, the other character(s) behave as an aid or an obstacle to your overall need. In other words, they can help you to get what you want, or hinder you by interrupting or distracting you. While the other character(s) may do either at different times, the important thing is that what you really want to do—your scene objective, the desired goal—doesn't change. If it is "to finish my work," it is the primary thing you will be striving for throughout the scene. Other examples of situational objectives might be "to get comfortable" or "to have my dinner" or "to enjoy myself."

Also, if you are alone on stage at the beginning of a scene, your need is situational, unless you are waiting for another character to arrive, or if you are on the telephone, in which case you probably have a relationship objective. In Jason Miller's play *Lou Gehrig Did Not Die of Cancer*, a housewife is at home putting on makeup, and generally getting ready for her opening night in a community theater. Her frustrated husband comes home after coaching a Little League base-ball game. He walks in complaining about one of the kids on his team, and in short order the two of them get into a high-pitched argument, eventually covering everything that's wrong with their marriage, including why they are childless, her disappointment in him, and his dysfunctional relation-ship with his father. A common trap for the actress playing the role of the wife is to prioritize the fight with the husband. Throughout the scene, her primary focus should continue to be on physically getting ready for the theater! If she stops for a moment it is only to emphasize a point she is making. Her objective is situational—"to get ready to go"—whereas her husband has a relationship objective—he wants to get his wife to forget her "theatrical" ambitions and stay home with him that evening, although he never verbalizes this. Maintaining their separate objectives throughout the long scene frees each actor from emphasizing what might appear to be too much exposition, which would make the scene deadly and kill the laughs. This is an important point, and of immense help in determining the right objective: knowing that the objective is situational unburdens an actor's performance, and frees him or her tremendously.

A *character objective* is something the character wants all through the play in one form or another in all of the scenes. Although not so common, some examples are: the young novice Agnes, in *Agnes of God* by John Pielmeier, whose pri-mary need in all scenes is "to obey"; Maggie (who is based on his wife, Marilyn Monroe) in Arthur Miller's *After the Fall*, who wants "to find a safe haven"; Edmund in *A Long Day's Journey into Night* by Eugene O'Neill, who, while waiting to be picked up and taken to the sanatorium from which he believes he will never return, wants "to make peace" with his father, his mother, or his brother.

Such character objectives will sometimes overlap with the life drives of a character (see page 181), but not always. Also, they should be defined differently from the "play objective" (see page 123). The character objective exists when there is no other logical way to explain what the character wants in a particular scene, besides the overriding objective he or she has in every scene. And yet the actor can find different ways to express the character objective in each scene.

You have to be sure that the objective is something you really want and could achieve. If, for instance, you choose as a character objective "I want to shake up the world," that would be pretty difficult to do in a scene. You have to bring it down to the point where you can understand it in more concrete or practical terms.

On the other hand, if your objective is too small, such as "I want to get the other person to leave the room"—which might seem apparent as an objective in a scene —you will find yourself asking what you have really accomplished by achieving that objective. You will immediately see that there has to be some larger issue at stake. What will you really gain if you succeed in having the person leave the room?

In one of the final scenes of John Van Druten's classic romantic comedy *The Voice of the Turtle*, Sally is distracting her friend Olive so that Bill, the object of both their affections, can escape from the apartment. Sally's need is not the obvious one just stated: "to help Bill escape without being noticed." If the actress digs deeper, she may find that her objective is "to hold on to both of them." At this point, Sally is as concerned over her friendship with Olive as she is over her new love affair with Bill.

If the objective is too large, you can bring it down to size by asking yourself, "*How* do I get that?" And if it is too small, you have to ask yourself, "*Why* am I doing this? In order to get...what?" Being able to fit the objective to the scene is another subtle and important technical tool.

Also, you never want to enter into a scene believing or knowing that you will fail. Technically, what the actor is doing here is playing the *obstacle* rather than the objective. No one enters into a conflict with a wish to fail, even if the odds seem insurmountable. Another error actors sometimes make is to allow an action or actions in a scene to take over, losing sight of the objective. In an argument, the objective is "to win," but often an actor gets caught up in arguing for its own sake. In Ibsen's *Hedda Gabler*, Hedda is interrogating her old school friend, Thea, driven by her objective, "to find out what makes her tick," and yet the scene consists of a variety of actions, such as charming, empathizing, even bullying. It is the actress's job to keep sight of her objective—even when unexpected information is revealed, such as Thea's relationship with Lövborg, Hedda's old flame.

In any one day of a soap opera, there is so much verbiage—written exposition—and it is all going to be repeated the next day, and in the following weeks as well—that perhaps the best objective is "to wait for my lunch break." I'm serious! The actor needs the scene objective for focus, and it is supposed to remain in the subtext. In the case of soap opera's dense scripts (dense in two senses of the word), a physical objective can be what saves the actor from getting all tied up in the words. And you want to avoid choosing obvious objectives like "to convince," "to seduce," or "to plead," since the dialogue is already doing that.

On the other hand, in nighttime dramas, other kinds of situations occur that demand a larger objective than what is apparent in the text. In any script of *Law & Order*, for instance—a hit show that provides New York actors with a great deal of work and seems as if it may keep on running, or at least re-running, forever—there are very familiar scenes, such as the obligatory cop interview scene. A potential witness is being interrogated by the police, who are looking during the first half of the show for the perpetrator of the crime that we have been shown at the beginning of the program. The second half of the show takes place in the courtroom. The interrogation scene is usually about one and a half pages long, and will always contain one moment in which it "turns on a dime," about halfway through the dialogue—meaning that the interviewee suddenly tells the truth, which signals that the scene is about to end. Up until that point, the witness may have been trying to divert the cops, or was reluctant to respond or was putting up a smokescreen, for whatever reasons. If it's a one-scene role, all the rest of this character's existence is left up to the actor's imagination.

To find the objective for a formulaic scene like this, you would want to look at the beginning and end of the scene, although with virtually every scene written for nighttime drama, the scene has no beginning, but starts sometime later in the situation. The first line is usually that of the interviewee responding to an unheard question by a cop, which the actor has to imagine: "She left about two in the morning." To fill in the circumstances of the scene for yourself, you can choose that you were at your job as a coat-check girl in the club when the cops came in and took you aside, away from your post, and that this is how the scene actually began. You are then expected to respond to their questions normally and calmly, even though a murder was committed right under your very nose. After about two minutes of dialogue in the form of questions and answers, you confess that the girl you replaced in the coat-check room was indeed missing on the night in question. She might have had something to do with the crime! And now she's fingered! She is the possible perp! The point is, how do you find your objective?

To find an objective that will work for you, you first tell yourself, "At the beginning of the scene (unseen of course), I am at work, and the cops come in. At the end of the scene I've given them the information they were after, and the cops leave. A good possibility for an objective is simply 'to do my job.' I am interrupted by the police and I am reluctant to respond to them because they are interfering with my making a good impression on the boss. Going a bit deeper, I can imagine that I am only a trainee and that I want to do well so that I can become a permanent employee." In either case, because of the cops, the character failed in her objective. By thinking about the scene in a larger sense and looking beyond the interview scene, the actress will give herself higher emotional stakes and will help not only in finding a background for her character, but potentially finding very original, moment-to-moment behavior in the scene itself. The point is that the actress cannot only stick to the text, and say, for instance, that her objective is "to cooperate with the police," or "not to cooperate with them." After all, in the first half of the scene she doesn't want to answer their questions. And in the second half of the scene, she tells them something that might get her colleague in trouble, so maybe she is sorry she cooperated with them. Since the interrogation was nothing that was planned anyway, none of this can be her objective.

By trying to find a subtext the writers did not suggest, you can find something that would make you a more interesting character, and help you to avoid playing a stereotype, such as a gum-chewing floozy who works in a sleazy nightclub.

It is actually more difficult to find the objective in narrowly written material, such as television episodic scripts, than it is in brilliant plays like those of Chekhov, O'Neill, or Shakespeare, which is why I advocate acquiring first-hand knowledge of the great writing of both the past and the present: the more you become familiar with real playwriting, the easier it becomes to rise to the occasion when you are forced to find your character in the mediocre scripts that television provides.

I once asked Herbert Berghof why he assigned such complex material as Maxwell Anderson or Jean-Paul Sartre to new and beginning students. His reply was that since as a teacher he was forced to observe clumsy acting from beginners, at least he could listen to great language! And, likewise, the students were introduced to great writing, and received the gift of his lectures afterwards.

The Beat Objective

The *beat objective* is a small objective that can be found inside a scene and furthers the scene objective. It is a piece of a scene. The use of the word "beat" started with the Stanislavsky System, and was probably a Russian-accented pronunciation by the master himself of the word "bit," by which he meant a small portion of a scene. Nevertheless, "beat" has stuck in English terminology, and is very often confused with its musical connotation or its supposed connection to the rhythm of a scene. And it is often inappropriately applied in such instructions from a director as "Take a few beats [meaning a few moments] before you walk in."

A beat ends with a transition that takes you to the next beat, or event, in a scene. And the person in the scene who leads the transition—that is, the person who wants to go on to something else—is the "leader" in the scene (see page 89).

After much experimentation in trying to teach the best way to build a "score" (another word with a musical connotation), which is the list of beat objectives—to be marked in the margins of a script—I discovered that a typical "beat" in a stage play lasts about a minute (about two-thirds of a page in a published play) until it wears out in either failure or success. This brief stretch of time forces the actor to sustain the small objective and prevents the spoken dialogue from taking the actor off track. It helps to clarify what is truly going on beneath the words in a contemporary scene.

If a beat objective lasts for a minute, you would have five beats in a five-minute scene. However, at the beginning of every scene there is another, even smaller beat, of usually a few seconds' duration, that is the "springboard" or the *adjustment* to the previous events. That first tiny beat will help to put you into the situation within a flow of circumstances, whether you are entering the scene or are already on stage; whether the scene is a continuation of a previous scene that has been taken out of context, such as a scene for class or a film scene, or if there has been a break in time and/or place between the scenes, or if the scene is the opening scene of a play. The beat lasts a moment or two and could end after a simple exchange of dialogue or action. For instance, suppose you are outside knocking on a door, and someone inside the room says, "Come in." The beat is then over and your objective has succeeded: "to find out if someone was there." Now what? The second beat, which may begin with your entering the room, will be the first minute-long beat.

If the scene begins with you on stage, and your scene objective is "to get cooperation" from the other character, your focus is on the relationship, and your first beat of adjustment might be "to check to see how the other person is feeling, and if it's a good time to begin," or "to see if you have his or her attention." This requires a glance at the other person, and the tiny objective could be accomplished in a very brief time, perhaps without a word of dialogue. To continue with the score, a second beat might be "to lay my case on the table." The third beat might be "to appeal to the other person's goodness," and then, fourth, "to try to strike a bargain." And the fifth beat could be "to demand loyalty." The final beat in such a five-minute scene could be "to threaten the other person." For each beat objective you will determine whether it ended in failure or success, either of which sends you on to the next beat. The moment between beats is the *transition*. At the end of the scene, you will discover whether you have succeeded or failed in your overall scene objective. Importantly, you cannot be swayed by the possible circuitous routes taken by the dialogue: maintaining each beat objective until it is over insures that the structure of the scene is not lost.

Defining and jotting down the beats is ideally done *after* you have experienced them in rehearsal. In other words, you have felt where the transitions happen, due to the pressure of trying to achieve the scene objective, and knowing that they do not depend on the dialogue's twists and turns. I remind my students to begin building the score for a scene for class late in the rehearsals, after they have completed at least three of the five required rehearsals. The scoring process can be a major help in learning the lines as well.

In a screenplay or television script, you are often compelled to break down the beats early without the benefit of rehearsal, and you need to learn the lines beforehand. The length of the beats in a filmed drama is different from what it is in a play, since the words are at a minimum and the action is described in greater detail.

Here is an example of a series of beats for a scene (below) that is almost entirely made up of action. I have represented the transitions with slash marks. (Marsha and Tad are strangers to one another but both are being victimized by a maniacal killer.)

> *The door is closed; the room is empty and quiet. / The door is kicked in. / Marsha, backing in, drags a semiconscious Tad into the safety of the room. She is in pretty bad shape. / She finally reaches a spot near the closet and lets go of him. / Tad just lies there. Marsha settles back, catching her breath. /*
>
> TAD
>
> …thanks…/
>
> *Marsha turns to him, surprised he is awake. /*
>
> MARSHA
>
> You're welcome…

I can count seven beats for Marsha in just one third of one page in a screenplay, including a beat before she even appears, which might consist of her having to position her-

self in such a way as to be able to (1) "kick open the door."
From there, the second beat and the subsequent ones can
be defined as: (2) "to find a place to hide"; (3) "to see if I
have the strength to do it": (4) "to let go"; (5) "to rest"; (6)
"to discover he's alive"; (7) "to begin to form a relationship
with him." Her scene objective—or throughline—is "to escape."

Unlike a stage play, the actor has no control over the amount
of time the scene lasts. In the final cut, the scene above could
take anywhere from two to ten minutes!

You also choose smaller beats for television scripts than
you would for a play, even when there is a barrelful of words,
as in a soap opera:

> JOHN
> Teresa, I will not forget about who's feeding you this trash,
> and that's my problem. And no matter how guilty Tiffany
> feels about Rock, she wouldn't…/ It's Betty, isn't it? She
> forged the so-called document to try to turn you…

> TERESA
> Then why did she tell me to call the insurance company and
> trace it if I wanted to?

> JOHN
> Because she knew you wouldn't take her up on it! / Honey,
> don't be naïve. This is what Betty wants. Think about it.

And on and on…

I've defined three beats for the character of John in this
small portion of a soap scene, although you can count four
inner objects: Tiffany, Rock, Betty, and the insurance company. Because each beat's transition is like putting your foot
on the gas pedal and giving the engine another spurt of fuel,
the beats in this case are required to help the actor keep up
his energy for the words,. Definitions of John's beats could

be: (1) "to maintain being an authority figure;" (2) "to get at the bottom of it"; (3) "to appeal to her better nature." The scene objective for John in this case, because it is soap opera, could very well be "to get to an appointment on time!"

Instead of the above verbs, by the way, it is more common to see scribbled on actor's scripts, soap and otherwise, descriptive adjectives instead of objectives. For instance, the three beats above might be designated as being "forceful," then "softer," "nicer," and so on. Such notes not only create a mechanical reading of the contrived lines, but are uninspired, adding insult to injury.

When you score the beats, you always want to start at the beginning and work your way toward the end of the scene, remembering what happened in the last rehearsal, if you have had any. Even if you have put the scene aside for awhile and are starting to work on it again, always review the score from the beginning. If you start in the middle, you will run the risk of intellectualizing. The beats and the score are logical to you, the actor, personally, and not necessarily to anyone else.

I remember doing a scene from William Inge's *Picnic* when I was a student in Uta Hagen's class. I felt I had accomplished what I wanted to do with it, and Uta said it was excellent. The following term, one of my classmates was handed the same scene, and she called me up and asked me for my score, which she wanted to use. Even as a young student, I understood that somehow this was not correct. I don't mean morally; I simply understood that my score would have nothing to do with her, or her interpretation. The score was only logical to me. In other words, the score is only meaningful to the person who composes it—even though a musical score can be played by any instrumentalist who can read music, each will have an individual interpretation. The words we use in labeling the beats come out of our unique and personal vocabularies.

When I was a young mother, I helped a lay analyst achieve

his doctorate in psychology by testing his patients for him. His hypothesis had to do with the Freudian concept of "transference." He formulated the tests, which were bell curves, by using a different and personal list of words for each patient, culled from their very own vocabularies. His contention was that each person uses particular words or phrases that have emotional power only for him or her when describing someone or some event.

But why is the score necessary at all? And do you have to use it every single time? Not everybody needs to break everything down into beats, but it is an excellent practice early on in your training, and makes you aware of the construction of a scene. And it can help you to give form to a scene, because you will always be building upward, instead of remaining on a plateau, or slipping downward and petering out. Also, an experienced actor can use the score to help overcome some baffling hurdle in a scene. These days, I use it to rescue me when I feel "stuck" as to the deeper meaning that lurks in the subtext, and to find the ideal scene objective. Breaking down the beats will clarify the character's psychology as well—for instance, the way a character "uses" the relationship to attain certain objectives.

The score is necessary for clarification, but, just like the scene objective—which you have been discovering is different and more deeply felt than what you thought earlier—it can change in the course of rehearsal. In any case, by the time you are in performance, the score should already be part of you, and, like everything else that went into putting together your performance, will be forgotten.

The actor's score would certainly have no meaning for the playwright. I have often worked with playwrights who don't know or care where the actor's transitions are. Playwrights are not interested in breaking a script down or analyzing it. They don't want to take a hammer and chisel to it. They already gave birth to it, and that is quite enough for them. It is the actor who has to analyze the story in order to breathe life into it, and to make it live in a way that may even be a revelation to the playwright.

The Play Objective

The play objective, unlike the scene objective, reveals itself in various ways throughout the text. An example: in Ibsen's *Enemy of the People*—superbly adapted by Arthur Miller—Dr. Stockman wants "to save the township" by solving the environmental problem of his town's water supply, which is in danger of pollution, and will spread disease if something is not done about it. He is opposed by many people for mostly economic reasons, and ostracized for his views. An actor playing the part may want in specific scenes "to protect my family," "to rally the people to my cause," and "to shame the mayor into being my ally." These are all different ways of achieving his objective throughout the play.

And, in a play where your character dies at the end, there is something about that tragic and fatal ending that has to be prefigured in the beginning of the play. My theory is that the "seeds of doom" are already there at the entrance of any character who dies in the final scene, whether that character dies through violence or illness or suicide. And, strange as it may seem, the death of a character may not mean the failure of his or her play objective.

For instance, in the case of characters who stand up and are martyred for a cause, such as Antigone in Sophocles' play of the same name, or Joan of Arc in any number of plays and films, their struggle began in very early adolescence, and their fate was similarly sealed. Their play objective was fulfilled. In Greek tragedy, the audience often learns the end of the drama before the play begins, because the Chorus informs the spectators about what they will soon see. Destiny and fate were considered unavoidable in ancient Greece, and tragedy overwhelmed those who tried to overcome the decrees of the gods. I believe that in modern plays, too, destiny has a hand in any character's tragic ending. However, it is not a decree of the gods, but rather an inherent psychological flaw, such as a destructive or suicidal bent, that determines the character's fate. In modern times, characters are "doomed" by certain character flaws or weaknesses from the start, which are then exacerbated by their environment and relationships. In Greek tragedies, obedience to the gods is paramount, rather than a flaw in character. The actor is aware of this but should not telegraph the outcome.

Constantin in *The Seagull* is suicidal from his first entrance, because he cannot admit his feelings of rage toward his mother, and will turn them against himself instead. Nina is the device that Chekhov uses to push him over the edge, but he was already on his way to his fate. And a choice may be that he *succeeded* in "getting his mother's attention" or in "finding peace." For each scene, however, Constantin's objectives can be characterized as follows: in act one, "to make an indelible impression with my play"; in acts 2 and 3, "to test my mother's love"; and in act 4, "to carry on with my work against all odds." He fails in each scene objective (normal for Chekhov's characters), and in the fourth act, when Nina shows up and then goes, leaving him utterly hopeless, he ends his life. Looking at it this way, we could say that he fails throughout but succeeds in the end.

Eddie Carbone in Arthur Miller's *A View from the Bridge*, which Miller thought of as a contemporary Greek tragedy, dies violently at the end, but from the beginning he has various personal problems that he is not aware of and that are his Achilles' heels—his vulnerable points. They lead to his making very serious mistakes that deeply offend his community and eventually lead to his death. He is unconsciously incestuously in love with his niece, whom he has raised as if she were his daughter, and deeply jealous of a young illegal Italian immigrant, a relative who has no papers but who is under his protection. When the two young people begin to form an obvious attachment to each other, Carbone betrays the young man to the authorities, and this ultimate weak act will prove his own undoing. His play objective could be "to maintain my position of authority at home and in the neighborhood."

In any and all cases, you must choose objectives with the idea that they will succeed! If the actor does not believe he can accomplish his objective, which the character would never have embarked upon if he or she didn't have faith that it would succeed, the actor begins to "play the obstacle." As an analogy, suppose you are standing on a riverbank wanting to get to the other side. You will have to determine the depth of the water, how many stones you will have to step on, the distances between them, and how slippery they are, to get to your destination. But, to make sure that you do not slip and fall, your primary focus must always be on getting to the other side.

Obstacles

Obstacles to objectives come in great variety, but you can divide them into two major categories: physical, such as aches, pains, heat, cold, lack of time, a pen that's out of ink, the absence of an important physical object, or being tied up during a robbery; and psychological, such as character traits that interfere with attaining one's objective, like stubbornness, hostility, being overbearing or neurotic; or vulnerabilities, such as fear, weakness, insecurity, or shyness. The obstacles should theoretically and practically increase the will to succeed in your objective, and not diminish it. There is always an obstacle: the inherent obstacle to attaining an objective is, of course, "I don't have whatever it is I want." Therefore, I don't always recommend defining the obstacles. However, when the obstacles are more apparent than the objective, it helps to ask "What is in my way?" and "What do I really want?" In *The Odd Couple*, by Neil Simon, Oscar lists all the things that Felix does that drives him crazy. What is it that Oscar really wants? It may very well be "to throw Felix out without feeling guilty!"

Playing the obstacle simply means mistakenly starting the scene with a sense of failure. Everyone goes for success. No one purposely goes for failure, at least not consciously. Even if a character has a "fear of success" syndrome, he chooses an objective that is capable of succeeding: for example, "to make you feel sorry for me," or "to prove to you I'm worthless." The objective is worded positively no matter how negatively the character is thinking.

To summarize, objectives, which constitute the driving force of the actor's—and the character's—life in a play or screenplay, are defined within three categories, and in the following order:

1. the scene objective for each scene;
2. the beat objectives within the scene; and
3. the play objective, which is the character's overall desire.

CHAPTER 8

Step 5: Following Up on Place and Circumstances: The Here and Now

IIIIIIIIIIIIIIIIIIIIIIIIIIIIIIIIIIIIIIIIIIIIIIIIIII

Place

One might think that the basic Stanislavsky System question, "Where am I?" should be one of the first questions an actor asks, but, as we've been discovering, searching for the inner objects and objective through the relationship is paramount at the beginning. And in film and television, you won't see the place until the first day of the shoot. In most contemporary plays, the setting is described in detail, sometimes by blueprinting what the stage should look like, while at other times it can be a beautiful piece of prose describing the place, the greater surroundings, the town, the city, and the country—helpful references for the actor, who may even be inspired to research further the setting given by the playwright. In classical plays, of course, the place is simply "The Orchard" or "The Bedchamber," since no scenery existed. Coincidentally, the same thing is true for soap opera and sitcoms, which take place in "The Living Room" or "The Bedroom." Yet you cannot just make choices about the place offhandedly or casually, or merely assume that you know about it. The physical place should support the actor's journey in becoming the character, or it will play no part at all.

In the classroom, I encourage students to create the place for the scene with thought and care, not just to push the furniture around or disregard it altogether. New students are usually lazy about creating the place for themselves. I try to encourage them to set up a "full" place, including pieces that may never be used in the scene. There is nothing so discouraging as to exist in limbo or in the middle of some mess that has nothing to do with the circumstances in the play. I also remind them to try to place the furniture at what would be logical distances, so as to avoid taking long walks, or talking to their partner from far away, or, conversely, being on top of each other. Learning to live within a setting is a basic requirement for physical freedom, whether it is "realistic" or imaginary, or a combination of both. The place is where your character lives, and it should be as personal a choice as any other. Your choices regarding the physical place may either satisfy your character or embarrass him or leave him depressed, adding yet another emotional dimension to the character. For instance, in *A Streetcar Named Desire*, the same small apartment in New Orleans is a "palace" to Stella and a "dump" to her sister Blanche. The place she is in as she perceives it to be adds to Blanche's anxiety throughout the play.

While planning the place for your scene, do not forget the "fourth wall." This is the invisible wall or walls (if you're working on an arena stage) through which the audience views the action. The fourth wall separates you from the audience, and the theory behind it is that it will give the actor *privacy*. The fourth wall is your personal business, and it can include imaginary elements that you feel your character would relate to either happily or fearfully. For instance, it could be a wall of sunny windows looking out at a beautiful green lawn, or one of cracked plaster stained with blood smears. Since it is invisible, each character in the play can have a different "fourth wall." It is there in your mind, though you may never actually look at it. You can build it in your imagination in fine detail, but in the end what gives you the greatest privacy is what you are doing in the place in a fully justified way, and how occupied you are in doing it.

Once when I was practicing a scene for Uta Hagen's class with a fellow student, she insisted that we go over the fourth wall together. Although I understood then that it wouldn't be necessary to do that—unless we were both going to use some specific imaginary object on it, such as a window that the two of us were to look out of, or a mirror we might each peer into—I agreed to it. She quickly went over a list of items: in this corner, a window; next to it a sideboard with a vase of beautiful flowers on it; next to that, on the wall, a large painting of a landscape, then a bookshelf, then Uta, then in the other corner... "Just a minute," I interrupted her, "Did you say Uta was on the fourth wall?" "Yes!" she replied, "Uta is always on my fourth wall!" So much for privacy!

As a student, I always enjoyed imagining the exterior of the house my character was living in, the street it existed on, the neighborhood, how long I had lived there, and whether I had been happy or unhappy to be there, even if there were no references to this in the play. Later on in rehearsals, I would add other details, such as what floor the apartment might be on, who the neighbors were, and so forth. The playwright rarely gives details like these, and it's up to the actor to fill them in. Exceptions to this are such plays as Neil Simon's *Barefoot in the Park*, and *Prisoner of Second Avenue*, both set in New York.

Likewise, doing research about a town or country that your character is living in can be inspirational and help tremendously in your interpretation of the events. The great actress Laurette Taylor would travel to the actual location where the play was supposed to be taking place, before rehearsals began, just to soak up the atmosphere. The movie locations are helpful to the actor in the same way.

As for exterior settings on stage, the actor needs to visualize for himself all the surroundings, including the sky, the horizon, what's underfoot, the weather, smells, and sounds, since not all of this description will be given by the writer, unless she is Virginia Woolf writing a novel. I recommend to acting students that they visit the public place—a park or a restaurant, for instance—where the scene is taking place, and observe two or three things among the sights, sounds, or smells in the atmosphere, to incorporate when they do the scene in the classroom.

It is a great privilege for the stage actor to be able to imagine and re-create reality, and thereby build the illusion for the audience. I had a very weird but pleasant experience once when, in the middle of a scene in Neil Simon's *Plaza Suite*, which I was performing in Chicago, an airplane flew low over the theater, drowning out the dialogue for a moment. I must have jumped up and rushed over to the window of the set, because I suddenly found myself looking out at the backstage of the theater and became startled. Turning around, I saw my fellow actor staring at me, frozen. I giggled at the sudden awareness that I had entirely forgotten I was not in the Plaza Hotel in New York City, but in a theater in Chicago.

Conversely, in one of my earliest experiences acting in a film, Robert Rossen's *Lilith* (1964), I became petrified with self-consciousness when directed to simply walk down a grassy path toward a car in the distance. Thank goodness the camera was behind me, because in the first take I would have looked glazed and numb. For the first time in my life as an actor, the place and its sights, sounds, and smells were actually there. I had nothing to do but walk. No longer required to create the illusion for myself, I was so unoccupied that I felt stultified. Afterward, I came to the conclusion that the way to insure that one is occupied in a film scene is to "plant" oneself in the actual environment, and make a conscious effort to focus on the textures of what's really there. For instance, I should have been listening to the ground crunching under my feet, the trees rustling in the wind, birds singing, the feeling of the air on my bare arms, and so forth. In film, the actor's function is to *be there*, maintaining a continual awareness of and connection with the physical place. I advise actors to be sure to "connect" with something in the physical place during their preparation, and before each take.

In the theater, of course, exterior surroundings and environment are placed there by the actor through his or her imagination, even when the set is realistic; and the actor makes truthful behavioral adjustments, such as cooling off in the "heat" or bundling up in the "cold," all the while staying focused on what he or she is doing or saying. A great actor can create the illusion so completely that I'm sure everyone in an audience, at one time or another, has actually experienced the "weather" such an actor imagines.

Unlike my experience in *Lilith*, there are instances in filmmaking where actors have to suffer extreme conditions while pretending they don't exist: acting as if it's a hot day on the beach, and sitting there in a light bathing suit when it is actually the middle of winter; or pretending to be freezing, all bundled up in a parka, scarf, hat and gloves, while the scene is being shout under a broiling sun. At such times, making a film becomes an endurance test for the actors.

During the first rehearsal, it is necessary to make a preliminary plan of the place in which the scene is occurring, so that you can incorporate movement soon thereafter. In the theater, it is traditional at the first rehearsal for the director to show the cast a three-dimensional model of the set with pieces representing the walls, doors, furniture, and other elements.

I tell my students that it is essential to begin considering the physical life of the scene at the outset. If you wait too long, much of what was discovered in the emotional and psychological life of the character will be in danger of evaporating. Many a time, as a student and later as a teacher, I have seen acting students go through a scene, jumping with nerves that shatter their freedom and privacy, only to discover that they had never really gotten up on their feet before that day in class. Also, one must allow oneself to go through an awkward stage, "discovering" the place and trying out the activity (see step six) while still reading the scene, in order to gain comfort and freedom later on.

In a lecture given by the Moscow Art Theatre's Angelina Stepanova in 1965, she related anecdotes about Stanislavsky that illustrated how he had come to emphasize physical behavior related to the place and activities as equal in importance to, and even surpassing, the exploration of the character's psyche in building a character. I know that I like to get up and move around early, as an actor and as a director.

Blocking

While rehearsing a scene for class, there is no need to set blocking (the moves). Blocking is something for the director alone to consider, so he can suit it to his vision of the play or, in film or television, work it out in collaboration with the cameraman's choices. Most American stage directors these days, with the exception of those who direct musicals or classical plays, rely on the actor's impulses for a long while before finalizing the blocking. Rightly or wrongly, they leave the actor free to follow his or her impulses during early rehearsals. In such cases, the actor must make the most of his or her freedom by remaining true to the character. But you should never allow yourself to get involved with the final blocking of the scene. Let the director set the moves.

According to Stanislavsky, there are only two real reasons for a move: your character is either going toward an animate or inanimate object for a purpose, or else moving away from an object (and toward some other object) for a purpose. A simple and obvious example of a reason for a move is that when you are leaving, you must move to the door. A slightly more complex reason for moving might be that when you are threatened, you move away from whatever threatens you, and go where you feel safer. All blocking is based on moving toward or away from objects.

Sitting or standing during the course of a conflict is also closely related to the actor's impulse. If you as the character feel superior to or above the other character, you may have an impulse to stand when that character is seated; you will, in effect, be lording it over him or her. On the other hand, if you feel inferior to or beneath the other character, you may sit down or remain seated when that character stands. Or, if you feel equal to the person, you will have the impulse to face the other character eye to eye, either seated or standing. This sort of body language is automatic and spontaneous, and I have observed it throughout my teaching experience. However, if you're not comfortable or if you are unfamiliar with the place where all this is happening, you will not be free to follow your impulses or you will ignore them, afraid to step out into limbo. Freedom of movement is what every actor wishes for. And it must begin with the place. Whenever a student is frozen and self-conscious, you can be sure that he has have not considered "where" he is in the necessary physical and personal detail.

On rare occasions, film directors will set the camera to suit the actor, rather than the other way around, thus allowing for a more organic blocking. I directed a short film called *Working for Peanuts* a few years back, and I provided my cast and crew with a unique experience by taking the time to rehearse the actors thoroughly in the scenes and showing them to the entire crew *before* deciding where the camera would be placed, and what and how many shots would be made. The time I took to rehearse saved more than twice the amount of time that would have been needed if the actors and I hadn't been ready. I had a professional union crew, and they all confided to me by the end of our one week of production that they had never before been as involved with the content of a film they were hired to shoot.

Whenever I am on a movie location or a television or movie set, I explore it thoroughly. Sometimes I try to relate by physically touching every part of it, so that I will feel grounded when the camera is turned on. This replaces the stage actor's occupation with imagining the place and endowing the set with personal and physical properties. If you as a movie actor don't familiarize yourself with the set, you will become just as "hung up" as any stage actor might who has not "owned" the stage set by investing it with imaginary qualities. By "hung up" I mean awkward, not knowing what to do with one's hands or feet, which is distracting to the actor and the audience, to the point of not being able to concentrate on the action.

I remember a poignant experience from my days in Mexico working on the western *Buck and the Preacher* (1971), directed by Sidney Poitier. Every morning at the crack of dawn, we would form a caravan of cars to drive across the Durango desert to the chosen locations. For about a week, we traveled past a movie set that had been built for a previous film and was still being used by more than one movie production company. When no film was shooting, otherwise homeless Mexican Indians would inhabit the half-built structures, hanging up their clothing and utensils, even planting a small farm, and raising a few cows and chickens. That's how real the set was to them.

Circumstances

Circumstances are the surrounding and immediate facts of the scene that have a direct influence on the scene itself. They are to be broken down into three categories:

1. *Past Circumstances*: Where have I come from? Or, if I begin onstage, what have I been doing?
2. *Present Circumstances:* What time of day and what day of the week is it?
3. *Future Circumstances*: Where am I going afterward? Or, if I remain onstage, what do I plan to do afterward?

Fully deciding the circumstances in all three categories will inform you of the reason why the scene is taking place *now,* thus giving it immediacy. All life on stage should have life-and-death urgency, even the most casual exchange. Rarely are all three sets of circumstances dictated by the author.

It is not enough to know the present time and day. If you are without past or future circumstances, then what is happening in the present could take place at any other time, before or after; and that would diminish the urgency or immediacy of the conflict. The scene would then be "general," which is just another word for boring. While watching a scene from the audience, if you find yourself mentally going over your grocery list, or watching the other members of the audience, or examining the architecture of the theater, you can be assured that the scene taking place onstage is lacking immediacy, which means that some or all of the circumstances are missing, and that the actors are only concerned with how natural they are being in their moment-to-moment existence. Incidentally, Herbert Berghof despised the word "natural"; he said it was the other side of the coin of theatricality, only instead of imitating theater, the actor imitates life. "We do not want to be 'natural' on stage but 'real,' " he would say over and over again. This means being thoroughly aware of the facts surrounding the scene, justifying the raison d'être of the scene, and being really involved.

Moments before your first entrance, especially, you should stand in the wings preparing to go on by reviewing all of the preceding circumstances from a point of perhaps an hour or two before, and then review how you arrived at your place of entry—that is, whether you walked, drove, or were driven. Just before entering, it is a good idea to "contact" or connect with something about the imaginary place, using a sight, sound, smell, or feeling, which will also be imaginary. This locks in the previous circumstances and prevents you from worrying about the future.

If you begin the scene already in the place, the best preparation is to review what happened in the previous circumstances, whether written by the playwright or imagined by you; and then to remind yourself of the time—once again, either determined by the author or by yourself—before focusing on your primary object, which could be the other actor, or an object on the set.

As actors, we are committed to the "here and now." Therefore the two preparations described above for beginning a scene are effective because they help to establish a flow of circumstances: if you are offstage, you need to establish *where* you are, and if you begin on stage you need to set yourself in the *time*.

And if you are occupied with the character's previous circumstances, you will more easily be able to overcome the nerves that go along with the first entrance and the tendency you might have to "sneak" in because of them. How often have I watched actors standing in the wings mouthing their lines? It is a sure way to increase rather than relax your nerves. "Where am I now?" and "How did I get here?" are the correct questions to put your mind to, not what is going to happen after you arrive. At the same time, being occupied with circumstances should tone down the few actors I have observed who like to make grand entrances, as in the old days. Similarly, if you know where you are headed when you exit, you will be able to stride with purpose to the door.

The preparation described above is very important for stage work because in the theater, the first entrance is potentially a nerve-wracking experience for all actors, to a greater or lesser degree. Although the pressures are not nearly so great in front of the camera, knowing how to prepare to create a flow of circumstances can cut down the number of takes the actor may be required to do to "get it right."

There are few times in movies or television when an actor really impresses me with an entrance or an exit. In the old films, I think of Spencer Tracy, purposefully coming into and going out of any scene. Robert De Niro has impressed me with the seamless continuity of his on-screen life. When he walks out a door, I can almost feel where he is going. He never makes an exit just going nowhere, and neither should you!

CHAPTER 9

Step 6: Planning the Activity

IIIIIIIIIIIIIIIIIIIIIIIIIIIIIIIIIIIIIIIIIIIIIIIIIIII

An *activity* is a physical task that is secondary to the primary or scene objective. Uta Hagen called this the "while life," because the activity or activities are going on while the conflict of the scene is being played out, and can be either suggested by or actually written into the script by the author—such as scenes where the characters are eating in a restaurant or being served tea in a drawing room or working in an office. Sometimes called "business" or "stage business," the activity along with the place insures the actor's physical freedom. For all scenes, the actor should choose activities, even when the character would be restricted from doing them. Otherwise, it would seem as if the characters are in a particular place and time only to have a conversation. If talking were the only thing they were doing or all that was on their mind, the result would be very boring. When activities are not suggested in the script, the question to ask is, "What would I be doing in this place at this time if the other person or persons were not here?"

Physical freedom is essential for the actor. Even to the audience, physical freedom or the lack of it is an obvious and fundamental difference between the professional actor and the amateur, who often appears wooden and awkward. All of us have suffered from painful self-consciousness when we started out in our training. The mere fact of being observed will cause anyone to tense up—as it will in everyday life—and the student actor standing up in front of a class for the first time may feel as though he or she has become paralyzed, mute, deaf, or blind. Our senses shut down and we freeze!

It is important to note that there is a marked difference between nervousness and tension. Throughout our careers, any of us can become nervous in auditions or on opening nights, but this does not necessarily interfere with our performance. In a class scene, when a student is painfully nervous, I attribute that nervousness to unused energy, which is usually due to a lack of occupation—that is, the student has not found a way to be occupied with something in the scene; there was no planned activity, or there were missing circumstances that he or she neglected to consider. When the nervousness develops into tension, we become blocked.

As a teacher, I worried for many years about how to relax new students or how to get them to stop posing. At first, understanding that "acting is doing" helps, but then I teach them to regard "doing" as more than what the text suggests, in order to ensure the ultimate goal of attaining privacy and physical freedom. A justified continuous activity has to be considered, whether the scene permits it or not.

Even the advanced, experienced actor who has found all that is necessary psychologically and emotionally in a role will fail to convey it beyond the footlights or to maintain his own personal involvement if he is at a loss for what to do with his hands.

But an activity should not be just busyness! All physical action has to have a psychological source and a purpose behind it. The physical "business" you bring to the scene, where none is indicated, must be logical.

For example, if you are not in your own home or office, and you are a visitor or a guest, perhaps you are thinking of making a call on your cell phone. Or perhaps you want to count your change. Or perhaps you are very interested in the place, and would like to check things out. The latter possibility suggests that you might be looking around to see what the place is like, even if you are just standing in one spot. On the other hand, if you are at home, the possibilities for activities increase. There are always countless chores that need to be done; and just knowing they are possibilities, whether you do them or not, will help to free you physically from feeling awkward or tense as an actor.

Since the activities are secondary to what is primarily going on in a scene, they can be "arrested"—stopped temporarily, to be resumed or not, as the circumstances dictate, but they should never overshadow the events of the scene!

And if you choose something merely for the sake of doing stage business, you will probably be doing either too much or too little, since it is difficult to gauge how much you should be doing when there is no logical reason for it. I have watched scenes done in class in which one or both students are so busy as to be distracting, because clearly they have not justified what they are doing or why they are doing it now, in the present moment. Also, when you add a physical activity to a scene, you have to be very careful that it not be something that would require dialogue, when there is no dialogue to cover it. For instance, you cannot serve a meal to someone who makes no mention of it whatsoever, and which your character also never mentions.

You have to rehearse the activity in conjunction with the scene. I recommend that my students practice with the necessary physical objects from the second rehearsal on. I have seen students in class drink water that is supposed to be vodka in such quantities in a five-minute scene that they would be on the floor if it really were vodka. Unless the activity is practiced early in rehearsals, even though it may feel uncomfortable to handle objects while holding the script, you will become extremely self-conscious and nervous about it. How often have you seen an actor on stage holding a glass of wine and not taking even one sip? This is because he did not practice with it early enough, so that it could be integrated into his life in the scene. Also, if you are dealing with objects that you are not at all used to, such as when you play a doctor or a concert violinist, then you want to learn how to handle and work with those medical instruments or that violin immediately.

Often, theater directors who are insensitive to this problem will not introduce the physical props into the rehearsals until the set is built and it almost time for the tech and dress rehearsals. In these cases, the actors should take it upon themselves to improvise with whatever is at hand earlier.

An activity can also lead to inspiration when it becomes punctuation or an emphasis for the character's psychological life; for example, in a domestic scene between a husband and wife who are fighting while she is cleaning up and he is making himself a sandwich. The intense conversation they are engaged in will often arrest the activity, which is secondary to their discussion. However, during the course of the scene, the wife may remove her husband's plate before he has finished eating that sandwich, or the husband may slam the refrigerator door after he has gotten out the ham and cheese. Or the wife under stress may actually throw a dish she's been drying to the floor and smash it. Usually, these actions are not written into the script, but they can become inspired choices for the actor purely out of a spontaneous impulse. In rehearsals, such behavior will often excite the director, who will undoubtedly say, "Keep that in!"

In my first year of summer stock, I played the waitress in Noel Coward's one-act play *Still Life*, on which David Lean's classic black-and-white film, *Brief Encounter* (1945), was based. The set wasn't completely built until the day before we were to open, and only at the dress rehearsal did I discover too late that there was a step down to where the lovers sat at their table. Carrying a tray with two pots of tea and cups and saucers, I tripped going down the step before I reached the table, but caught the tray and its contents just in time. When I turned to go, I tripped again. I became rattled, and the same thing happened again and again as I was called to their table and then back to the counter, and it caused a great deal of hilarity among the people watching. In addition, a staircase had been newly built, stage left, which I had to climb hurriedly later in the scene to get to the railway station to deliver an urgent message. Racing up the stairs for the first time, I fell and slid down, got up, and continued on my way. More laughter. When the dress rehearsal was finally over, my director yelled, "Keep that in!" Needless to say, I was black and blue by the time the week's run ended. The moral of the story is: demand that the set and the props be ready before the dress rehearsal or you will be forced to be the comic relief, whether you want to or not!

Actors who started out in the theater do so much better with physical activities on film than actors who have had no stage experience. Theater actors have the advantage of always being quite aware of a character's physical life, because on stage, the actor is constantly observed from head to toe, and has had to get used to an entire, continuous physical life.

When I taught acting technique classes at HB Studio, I found an organic way to introduce the students to secondary activities. One student would begin with a chosen physical task that was the objective. I then added a partner to the place who had a physical task to do as well. Each person's physical business was his or her primary objective. Then, over the next week or two, I added a conflict as the primary objective for each of them, but I asked them to retain the tasks they started out with, which were already justified in the place and by the circumstances. The one-time physical objectives automatically became their *activities*, and were secondary to the conflict. And they were almost surely going to be interrupted, and probably not completed. In some cases, depending on the intensity of the conflict, the students hardly even got started with the physical task. Nevertheless, it provided them with the freedom to exist in the space.

I remember one young woman having difficulty with the

concept of activities. She was so fixated on her main objective that she would stand frozen and not even attempt to do a physical activity. I encouraged her to try to go on with her chore, and not to focus too much on her partner. The conflict: her husband was leaving her and breaking up the marriage. Her objective: to get him to stay. Her activity: to fix up the room (justified in the given circumstances). She tried forcing herself to continue with rearranging the furniture, trying one thing and another, and at times the activity seemed inappropriate, given the very serious situation between her and her husband. Occasionally, she would stop what she was doing, correctly so, and plead with him to stay. He would say no, and give her all the reasons why he was leaving her. Finally, she had to give up and let him have his way. As he was heading out the door, however, she said, "By the way, could you screw in a light bulb in the hallway on your way out?" The whole class burst out laughing, of course, and I said, "Well, there you have it! You have a justifiable physical activity... only now you've made it your overriding need." The point is that the actor must find the balance between a secondary want and a primary need.

Even if two characters are eating in a restaurant, and the conflict between them intensifies, they will stop eating and drinking in order to deal with each other. They may later resume their meal at a moment when the conflict has died down, perhaps temporarily, just as one might in real life. Recently, I was watching two of my most promising male students performing the Chinese restaurant scene in which the robbery plot unfolds in David Mamet's *Glengarry Glen Ross*, and I found it to be inactive and talky, because they had conveniently chosen to have finished their meal before the scene began. I suggested that they do it again the following week, and actually bring in a meal to eat during the scene. When they did the scene again with the added activity of eating their lunch, it was mesmerizing, and the actors were able to find the many levels in their respective characters.

When there is no physical activity apparently going on and no handling of actual physical objects, and yet the scene is working very well, it is because the actor has chosen an activity, but is in fact arrested from doing it. In Harold Pinter's *The Collection*, one man enters an apartment to accuse another man of sleeping with his wife. The second man has tried to keep the first out, but he forces his way in. In one very successful performance of the scene, the man who has forced his way in barely moved once he was inside, except to do something indicated in the dialogue, such as getting a drink from the bar. During the long verbal exchanges, he stayed still in one place, and yet he was perfectly relaxed. This caused the second man, who had been reading the paper before the interruption, to be still also, while verbally defending himself. The scene built in intensity, and the accuser finally threw the other man down onto the floor. Both actors understood what it was they might have been doing if the conflict hadn't prevented it, and it helped them to stay still and occupied without self-consciousness, and thereby to create greater suspense.

However, in a movie, physical tasks such as climbing a mountain, driving a car, or flying an airplane should naturally take precedence over any dialogue, if you want to be real and not ludicrous, as some badly directed action sequences are. If you are climbing a mountain, for instance, the necessary physical actions—the use of tools and equipment, making sure of your footing, and the constant vigilance required—would certainly have to be your main objective, even if the climbing partners are at loggerheads over climbing techniques or what to do next, or if one of them is planning to murder the other and make it look like an accident. The objective in a mountain-climbing scene would have to be simply to climb the mountain and to get to the top, and to safety, therefore making any conversation between the climbers secondary. Also, it is very common for members of a movie audience to cringe while watching a scene inside an automobile, when the "driver" spends most of the time looking at his passenger during a conversation. It is obvious that the car is being pulled along or, as in the old days, standing still in front of a screened projection of moving scenery. The main objective in such a scene should be driving, and getting to where you are going.

There are scenes in plays and films where one person is sketching or painting another, who is posing or modeling, either in an art class, or in order to have a portrait painted. The film adaptation of Oscar Wilde's *The Picture of Dorian Gray* (1945) comes to mind. In the opening scene, Lord Henry has come to visit Basil, who is in his studio painting a portrait of Dorian. Basil's objective is to paint; the conversation that takes place is secondary for him. For Dorian, the original reason for being there was to pose for the artist, but the conversation with Lord Henry, whom he is meeting for the first time, turns out to be so interesting that he is distracted. For Lord Henry—whose secondary activities include smoking cigarettes, inspecting the studio, and sitting around watching Basil paint—getting to know Dorian is primary. The fine distinction between primary and secondary activities is a necessary one for each actor to make in order to ensure his freedom and the correct construction of the scene.

In William Snyder's play *The Days and Nights of Beebee Fenstermaker*, a young lady, Beebee Fenstermaker, has taken up painting. Her neighbor and, as it turns out, her only friend, Nettie Jo, comes to her apartment at a regularly appointed time to model for her. While Beebee prepares her materials and then sketches Nettie Jo, a conversation goes on, revealing that Nettie Jo has gotten engaged and is planning to leave the city. This development will leave Beebee all alone. Needless to say, the sketching gets constantly interrupted, sometimes because Nettie Jo becomes animated and won't sit still, and sometimes because Beebee loses heart in the task itself, until finally the sketch pad and charcoal are put away altogether. Unlike the previous example, the painting and posing are secondary for both characters in this case. Beebee's objective is not the physical task of painting, but rather "to look for a way to fill her time" because she is bored, and it's only an excuse to invite her friend over. Similarly, Nettie Jo is coming in to pose for her friend as an excuse, because her real objective is "to break the news" about her engagement.

When an actor is "hung up" and feeling awkward on stage, or in front of the camera, he may fold his arms over his chest or put his hands in his pockets or lean on the furniture or pose in some way—the latter is more common in English theater than American. Even for a close-up in front of the camera you need to have a sense of physical freedom throughout. Just because a camera is trained on your face doesn't mean the rest of your body is absent and inactive. You have to remain involved, and to know what your activity is or could be. Herbert Berghof once warned a student who was playing Brick in Tennessee Williams's *Cat on a Hot Tin Roof* to keep his entire body active, even though his character has a broken leg in a cast and is using a crutch. Herbert told him to be aware of sensations in the unused leg, and reminded us all that we can never allow our body, or any part of it, to become inert on stage, or we risk being lethargic throughout.

A spear carrier on stage in a classical epic or a chorus member in a musical is usually directed to stay in a certain place and not to make too much movement so as not to distract the audience's attention from the scene that is going on at center stage. However, if the actors in these situations look frozen, they will be distracting, because nobody stands rigidly in one place without doing anything. The actor will be physically involved if he knows what he might be doing, even though he is not doing anything. And he should be mentally involved with the inner objects as well, having fully considered his past, present, and future circumstances, in order to avoid "counting the house."

Rarely do directors ask you to do something with an object, such as putting down a glass, at a precise moment, perhaps on a certain word. However, it does happen, and if you have to do something that specific, it can be justified as a part of the entire activity. Actually, correct timing happens automatically when you are doing a justified activity, and not just doing business for the sake of doing it, or simply obeying a physical direction.

Tennessee Williams is a taskmaster when it comes to a tiny physical action having to occur at precise moments: In *The Rose Tattoo*, Mangiacavallo accidentally tosses a condom out of his pocket during a scene with Rosa; and in *Summer and Smoke* Alma accidentally drops the card while unwrapping a gift from Nellie. Yet the actors must never anticipate the event or even be aware it's happened until a line has been spoken pointing it out to them. This becomes a staging problem that needs to be solved. The physical activity causing the event requires full involvement, even while the primary objective is taking precedence.

I was working with a student in a technique class who was busy, busy, busy running around during a scene. At one point his shoelace came undone, and he knelt down to tie it, and then continued with the scene. Afterwards I said, "You were not really involved in what you are doing, except when you stopped to tie your shoelace. That was the best moment in the scene, because you actually had something to do, and you had a reason to do it."

CHAPTER 10

Step 7: Delving into the Prior Relationship

||||||||||||||||||||||||||||||||||||||||||||||||||||

How did we meet? What happened along the way? What events brought us to this point in time? In a two-person scene, you may already know some facts about the prior relationship from the play, but usually you'll find that very little is written about it, and, sometimes, because the playwright is avoiding writing exposition, there is nothing at all. Therefore, how the relationship between the characters may have begun and what happened along the way are choices for the actors to make, through mutual discussion, and using their instincts. Exploring the background of the relationships helps to add layers to the performances, and will allow the actors to work together more cohesively.

As a young theatergoer, I was struck by the electricity that was always in the air when watching husband-and-wife teams perform on Broadway: Fredric March and Florence Eldridge in *Long Day's Journey into Night*, Hume Cronyn and Jessica Tandy in Donald L. Coburn's *The Gin Game*, Eli Wallach and Anne Jackson in any number of plays, including Ionesco's *Rhinoceros*. Theirs were built-in prior relationships that caused the sparks to fly.

In the theater or the classroom, some actors and directors, in addition to discussing the first meeting of their characters, or an event from the character's childhood, or their relationship as siblings, choose to develop the prior relationship through improvisation. I warn actors, however, that the appropriate time for an improvisation is only after they have rehearsed enough to become familiar with the scene in the play, and already are experiencing some vulnerability to each other. Otherwise, improvising may turn out to be just an intellectual exercise with the actors objectively "writing" ideas. Nothing can be more deadly than a forced or mentally directed improvisation. However, after they have gained a deeper sense of each other, the actors and/or the director will be able to choose the correct premise for the improvisation, and can act with spontaneity. Here are two examples of what a good premise might be:

In *A Hatful of Rain* by Michael Gazzo, the brothers, Johnny and Polo, have a competitive and volatile relationship. Johnny begs his younger brother Polo for twenty dollars (remember, this was 1955) to pay off a loan shark, and Polo refuses at first, telling him to "go rob someone in the subway." When Johnny gives up, and tells Polo that he is going to face the thugs who are coming after him, Polo does an about-face and wants to help him. A useful premise that would bring emotional energy into the scene is for the actors to improvise an event from their boyhood, at home or in a playground or ball field, where they are competing in a game and it escalates into a brawl, demonstrating how Johnny bullies Polo. Improvising a scene like this can help justify Polo's deep-seated resentment toward his brother, and permit both actors to more freely play the brutal behavior they indulge in toward each other.

In the case of siblings, I recommend always making an immediate substitution from your own family, because the dynamics of interfamilial relationships in plays and screenplays are so complex (see page 65). If you haven't got a brother, you can substitute a sister, or even a parent.

In Edward Albee's *Who's Afraid of Virginia Woolf?* the married couple, George and Martha, battle from the beginning of the play, but they reach the pinnacle of rage in the middle of act 2, at which point they famously declare "total war!" Starting with the premise that they had a loving relationship at the beginning of their marriage, the actors could improvise a scene of the couple coming home from their honeymoon and settling down in their new home. The two actors could then experience their early affection for each other, which would help to bond them, and at the same time inspire them to look for all the pitfalls and disappointments that might have happened in the relationship that brought them to their present circumstances. Their fighting would then be coming from a source and a background, and it would have justification, as such things do in real life. It could prevent the actors from simply "exercising what's left of their wits," as George says in the play. Even without an improvisation, the actors can work on the details of these prior relationship circumstances in their imaginations.

Quite rare in the theater, although they appear often in screenplays, are flashback scenes, such as the ones in Arthur Miller's *Death of a Salesman*, which portray the brothers, Biff and Happy, as young teenagers in their backyard. Here, their prior relationship, and how their father favored the older Biff over the younger Happy, is made quite clear by the writer, who gives the actors the opportunity to play it out, so that discussion and/or improvisation in this case would be unnecessary.

There is also no need to invent or imagine what the prior relationship was when you play historical characters whose backgrounds are public knowledge and can be researched, such as that of Helen Keller and Annie Sullivan in *The Miracle Worker*, by William Gibson; Anne and her family in *The Diary of Anne Frank*, by Frances Goodrich and Albert Hackett; or Eugene Gant—who is actually Thomas Wolfe, the author of the original autobiographical novel upon which the play is based—and his mother in *Look Homeward, Angel* by Ketti Frings.

When playing real-life characters, actors will benefit from reading biographies and looking at old photographs. I remember what a treat it was to study old faded photographs and read the memoirs of the 104- and 106-year-old Delaney sisters in the play *Having Our Say,* by Emily Mann, when I was coaching the actress Diahann Carroll in preparation for the television version. Feature films and television movies, much more often than plays, may take as their subject historical, political, literary, and entertainment figures. Although most of the research into the origins of the characters' relationships has been done by the author, and probably written into the scenes, it behooves the actor to do his own work, looking for personal clues. What you won't have to do for these types of scripts, however, is use your imagination when it comes to actual background facts.

Bear in mind, however, that the author has written a fictitious character, based on history, often very loosely at that, and therefore not technically historical. The words the characters say are usually invented by the author, although real words are often interspersed with the invented ones. Scenes are also invented, and the situations in them, based, again, on historical material, are therefore works of fiction. So lots of imagination, substitutions, etc., are called for—but not, I repeat, when it comes to the actual elementary facts.

Secondly, you do have to use your imagination to project yourself into the imaginary, quasi-historical situations and circumstances and background in the play or film. To take just one example, *The Diary of Anne Frank,* by Frances Goodrich and Albert Hackett (very successful both as a play and as a film made in 1959), is a highly fictionalized account, as anyone knows who has read the actual diary, or accounts by Miep Gies and other people involved with protecting the Franks in hiding, or seen documentary films about Anne Frank. And such characters as the elder van Daans (Lou Jacobi and Shelley Winters) are completely fictionalized, even to their names, as is the dentist Dr. Dussell (Ed Wynn), whose name and personality in real life were also different from what they are in the play. The account in the play of his personality and how he got along with Anne is complete fiction, written for dramatic purposes. It works beautifully in the play, but it is not history, and the actor cannot go to a biographical account for actual background information. In any event, when taking on a real-life character, the actor must go about personalizing it, just as he or she would with a purely fictitious character. It will always be your thoughts and experiences and your personal interpretation that will bring him or her back to life!

One more exception in which you will not have to use your imagination to come up with information on the prior relationship is in the writing style of the television soap opera, where every inconceivable fact about what went on in the characters' former lives is told and retold. Also, it would be difficult to make something up, since it is common for the writers to suddenly bring up some background fact, at the last moment, that would never have occurred to the actor.

I was once coaching an actress who had been appearing in the soap opera *Guiding Light* for seven years, playing a "good" girl, a hardworking journalist, as I recall, and so responsible and trustworthy that she was becoming horribly bored with her character. To try to inject some freshness for her, we analyzed and broke down some of the episodes, and occasionally discussed possibilities for her past life, when it seemed appropriate to justify some of her story line. Suddenly, one day, she was handed a script revealing that she had been a prostitute in her young adult years! She was bowled over. We were stumped as to how to deliver the speech containing this revelation to her longtime paramour, and to justify never having talked about it before. We made the decision (in the subtext only, being careful not to create any overt reaction) that she had had amnesia, and had just that day flashed on the memory!

CHAPTER 11

Step 8:
The Character Chart, Part 1:
Writing a Preliminary
Character Background

||||||||||||||||||||||||||||||||||||||||||||||||||||

Introduction

According to Michael Chekhov, master acting teacher, and nephew of the great playwright Anton Chekhov, to create a character, the actor "must strive for the attainment of complete harmony between . . . body and psychology."

I learned as a student how to build a *character chart* in three parts, and it remains a wonderful tool for organizing all the discoveries one makes in the course of studying a play.

In reading the script, you will have figured out what the author thinks of the character. You will have read as well what the other characters say about your character. Except for taking account of such essential facts as the character's name, gender, age, and vital background information, my advice is to ignore all of the above! What may be more difficult to ignore is what you yourself have begun to feel about your character, but you must at first!

As you have already gathered in this book, the Stanislavsky philosophy differs from earlier acting techniques in that you do not want to start out with a preconceived image. If you begin to envision how your character will look, sound, and move before you have even mixed the colors on the palette and put brush to canvas, you will be starting at the end and working backward, which is much more difficult than starting at the beginning and working forward.

Years ago, the brilliant actor Paul Muni, who was one of the ensemble members of the Group Theater and went on to have a memorable Hollywood movie career, returned to Broadway to play Henry Drummond, the part based on Clarence Darrow in Jerome Lawrence and Robert E. Lee's *Inherit the Wind*. I had the privilege of seeing him live on stage. I was a student then, and I will never forget his towering performance, which awed me with its minute details, such as how he would place his pencil behind his ear when getting ready to interrogate a witness. In an interview that was printed in the playbill, he was asked how he went about creating his characters. "I build my character the way my grandmother bakes an apple pie," he said, "First she gets all the ingredients and utensils together, then she puts on her apron and bandana...and then she bakes the pie!" If there is one part of the Stanislavsky-based modern acting technique that is mysterious, it is the moment when the character you have been working on suddenly emerges, like that apple pie that comes hot out of the oven. In an ideal rehearsal period, the moment comes usually before you know it (see step 11).

I fully believe that all of us have experienced, in one way or another, everything any written character has experienced, and we have done so by the time we were twelve years old! Each of us has within us the potential for all the characters ever written. Obviously, we have not actually lived through love relationships, marriage, betrayal, loss, divorce, murder, suicide, revenge, etc., by twelve years of age, but I contend that we have experienced these things emotionally and "lived" them in our imaginations. That is why, in order to build an original character, not one that is preconceived or a cliché, we can begin with ourselves.

I know that it would be impossible for us not to gain some sort of image for the character after we have finished our initial reading of the script, especially in our times, when we have an avalanche of media at our fingertips, every day of the week. But we must learn to put that picture on a shelf, and try to begin afresh, from the beginning. In my classes, I have sometimes illustrated this point by referring to Garson Kanin's classic comedy, *Born Yesterday*. I say we must start our journey as if we were born yesterday! Imagine how much harder it is for us to do that than it was for Eleonora Duse, and yet she complained about stereotypes, and declared that we would only have something original to say if all the theaters of the world burned down and were not rebuilt for fifty years! Yes, there are universals of human psychology, but each one of us is an individual, and the path we should want to take is the one that leads us to use our own particular sensibilities and personal experience in interpreting the role we are playing.

To start with, the actor needs to begin by putting the emphasis on the "I" and not on the "Who" when asking the classic Stanislavsky question, "Who am I?" When I began acting school, my classmates and I were drilled in the use of the first-person "I" instead of the third-person "he" or "she" while discussing our scenes and characters with the teacher. This rule served as a first step in beginning to personalize the character.

To help us do this, we constructed a character chart, consisting of three sections:

1. Background
2. Character Traits
3. Life Drives

The latter two sections will be discussed in steps 9 and 10.

Background Questions

If we consider the chart a map, as the name implies, the character background is the first leg of our journey. A preliminary background, subject to revision as necessary, can be composed immediately after you have read the play or screenplay. All you have to do is to answer the following eleven questions:

1. Where was I born?
2. What size family did I come from?
3. What was/is my father's occupation?
4. Is my father living or dead?
5. What was/is my mother's occupation?
6. Is my mother living or dead?
7. How far did my education go, and what is the highest degree I earned?
8. What occupation(s) have I had?
9. What is my marital status?
10. Do I have any children?
11. If I have any hobbies, what are they?

Some of the answers to those questions will clearly be found in the play, and, of course, will be used by the actor, but where not all of these facts are stated—and in most plays they are not—you should rely on your instincts. The answers to the questions can be thought about, even guessed at, early in your exploration of the part, and you are free to change your mind about them as often as you wish all through rehearsals. As you progress in the role, if you now begin to feel you were one of many children, although you originally thought you were an only child, you can erase your first response and put in the new one. That is true for every "fact" not given by the playwright.

As you can see, the answers asked for are *factual*, and not philosophical or psychological. An all-too-common propensity among acting students is to write long, involved, and ulti-mately confusing theses on the character's origins. How often have I asked for a simple fact about a character's background and heard instead a psychological prognosis of the character, as though written by a clinician in a mental health institu-tion?

In opposition to this all-too-intellectual approach—which is, I'm sorry to say, often proposed in other acting classes—I frequently joke with my students by announcing that in my class, they will learn to be actors, not writers, and in order to do this, they will use the "Joe Friday" method of acting! He was the detective played by a deadpan Jack Webb in the popular old television show *Dragnet*, who repeated the expres-sion week after week, "All I want are the facts, ma'am, just the facts!" Webb didn't want the witnesses to get emotional dur-ing his interrogations, or to express attitudes and opinions, which would only muddy things up for him. This should also be true for actors working on their characters.

As you begin your exploration, it is not a good idea to "psy-choanalyze" the character, whom you are not yet in a posi-tion to know. Most actors are probably not equipped to be lay analysts anyway, unless they have studied psychology. And you risk wiping out the character's humanity, as well as com-promising your own neutrality and openness. It is impossible to be subjective and objective at the same time! As Herbert Berghof said, in another pithy statement that my very young ears heard and have never forgotten, "You can get to midtown from downtown, and you can get to midtown from uptown, but you cannot get to midtown from downtown and uptown at the same time!" In other words, concentrate on working on the character using the steps outlined here, and you will get to where you want to go; but do not psychoanalyze the char-acter, unless you feel much, much later on in the work that it would be helpful or necessary.

If you "psychoanalyze" one of Chekhov's characters, for example, you run the risk of overlooking what is so inherently funny and pitiful about the character. It is hard enough for American actors (and directors, I might add) to see what is humorous in the Chekhovian characters anyway, but to get overly serious and clinical about their unconscious problems at the beginning of your work only darkens the mood more. Later on, if and when it proves necessary and enlightening, the actor may want to understand the character's psychology in greater depth.

Starting out with the subjective "I," actors should only fill in the vital background facts in the chart as if they were the character filling out the top portion of a personnel or jury-duty form. No other character's name or events that are part of the plot should be included, or, indeed, anything beyond the bare factual answers. After the eleven basic questions have been answered, feelings connected with them will arise, which will no doubt be of help when making other decisions about the character. I have often referred to the character background itemized in this way as a "pressure cooker."

Instead of letting out steam, this procedure builds up the pressure as you continue on your journey. How you felt about your parents and siblings during your childhood, or about your children, or when you got your first job, or if you were treated badly or abandoned as an infant, will all be brewing throughout the rehearsal process, most of it unconsciously. One cannot expect to know how much the character's past experiences, good or bad, have influenced and produced the events in the play prior to the practice and personalizing of those events, unless, of course, it is an intellectual choice only, which you should avoid making. The character has to be born all over again, and in you!

When I am coaching an actor in preparation for a role in a play or movie, I give that actor the assignment to think about and answer the eleven questions after the very first session, the first read-through of the play or screenplay. Since this can never be done too early, and since the simple facts asked for can be easily changed throughout the work on the role, it literally keeps the actor's hands busy, as well as serving to distract him or her from jumping to conclusions about behavior, or worrying about memorizing the lines too early, and potentially setting "line readings."

I know that to many actors this last statement regarding the lines is a controversial one, since there is a widely held, yet erroneous, belief that "I cannot begin to work on my role until I know all my lines," when, in fact, the opposite is true! As I have stated earlier, learning your lines organically and as gradually as time permits, as you would in the theater or for the classroom, will better prepare you for the overnight cramming you will have to do for a job in the media. Only with complete faith in this system will you be able to organize your time, no matter how brief, to learn the lines in such a way as to be able to begin to build a full-fledged character while studying for the next day's shoot. In any case, when filming a movie, your character is "accumulated" throughout the entire shooting schedule (see page 215). The character you are creating may not feel as fully formed to you in the first shooting days as it will later on, but it will be cut together satisfactorily by the editor.

Here are two examples of the biographical background section of the character chart, both from *The Glass Menagerie* by Tennessee Williams. Laura Wingfield presents us with an unusually complete set of character background facts that are written into the play, right down to hobbies:

1. **Where was I born?** Louisville.
2. **What size family did I come from?** I have one brother.
3. **What was/is my father's occupation?** Telephone repairman.
4. **Is my father living or dead?** Not sure.
5. **What was/is my mother's occupation?** She sells magazine subscriptions over the telephone.
6. **Is my mother living or dead?** Living.
7. **How far did my education go, and what is the highest degree I earned?** I graduated high school and registered but failed to take a business school course.

8. **What occupation(s) have I had?** None.
9. **What is my marital status?** Single.
10. **Do I have any children?** No.
11. **If I have any hobbies, what are they?** Collecting glass figurines.

In this great play, the remarkable fact is that an actress doesn't have to invent anything. And, as you can see, there is really no room in the list for mention of her physical handicap, her low self-esteem, or her crush on Jim O'Connor, the gentleman caller, or even for her attitudes towards her mother and brother. There is no need to list these things because they will be discovered and personalized throughout the rehearsals and performances of the play, and, even more important for retaining subjectivity, Laura herself would never reveal to the public the feelings she has about them! It would also be quite insulting to Laura to diagnose her with any serious mental, emotional, or psychological problems brought on by her mother's depression and need to control, or her brother's frustration, when in fact she is the clearest thinker in the play. If you were not to give her credit for this, and instead psychoanalyzed her right off the bat, you would never get to the heart of the character, or understand her. Any such analysis, in fact, would probably culminate in the cliché of Laura as only shy and retiring, and nothing much more.

On the other hand—and this is more usual in dramatic literature—none of the details about the background of Jim O'Connor, the gentleman caller, are given in the play, and filling them in requires the actor's imagination. The facts that are given are these:

7. **How far did my education go, and what is the highest degree I earned?** I am a high school graduate, taking some courses in public speaking.
8. **What occupation(s) have I had?** I work in the shoe factory.
9. **What is my marital status?** I am engaged to be married.

10. Do I have any children? No.

And we might easily guess from his conversation the answer to the question:

11. If I have any hobbies, what are they? Sports.

But we are told almost nothing about his family, so we have to make the answers to those questions up. Here are the possibilities:

1. **Where was I born?** Louisville.
2. **What size family did I come from?** Being an Irish Catholic, I probably come from a big family, and am probably the oldest child, and have brothers but no sisters.

The answer to question 7, "How far did my education go, and what is the highest degree I earned?" suggests the answers to questions:

3. **What was/is my father's occupation?** A longshoreman (or perhaps a policeman).
4. **Is my father living or dead?** Living.
5. **What was/is my mother's occupation?** Housekeeper.
6. **Is my mother living or dead?** Living.

So there we have it: a simple recital of facts about the characters' biographies, without analysis, which is unnecessary at this point in the process.

Imagine if, in a play or screenplay, you were playing Hitler and took to analyzing him immediately—an easy but very dangerous trap to fall into in the case of a character we have all seen and heard in numerous documentaries, and read about in so many biographies. In his childhood, he was miserable, deprived of love, and severely abused, and he came from a dysfunctional family (as if that explained why he became an aberrant, delusional sociopath), and...who cares at this stage of the game? Eventually, you will get to the source of his psychopathic fits of rage at his subordinates, as Klaus Kinski did in *The Downfall* (2005), and this will add depth to the insanity, but you certainly can't start there. The actor's job, beyond listing the essential facts of Hitler's background, is to attempt to create for himself his *current* depraved point of view, through personalization, defining objectives, and developing the relationships that are in the text. However, nothing prevents the actor from eventually considering the pathology of a character like this, brought on by a deeply troubled childhood, and/or a series of early adult experiences, once you have "become" him—maybe not until just before opening night, or near the end of the shoot.

In the 1960s, I played Gittel Mosca in William Gibson's *Two for the Seesaw*. A week or two after the opening, I was interviewed by a Baltimore newspaper and was shocked to hear my own replies to questions about Gittel's past life, which I described as under the shadow of her controlling, immigrant mother; and about her future, for which I predicted she would marry a much older, successful man, probably a widower, then spend her free time doing philanthropic work. Up to the moment of the interview, I had had no idea I knew all this! As an analogy, human beings do not go into therapy until after the harm has already been done to them.

To return to Laura Wingfield, just the facts that her father was a telephone repairman and that she doesn't know where he is or even if he is still alive, and that her mother sells subscriptions over the phone, suggest no doubt that she grew up poor, and this, coupled with her handicap, could certainly create a lack of self-esteem. Her hobby of collecting little glass figures suggests that she relates to fragile things, and wants to avoid harshness. And so on and so forth.

In answering the eleven questions about character background, you may be inspired by the background of someone else whom you know, or you can use facts from your own background. As I've mentioned before, becoming a character is in some ways mysterious, happening usually without your awareness at first, and yet the actor is always at the helm, making choices all along the way. It is essential, therefore, not to impede this process through intellectuality, but to rely more on instinct and on your imagination.

Here are five more examples of well-known characters from theatrical literature and the background portion, which is the first part of their character charts:

For Juliet in Shakespeare's *Romeo and Juliet*:

1. **Where was I born?** Verona, Italy.
2. **What size family did I come from?** I am an only child.
3. **What was/is my father's occupation?** A wealthy nobleman.
4. **Is my father living or dead?** Living.
5. **What was/is my mother's occupation?** She runs the household.
6. **Is my mother living or dead?** Living.
7. **How far did my education go, and what is the highest degree I earned?** I can read and write.
8. **What occupation(s) have I had?** None.
9. **What is my marital status?** Single.
10. **Do I have any children?** No.
11. **If I have any hobbies, what are they?** Dancing, embroidering, sewing, drawing.

For Uncle Vanya in Chekhov's play:

1. **Where was I born?** On a country estate not far from the city of Kharkov in Ukraine.
2. **What size family did I come from?** One sister.
3. **What was/is my father's occupation?** Landowner and gentleman farmer.
4. **Is my father living or dead?** Dead.
5. **What was/is my mother's occupation?** Head of the household.

6. **Is my mother living or dead?** Living.
7. **How far did my education go, and what is the highest degree I earned?** Self-educated.
8. **What occupation(s) have I had?** I manage the estate.
9. **What is my marital status?** Single.
10. **Do I have any children?** No.
11. **If I have any hobbies, what are they?** Debates and discussions.

For Catherine Sloper in *The Heiress*, the play and film by Ruth and Augustus Goetz, based on Henry James's novel *Washington Square*:

1. **Where was I born?** New York City.
2. **What size family did I come from?** I am an only child.
3. **What was/is my father's occupation?** Doctor.
4. **Is my father living or dead?** Living.
5. **What was/is my mother's occupation?** Housewife.
6. **Is my mother living or dead?** Dead.
7. **How far did my education go, and what is the highest degree I earned?** I had a high school education at an exclusive private school.
8. **What occupation(s) have I had?** I run my father's household.
9. **What is my marital status?** Single.
10. **Do I have any children?** No.
11. **If I have any hobbies, what are they?** Embroidery, needlework.

For Tom Ripley in *The Talented Mr. Ripley* (1999), Anthony Minghella's film based on Patricia Highsmith's novel:

1. **Where was I born?** New York City
2. **What size family did I come from?** I am an only child.
3. **What was/is my father's occupation?** Janitor.
4. **Is my father living or dead?** I don't know.
5. **What was/is my mother's occupation?** Housewife.

6. Is my mother living or dead? I don't know.

7. How far did my education go, and what is the highest degree I earned? I had an elementary school education and some high school, studied music, especially piano, largely self-educated.

8. What occupation(s) have I had? I was on the janitorial staff at Princeton University, and an attendant in a washroom at a concert hall.

9. What is my marital status? Single.

10. Do I have any children? No.

11. If I have any hobbies, what are they? Music.

For the unnamed heroine played by Joan Fontaine in Hitchcock's *Rebecca* (1940):

1. Where was I born? A small town in the United States.

2. What size family did I come from? I am an only child.

3. What was/is my father's occupation? Small-time merchant.

4. Is my father living or dead? Dead.

5. What was/is my mother's occupation? Housewife.

6. Is my mother living or dead? Dead.

7. How far did my education go, and what is the highest degree I earned? I went to a girls' finishing school.

8. What occupation(s) have I had? I am a lady's traveling companion and general servant.

9. What is my marital status? Single.

10. Do I have any children? No.

11. If I have any hobbies, what are they? Traveling, reading.

The American playwrights David Mamet and Edward Albee and the British dramatist Harold Pinter write plays that derive from the Theater of the Absurd of Samuel Beckett and Eugene Ionesco. They are actually absurdist themselves in many ways, although in quite a few of their plays the characters seem to exist in a more real context than in either Beckett's or Ionesco's abstract pieces. Still, the settings and incidents often take on an almost surreal quality of eerie timelessness and isolation, as if the characters were alone in their own universe.

One of the hallmarks of absurdist plays is that they have no exposition, not even an implied one, and any past life the characters have has to be invented, in large part, by the actor. Where do the characters in Beckett's *Waiting for Godot* come from, where are they going, and what were their lives like before the play begins? Basically, we have no idea. We are presented with characters that have no past that we know about. The same thing is true in many of Ionesco's plays. And it is almost equally true in Pinter and Mamet. Pinter's *The Homecoming* and *The Collection* are purely absurdist plays, although they seem very realistic, certainly more so than such farces as Ionesco's *The Bald Soprano*, set in a middle-class English home. Ionesco was inspired to write this play by trying to learn English from records. Finding the phrases useless and ridiculous, he decided to write a play in which everyone repeats meaningless phrases as if they were making real conversation. The same quality of odd, bizarre conversations that seem, at least at first, to have no context, is true of a few of Mamet's plays, not to mention Tom Stoppard's *Rosencrantz and Guildenstern Are Dead*, and others.

Unlike realistic plays, absurdist pieces may seem on the surface to be harder to analyze, but in fact these playwrights may leave more room for the creative imagination of the actor than plays whose characters' backgrounds are accessible. You have to supply a lot that the authors do not, and remain flexible throughout.

Choosing the background for the character in the above simple way, by answering "the eleven questions," is freeing. It gives you the precise feeling that you are starting at the beginning, and that you are preparing to give birth to a character, rather than having to step into one that has been fully formed. The word "simple" in acting is actually a complex term. It involves the opposite of judgments and complications, and the greatest compliment you can give an artist in any field is to say that he or she has been simple in his or her art. The very aim of the artist is to clarify things for the audience by shining light on the truth of the human condition. If instead the artist, especially the interpretative artist, gets in his or her own way with all sorts of opinions, analyses, and, heaven help us, ideas, we the audience, remain in the dark. An appropriate quotation from W. H. Auden comes to mind: "All that was intricate and false; the truth was simple." For actors, to be simple is not easy. It takes hard work and commitment.

CHAPTER 12

Step 9:
The Character Chart, Part 2:
Deciding on the Character Traits

|||||||||||||||||||||||||||||||||||||||||||||||||||||

The second part of the character chart is a definition of traits: a psychological outline of your character's vulnerabilities, standards, moral outlook, peculiarities, and attitudes. The list of traits that you write down will consist of adjectives and descriptive phrases, no fewer than ten and as many as you want. Don't be concerned if the words have overlapping meanings, such as "demanding" and "bossy." Shades of meanings, as you will see, are useful when you are describing a character.

When working on a play, this section of the character chart should ideally be constructed about midway in the rehearsal process, or even a little later, certainly after you have learned the lines. When you list the traits, you will be using your instincts about the character—not your conscious mind, but rather the abstract and imaginative part of yourself. It is at this stage of rehearsal that the relationships between yourself and the others are beginning to cause reflexive responses and/or behavior in you, such as "quick to anger," "hurt," "a swell of affection," or "feelings of possessiveness." Waiting until this time to define the traits will ensure that your choices will not be intellectual but organic, arising directly from the situation and circumstances as you live them.

You realize by now that you must always be wary of trying to make any decisions too early in your progress. Ideally, you should make choices only when you are actually feeling them. You are then in a position to write the traits down as they come to you. For my students, the best time to do this seems to be after the lines have been learned, and after they have performed the scene once in class. And, of course, the character traits are also subject to revision and to additions as necessary—they are not written in stone, only on paper. You may think you are sure about a particular trait, and the next rehearsal may reveal to you that a different or slightly modified trait applies more accurately. This is where shades of language, subtleties and nuances can come into play.

Of course, "early" is a relative term when you compare rehearsals for the theater to getting ready for a guest spot on a nighttime television drama. In the theater, you are building a character who will live throughout the run of the play and one who moves the plot forward, whereas in the case of television drama, you are "him" or "her" for a day or a few days only, and your character is subject to the final edit. In order to avoid the trap of becoming a cliché in a nighttime television guest role, you will have to fit this step into your study of the scene(s) in the time at your disposal, but hopefully after you are at least familiar with the lines and events. However, in the relatively more leisurely time allowed in movies, you can make a list of traits before you begin shooting and make revisions and additions, if need be, over the course of your entire schedule.

The list of traits on the character chart—and I recommend at least *ten* and as many more as you can come up with—can be made up of simple words, although a dictionary or thesaurus is a good book to keep handy as a reference. Words that describe a character are *positive* ones, such as strong, responsible, good, loving, or friendly and *negative* ones, such as mean, stubborn, violent, or stingy, as well as terms with less definite moral associations, such as shy, overly meticulous, lonely, or reclusive. You want to be sure that your choices are basic to the character, and not just temporary or passing attitudes adopted under pressure. For good practice in honing your instincts about *basic* character traits, make a list of your own traits, or someone close to you. Don't be afraid to list opposites, perhaps in pairs, such as "secure/insecure" or "superior/inferior." Those things may all be true of a character.

Below, I have written two partial lists of traits for two great characters in dramatic literature—Shakespeare's Hamlet and Ophelia.

Can the first list describe Prince Hamlet, who is dedicated to revenge and whose life ended in bloody violence; and can the second list foretell Ophelia's tragic suicide? The simple words chosen might in themselves describe any character, but it is the totality of the choices taken together that is specific to the character you are playing. Notice that in the following lists I did not include "vengeful" for Hamlet or "suicidal" for Ophelia, because these words do not describe their basic characteristics, but only indicate what is happening to them in the circumstances of the play—a very important distinction, and a challenge in the choices the actor faces. Also, the list does not contain opinions other characters have about them, such as "mad" for Hamlet and "fair" for Ophelia; or negative judgments such as "a procrastinator" for Hamlet and "childish" for Ophelia.

The actor must remain subjective and determine for him or herself whether Hamlet or Ophelia were basically always hallucinatory and on the edge of their sanity, or—the much more active and organic choice, and the one I recommend—that the play's circumstances made them that way.

Hamlet:

Passionate   Independent
Sensitive   Stubborn

Impulsive	Energetic
Temperamental	A leader
Educated	Ambitious
Only child	Given to obsession
Melancholic	Witty
Analytic	

Ophelia:

Loyal	Easily swayed
Young	Eager to please
Loving	Affectionate
Obedient	Afraid
Fragile	Easily hurt
Romantic	Emotional
Sheltered	A dreamer
Dependent	

If Hamlet is passionate and temperamental, as I interpret his character, he was probably also overindulged as an only child. So it would stand to reason that he would go "mad" and be driven to murderous revenge when his father, his throne and his mother are ripped away from him by his hated uncle. And if Ophelia is fragile, dependent, and obedient—a fair analysis—then the loss of her lover and the death of her father would lead her to become insane and eventually to commit suicide.

For illustrative purposes, here are traits for part 2 of the chart for the characters whose biographical background questions were answered in step 8. If some of the same adjectives are repeated for different characters, remember that it is the ensemble of traits that gives you a specific character. Of course, many more adjectives for each character could be added to the list, and you are free to make your own list for any of the characters below.

Laura in *The Glass Menagerie*:

Shy	Sweet
Kind	Endearing
Goodhearted	Intelligent
Honest	Lonely
Loving	A dreamer

Jim O'Connor in *The Glass Menagerie*:

Earnest	Ambitious
Well-meaning	Sociable
Forthright	Friendly
Conscientious	Basically shy
Honest	Inferiority complex
Polite	Eager
Well-mannered	Athletic

Juliet in Shakespeare's *Romeo and Juliet*:

Loyal	Dutiful
Feminine	Obedient
Young	Sensitive
Innocent	Sheltered
Goodhearted	Nurturing
Loving	Smart
Passionate	Artistic
Committed	

Uncle Vanya in Chekhov's play:

Obsessive	Touchy
Conscientious	Easily hurt
Critical	Childish
Passionate	Responsible
Unhappy	Temperamental

Judgmental   Lonely
Sensitive

Catherine Sloper in *The Heiress*:

Shy   Needy
Kind   Obedient
Repressed   Sweet
Gullible   Long-suffering
Naïve   Resentful

Tom Ripley in *The Talented Mr. Ripley*:

Observant   Repressed
Susceptible   Sensitive to his own needs
Resourceful   Strong ego
Eager to please   Needy
Flattering   Paranoid
Easily upset and hurt   Narcissistic
Egotistical

The unnamed heroine played by Joan Fontaine in Hitchcock's film *Rebecca*:

Shy   Honest
Kind   Loving
Well-meaning   Sweet
Goodhearted   Endearing
Conscientious   Intelligent

More about Negative Character Traits

In an interview for a book on actors, Kim Stanley—an inspiration to young actresses, including myself, in the 1950s and '60s—said that she would make a list of adjectives describing her character and then cross out all the words she felt were like her. Then she "worked on what was left." Although that statement was too general, and the phrase "worked on" needed to be explained, it inspired me to formulate a way of personalizing the character traits.

Once you have made a list that you are satisfied with, pick two or three traits that you feel *least* describe you. Look at each word carefully, and then search your memory to find an experience from your past in which your behavior could have been described by that word. You may not think that you're "hostile," for instance, but there has certainly been at least one incident in your life when you felt and perhaps even behaved in a hostile manner. Perhaps you were a witness to a horrible event where someone was hurt, and had murderous thoughts toward the perpetrator. In your next rehearsal, you can endow the other person in the scene with having committed that long-ago deed, in order to bring up the repressed hostile feelings.

The endowment gives you a point of view that could effect a change of behavior in your response to the other actor, which is what you are looking for. Obviously, the endowment is not going to change the object you are endowing, whether it is the other actor or something else; the endowment exists only in your imagination. In my classes, I used to introduce the use of endowments by discussing how you could be walking down any street in New York City, and some stranger might shout obscenities at you, or—as once happened to me—hit you on the head with an umbrella. I pointed out that the stranger had probably "endowed" you with some long-ago injustice, and that she was behaving in accordance with that endowment.

Other examples of traits belonging to your character that you may feel are foreign to you, or are reluctant to admit to, are "sloppy" or "naïve" or "ignorant." And you are certainly not "illiterate" or "uneducated." At first, the traits you have chosen to work on will begin to operate in you when you simply recall the times you felt that way. However, to lock them in so that they become an integral part of your character, you will have to focus on the one element in the past experience that you believe caused the feeling. If you're like me, and you have to play a character who is uneducated or even illiterate, for instance, you may feel that way when you are with a brilliant professor speaking about a subject of which you know nothing. You can then endow your acting partner with using a vocabulary that is difficult or impossible to understand.

This endowment is a "fact" that exists only in your imagination. Similarly, based on past experience, if you think you become "sloppy" when you are on vacation in a rustic cabin and expecting no visitors, you can endow the place in the scene with the cabin's remembered atmosphere—its smells, perhaps. Or, if you remember becoming extremely "shy" when, as a small child, you saw a naked person, you can endow your partner as having no clothes on.

Note that the above examples all refer to what I term negative traits. I have found it to be true that actors, like everyone else, would rather characterize themselves as having positive traits, such as "thoughtful," "sweet," "honest," "friendly," or "sensitive," and they always try to put their best face forward; it's only natural. So in order to round out your character, you will probably need to select two or three of the negative traits to explore.

Back in the days of my Technique classes, I assigned an improvisation exercise where the student would have to invent a character based on three negative traits. It was a profound exercise in emotion, since it is the negative traits that create greater vulnerability in you. For instance, no one kills or commits suicide unless he is full of rage, depressed, bitter, isolated, and generally miserable and unhappy. As an exercise for class, I much prefer to teach students to release emotions through the process of personalizing a character's negative traits using memories of past experience, rather than isolating an emotional memory for no other purpose than to cry.

Digging around in your past life in order to select endowments to expose buried or repressed feelings, and using them in scenes and improvisations, is valuable to your overall growth as an actor. Incidentally, there is a difference between repressed and suppressed feelings: repressed feelings are those of which you are not conscious because they have been pushed out of consciousness, and they may return under certain circumstances; suppressed feelings are those you consciously choose not to act on.

For instance, Nora's rage at Helmer over specific things he does is something she is aware of throughout *A Doll's House*, and she chooses to damp it down—this is suppression. But her knowledge that he really does not view her as an equal human being and marriage partner is something she has repressed, because it is unbearable. Her repressed feelings about him return to consciousness when his behavior becomes completely impossible, so that she is almost forced to acknowledge that he really has no respect for her as a human being. Those feelings were there all along, but she could not admit them.

By dealing with what is inside yourself, you will begin to agree with me that you have the potential for all characters. Too often, I have heard actors say, "I can only play characters that are close to me." Just as erroneous is the statement, "I can only play characters that are far away from me." The reality is that any fictional or historical character—historical characters are inevitably fictionalized, remember—should be regarded as a person other than you, and as a challenge. The choices that you make for the traits, positive and negative, have to be instinctual and personal ones. They can only come from somewhere inside yourself. Even the most horrible traits, such as homicidal feelings, are there somewhere. There can be nobody on this earth who has not at some time felt like killing someone else.

In class, I use the phrases "characters with a small c" and "characters with a capital C," the difference between them being that the first are those you can become almost entirely simply by making the situations in the play specific and real to you, whereas characters with a capital C will always need more consideration, work, endowments, and perhaps research, in order to enable you to embody them fully. In either case, however, you should make a full character chart.

A perfect example of characters with a small c would be the young American couple in Neil Simon's *Barefoot in the Park*, if the newlyweds are played by young American actors. Although Corrie is gay and carefree, while Paul is serious and responsible, they should be easy characters to play once the relationship and the conflicts are made personal. All Tennessee Williams's characters, however, could be regarded as having a capital C, because of their extremely erratic behavior and the dialogue's highly poetic nature.

As for the media, in teen comedy movies—to take one example—young actors and actresses with a comic flair don't have to go too far beyond themselves to seek out and find their characters (small c), whereas on television series, when so little is given, the actors need to do much more work in the initial stages, such as when making the pilot (capital C). The teen comedy or horror movie is usually typecast, and the script is rewritten during production to make it even more suited to the young actors' qualities and peculiarities. And nighttime television generally spews out only two-dimensional characters, especially for its guest spots, giving it a capital C difficulty for the actors.

Two Exercises

In order to help to sharpen instincts as to how to choose character traits, I used the following two exercises when I taught Technique at HB Studio.

1. Do a simple, familiar task twice, in the same place and with the same objects, but with two completely different sets of circumstances and conditions, or influencing forces: a physical state, an emotional state, and a room condition.

For instance, the student will enter the room to do a simple task such as getting ready to go out, using a coat, briefcase, cell phone, and keys. In the first exercise, he is in a hurry because he is late for an appointment. He is very unhappy due to certain circumstances such as the loss of his job. It is winter, and the room is unheated and frigid.

The second time, he has a hangover, but he has received some great news about a new job. It is summer; the window is open and it is hot in the room.

In both cases, the student knows where he is coming from and where he is going. After the student has completed the double exercise, I ask the class to pretend that he was two different characters, not just one person under different pressures. Because the conditioning forces caused very different behavior in each, they could judge him to be two different characters, just as we do in life when we have first impressions on meeting someone new. In the first exercise, words like "frazzled," "angry," "irritable," and "impatient" might describe him, whereas in the second exercise, the adjectives might be "giddy," "buoyant," "lazy," or "slow." I would remind the class that these were not basic traits, just the student's responsive behavior to outside forces. Nevertheless, this is still a lesson in searching for adjectives to describe a character.

2. Do an improvisation with a partner. It should revolve around a simple conflict. For instance, you want to go out, but your partner wants to stay in.

Do it again, only now choose a substitution for your partner, who should be someone important from your past life, such as a parent, sibling, teacher, or first love. And remember to search your past experience from five years or earlier, so that whoever you choose is "filed away" in a particular emotional slot. Present-day relationships are difficult to use as substitutions since judgments and feelings toward them fluctuate from day to day. I would also suggest finding a person from your past who changed your life in some way, and if it is

someone you are still dealing with in the present, try to recollect her as she was when you first met.

Before doing a repeat of the improvisation in class, while
you are relaxed and alone at home, write a list of adjectives
(traits) you think describe yourself when you were in the presence of this person. Make no revisions, but base it on your
memory only.

In class, the student would hand me his list before doing
the improvisation. I would not look at it, but instead I would
make my own list while observing the change in his behavior in the scene, trying to filter out what might be temporary
attitudes. I would just list the basic traits, based on the assumption that we actually do become different people in different relationships. I would then ask the student if he felt the
"substitution" worked for him. Knowing the student, I could
observe whether or not it had worked, or if it had worked in-
termittently. Then I would compare the lists.

The first attempt at this exercise was usually rocky, because
either the substitution wasn't working, or the list wasn't constructed well enough, and it was rare that my list and the student's list were comparable. But then, after doing the exercise
again, and then for a third time with different substitutions,
the students developed a facility in (1) the use of relationship
substitutions; (2) remembering their feelings more vividly;
and (3) finding the right words to describe characteristics.
Then our lists would match! Sometimes I would ask for the
class's observations about the "character" before I compared
the lists, and see how sharp we had all become in observing
and feeling traits.

CHAPTER 13

Step 10:
The Character Chart, Part 3:
Life Drives

||||||||||||||||||||||||||||||||||||||||||||||||||

What do people want out of life? Do we stop to think about what we want in our own lives, and try to put it into words? Though we may rarely do this for ourselves, we can do it for our character in a play. It is the third and last part of the character chart, and the wrap-up of the work on the character.

In an ideal rehearsal period, this part of the chart should only be considered close to opening night. As you are now *becoming* the character, you are ready to make a profound choice—and one that your instincts tell you began in early childhood or adolescence. Only after having succeeded or failed in the scene objectives, and having determined the play objective (see page 123), can we choose the character's objective(s) throughout life. You will be using your instincts to decide this, and you don't want to make a facile choice, or choose something that is overtly stated in the plot. If, for instance, a character complains about being alone and wants to be married, the actor should merely use these words as a clue to what the character really wants out of life: Does the character desire safety, security, or protection, for instance, or perhaps simply to be loved?

A character's life drive is different from what the "character objective" in the scenes in a play might be, and it is also different from the play objective. In *Agnes of God*, all of the young convent girl Agnes's scene objectives can be defined as "to obey," which is a character need, and she succeeds or fails to do this, depending on the scene. Her play objective could be "to become a good nun," failing miserably of course since at the end of the play she is put into a mental institution. Agnes's life drive, however, could be "to survive," because of what we know of the background of abuse perpetrated on her by her mother from her infancy on. Another life drive for Agnes might be "to find God."

The life drives, unlike the other objectives, do not necessarily end in success or failure, since they are not resolved at the conclusion of the play. The character lives on, after all (if he or she does), and a life drive should be what the character wants out of life for as long as he or she lives.

You may also be surprised to find that the character's life objective is often contradictory to what he or she is saying or doing in the script. Perhaps your character really wants harmony, even though the script gives endless scenes of conflict and disharmony. Maureen Stapleton, who played Amanda Wingfield in the first Broadway revival of *The Glass Menagerie*, said that she had finally discovered, after weeks of rehearsal, what Amanda wanted from life: peace and harmony. That is actually why she makes things so difficult for her children, and creates so many problems: she is looking for something that is unattainable for her, and she doesn't realize it. I didn't see the show, but I was told that she was riveting, even just sitting on the couch in her living room and contemplating what to do next, because everything she did, even thinking, was so active, and so driven, and her despair was almost palpable.

Instead of limiting yourself to only one objective, you should define two or three life drives. Putting into words what the character wants out of life has come out of all the decisions you've made thus far for your character and, in turn, infuses the character with a soul, an animating force that co-exists with and further influences your behavior in the play. In determining your choices, don't name the other characters or describe any part of the plot.

The life drives tend to revolve around such tropes as Happiness, Love, Power, Success, Greatness, Recognition, Excellence, Adventure, Sainthood, and so forth. Coming up with two or three objectives helps the actor to round out what may seem conflicting in the character's nature.

Two of Hamlet's life drives might be "to be a great king," since he has been trained for that from the time he was born, and "to find love and true companionship," difficult for a lonely prince. Because he dies at the end, he ultimately fails in one, and perhaps has succeeded in the other, having the loyalty and even the devotion of his one true friend, Horatio. But, as I stated above, the life drives do not need to be resolved. Ophelia's life drives might be "to find true love" and "to please her father and become queen," a drive her ambitious father may have instilled in her as she grew up at court.

Tom Wingfield in *The Glass Menagerie* may want recognition as a writer, as well as travel and adventures. Eddie Carbone in *A View from the Bridge*, the best of Arthur Miller's plays, wants recognition for a life of responsibility and hard work, and a feeling of success—the immigrant's dream.

Here again, keep everything simple. You can use phrases or one short sentence for each life drive: "What I want out of life is_____." Don't write a long essay on these life drives, because it will not help you. Short, incisive sentences will suffice. And if you choose the life drives when you should, late in rehearsal, then they will be absorbed and forgotten, as they ought to be. In fact, they may be absorbed and forgotten almost as soon as you put them down. Only the actor embodying the character can and should define them.

We all walk around carrying an awful lot of baggage, and

some understanding of ourselves and our behavior, and a lot of self-justification for it. But we never get around to voicing any of that until we are asked about it. You want to have all of the choices for the character in the subtext, just as we do so many things regarding our desires and the drives in our own lives.

Here are possible choices for the life drives of the characters already discussed in steps one and two of the character chart:

Laura in *The Glass Menagerie:*

(1) To escape; (2) to have an effect.

Jim O'Connor in *The Glass Menagerie*:

(1) To rise in the power structure; (2) to find happiness.

Juliet in Shakespeare's *Romeo and Juliet*:

(1) To be happy in love; (2) to live in harmony and at peace with the world.

Uncle Vanya in Chekhov's play:

(1) To be loved; (2) to feel that he has accomplished something and made a contribution, and that his life is not meaningless.

Catherine Sloper in *The Heiress*:

(1) To be happy in love; (2) to gain her father's love and approval.

Tom Ripley in *The Talented Mr. Ripley*:

(1) To be respected and looked up to; (2) to fulfill all his own needs, no matter what the cost to himself or other people.

The unnamed heroine played by Joan Fontaine in Hitchcock's film *Rebecca*:

(1) To earn an honest living and keep the wolf from the

door; (2) to earn the respect of other people.

Characters like Antigone or Joan of Arc, who are martyred at the end of a play, have begun in very early adolescence to attach themselves to the causes they espouse. At least one of their life drives is realized at the end of the play. Of those drives, an important one is always to obtain recognition for their principles, so that they will not have died in vain.

Antigone would have liked to be happy, and that is unattainable. She has deliberately sacrificed her life for her honor, going to bury her brother against the express command of her uncle, the king, who considered his nephew a traitor. In addition, she has had to live through the tragedy of her parents, Oedipus and Jocasta. As Apollo had prophesied, Oedipus had killed his father, not knowing who he was, and, equally unawares, married his mother, Jocasta. Antigone is one of the fruits of their incestuous union, and she has had to live with that, and with the horror people feel at the very sight of her. But she dies with her principles and integrity intact, and is an example to the world of nobility and honor.

It is important not to put plot elements into a statement of the life drives. For instance, you would not list as Joan of Arc's life objectives that she wants to save France or that she wants the voices she hears recognized as coming from real angels, or that she wants to be martyred so she can be a catalyst spurring the people to rise up and throw off the yoke of the English occupation and oppression. Instead, one of her life objectives might be "to be somebody" who is known beyond the little peasant farm and the village where she was born, and to make her mark in the world, and another, "to be happy."

In *Night Must Fall*, by Emlyn Williams, the main character is a serial killer, a psychopath who kills women and cuts off their heads. Determining his life drive—and therefore the way that he thinks—is an interesting exercise: could his drives be "to be recognized" and "to be fulfilled"? The other complex character in that play is the young woman, Olivia, who is attracted to and fascinated by him. This type of character exists today, and there are women who are attracted to danger, or who remain in abusive situations for any number of reasons. What are the life drives of such people as Stella Kowalski in *A Streetcar Named Desire*? She is fascinated by the danger Stanley represents, and deeply attracted to him partly because of his potential for violence. This is a difficult, contradictory situation for a character to be in.

Women like Olivia Grayne in *Night Must Fall* and Stella Kowalski may have life drives that put them in harm's way: "to seek adventure" and "to stand out in a crowd." They attach themselves to a more aggressive person because of their own limitations in finding outlets for their fantasies. The actor's exciting job is to research these motivating factors on a personal level, but not necessarily in a clinical way. And, of course, this is easier when you are already experiencing the character, as rehearsals are coming to an end.

Whether difficult to attain or fairly easy, the life drives are the heart of what the character wants, and what he or she struggles for. They are clearer in characters than they are for us in real life. And they make playing characters fulfilling and enjoyable.

CHAPTER 14

Step 11:
Becoming the Character

||||||||||||||||||||||||||||||||||||||||||||||||||||||

We have reached the most mysterious part of the actor's art, and that is when the character starts to reveal itself after all the work has been done. When and how it arises remains something of a mystery, but what is clear is that it results from all the organic, instinctual work done thus far, with its gradual revelations. The decisions you made about the character came from instincts you have had during the process described in the previous ten steps. Not working from a source and from the ground up is like buying a suit of clothes blindly, and having to try to fit into it, as opposed to taking measurements and buying the right-sized suit, made with care and hard work, one that you can fit into easily and that is really yours.

The oldest member of the Moscow Art Theatre during their 1965 visit, the distinguished Angelina Osipovna Stepanova (1905–2000), had worked with Stanislavsky and Nemirovich-Danchenko, and had been in the latter's famous 1940 production of *Three Sisters* as Irina, and in revivals of the *Cherry Orchard* playing Ranevskaya's seventeen year-old daughter, Anya. Now she was playing the governess, Charlotta Ivanovna, in the same play. I was fortunate to attend a lecture she gave to a group of acting teachers. You would hardly have believed the number of well-known acting teachers who were present: Uta Hagen, Herbert Berghof, Stella Adler, Lee Strasberg, Paul Mann, and Sanford Meisner were all there, among others.

I remember a particular anecdote Stepanova told that struck me at the time. Stanislavsky had asked her to play the queen in some project, and she was immediately terrified, because, except for Irina, she had only played working-class people and servants up until then. She didn't think she had the instincts to play a queen, but she didn't dare refuse Papa, so of course she set to work on the role. All through rehearsals, she felt she simply wasn't getting it, that she would never be able to play a queen. The company used to go to a nearby coffee shop after rehearsals, and one day they went as usual, and the actress ordered a cup of coffee. The waitress, apparently taken aback, did not move, and when Stepanova looked up at her, she said to the actress sneeringly, "You ordered that cup of coffee like you were a queen or something," and flounced off indignantly. Stepanova was overjoyed, because she knew at that point that all her instincts had been awakened, and that she was becoming the character.

I also realized, in a moment of clarity that came to me after years of teaching, that after the actor becomes the character without even realizing it, the next rehearsals contain a dangerous trap: If and when the success of having achieved our character is pointed out to us, we have to work hard to forget that fact as well.

As long as we remain conscious of "being somebody else," that will prevent us from seeing the world from that character's point of view. An analogy that I use in order to point this out to students is that your character can't be driving the car. You have to put your character in the back seat. I tell them to tell themselves it is "I" who am driving the play forward, looking ahead, aware of the pitfalls, and not the "he" or "she" of the character. Actors feel the difference when they "forget" they are playing a character and trust that they are the character. Once you have passed this test, you can relax: your performance is complete. Now comes the joy of "being" the character every night and matinee, for as long as the production lasts.

Essences

The decision you have made in the last part of the chart—the life drives—is one of the things that helps you to finalize the character; and to determine the character's essential nature, or essence. You can define "essence" as "whatever makes something what it is."

Essence exercises, which are helpful in the search for the character, were devised quite early on in the Stanislavsky System. The old clichés of "I am a tree, I am a tree" or "I am bacon sizzling in a skillet" come from the essence exercises. At the end of the rehearsal period, after all your work, when you are ready to perform, it may occur to you that your character is like a rock at the side of the road, or like a particular animal. This is not something you would have thought about early on, when such an idea might only be in your way. For instance, Tennessee Williams's description of Blanche du Bois as "a moth" is an impossible direction to follow, especially before you have really experienced the character in all her situations.

There are at least three different kinds of essences for the actor to think about using: inanimate essences—"I am a teapot" or "I am a doormat" (which happens to be the way some people describe themselves); animal essences—"I am a tiger" or "I am a lapdog"; and the "Who am I?" essence, for which you choose to imagine yourself to be another human being, either someone you know well or someone you may never have met, such as a movie star or a politician, but who is vivid for you.

The "Who am I?" essence is a very nostalgic one for me since it was that kind of fantasizing that compelled me to want to act in the first place. I spent a lot of my young life at the movies, because in pre-television days it was an inexpensive babysitting service for the working parents in the poor Brooklyn neighborhood I grew up in. When we were not in school, my brothers, my friends and I went to five movies a week. And it was in the darkened movie theater that my secret desire "to become someone else" was formed. Strangely enough, I didn't want to be up there on the screen, but just to be the characters in the stories, or to be one of the movie stars. I remember leaving the movie house and "putting on" that person, her clothing and her manner of walking and behaving; and I remained "her" for the rest of the day until I went to sleep that night. I probably looked foolish, because I would secretly smile her smile, try to talk like her, and, if I had just seen an MGM musical, I would kick the train of my imaginary gown away from my feet as I walked so as not to step on it. As it turns out, to my surprise, my childhood game of pretending to be another character can be a valid acting tool.

The "Who am I?" essence is very useful when I work with students, or with actors on a theater or movie project, especially if they seem to be in trouble and can't quite make that leap into character. They have explored and personalized the facts, the intentions, and the relationships, but are finding it difficult to stretch out and "be" the character. Their behavior is tentative, and perhaps they feel embarrassed. I tell them, "Why don't you substitute another person for *your* character? Who are you?" If the actor needs to be more authoritative or overbearing, for instance, I might suggest, "Can you be your own mother or father, talking to you when you were a child?" In that way, taking on the essence of another person— behaving "as if" you were that person, but without having to imitate that person in any way—can give the actor the courage to make the breakthrough. I actually use the "Who am I?" essence quite often: to play someone imperious, I might suggest, "What would the First Lady or Lauren Bacall do in this scene?" And the simple fun of stepping into the shoes of someone like that can inspire the actor to change her behavior with confidence. Since the very occupation of being an actor, especially a struggling one, often plays havoc with our self-confidence, taking on the essence of "the boss" allows us to slip more easily into characters who are in leadership roles. I recall vividly that when I was a new teacher at HB Studio, there were days when I consciously walked like Uta along Bank Street to the entrance of the school, to rev up the confidence to teach my class. By the same token, playing a victim or someone deranged or despondent can also be experienced by recalling those types that you have come across in your life.

If you haven't practiced inanimate or animal essences in the classroom, you may find it very difficult to use them as a rehearsal tool, just as you might with the exercises in Michael Chekhov's books. In one exercise, he suggests that you imagine a "center of energy" situated in the middle of your body, like a furnace, and use that center, when changed in substance and size and moved anywhere else on your body, to create a character. For instance, the center might be a small silver ball on the tip of your nose that will make you feel like a snob, or a balloon resting on top of your head that may make you feel flighty.

Uta Hagen devised an exercise that she called "as ifs," for use in classical plays, particularly ancient Greek classics, in which the events are so large that it is impossible to personalize them: slaughtering your children and serving them up to your cheating husband, as Medea does; or blinding yourself upon receiving the news that you married your own mother, which is what happens to Oedipus. Uta's suggestion is to use imagined physical events in such cases. You might act as if your hair had just caught on fire, or as if you had had acid thrown in your face. Although I have rarely had occasion to use "as ifs," I have recommended them at times in the case of contemporary media, such as horror or so-called slasher movies, or action films. If you are in a scene where a monster or

prehistoric animal is approaching you, you might more easily "believe" you are at a ballgame with someone throwing a
fastball in your direction. But some of us are more in touch
with our dreams and nightmares, and therefore can respond
to fantasies, and behave accordingly.

One of my very first coaching jobs was on a movie called
Valley of the Gwangi (1969) in which my student, Gila Golan,
had to run from prehistoric animals, and scream in horror.
Needless to say, there was nothing from her past that paral-
leled these events, even though she had been found as an or-
phaned toddler wandering in war-torn Poland. Using "as ifs,"
such as looking up and seeing a piano falling from a window
above her head, helped her to "react" to a pterodactyl flying
and screeching overhead, and in that way she avoided feeling
silly as well. In fact, whenever you are called upon to deliver
a grand reaction to something that isn't there or is hard to
believe, you can think of the times you used phrases like,
"I felt the ground opening up beneath my feet," or "I felt as
though I had been hit by a ton of bricks," or "I was walking on
clouds," and can make use of them in your imagination "as if"
they were happening. At the time you spoke them, they were
real sensations.

To use an animal essence is to take on the characteristics
of an animal and to put them into human form. The original
classroom exercise was to imitate the animal's behavior in detail, not just in a general way. You would have to go to the
zoo to watch the animal, or observe your own or somebody
else's pet. Then you got down on all fours and imitated the
specific movements, including the facial expressions, that are
characteristic of the animal. After performing as the animal in
front of the class, you would get up on two feet and turn into
a human being, and then ask yourself, "Who am I now?"

When I was a student, I played the animal essence of a
squirrel. I went to Washington Square Park and watched a
squirrel for a long time—the way it moved and jumped around,
and held its little paws in front of its face, begging for food

and twitching its nose. In class, as I moved into becoming a human being I realized that I had become Lucy in *I Love Lucy*! At least that's how it felt to me: my squirrel was the animal essence of Lucille Ball.

In the following session, when I had to do an inanimate essence, I played a bottle of Coca-Cola, just pulled out of the ice chest, wet and cold, its cap removed, and fizzling. When I "evolved" into a character, I felt just like a gorgeous, high-priced call girl.

Essences are to be chosen and used at the end of the rehearsal period. By then, you may understand what type of animal your character reminds you of, and you can endow the character with its essence. You will only be using what you perceive as essential to the animal. If your character is a fox, this may lead you to furtive, sidelong glances, and a wariness that allows you to notice everything around you, almost as if you have eyes in the back of your head. Maybe your character is an elephant, causing you to move slowly and somewhat cumbersomely, while remembering the distant past. Suppose your character is a goose: this may make you feel more in touch with your character's silly, waddling, goose-like behavior. And sometimes you don't have to actually enact the essence; thinking about it should be enough.

Marlon Brando reportedly claimed that he used the animal essence of a bear when he played Stanley Kowalski in *A Streetcar Named Desire*. Supposedly, Lee J. Cobb in his legendary performance as Willy Loman in *Death of a Salesman* also used a bear essence. I have seen productions in which animal essences were very apparent—too much so, in fact. In some scenes of the Moscow Art Theatre production of Bulgakov's adaptation of Gogol's *Dead Souls*, they were so obvious that at times all I could think of was the animals the actors had based the characters on.

"Essences" was at one time a popular parlor game, like charades. Each guest at a party chooses someone who is in the room or someone everybody present knows, and the other guests ask such questions as "What article of furniture would you be?" or "What musical piece would you be?" "Which planet would you be?" "What animal are you?" "What plant or flower or tree would you be?" From the answers, they try to guess who that person is.

Finally, embodying characters can encompass "the stuff that dreams are made on"—the use of music, colors, etc. When I coached the deaf actors in the National Theater of the Deaf, I was fascinated to discover that they thought of sounds as colors.

Impersonations

There is a difference between an impression done by a comedian, and an impersonation done by an actor who is playing the role of an actual contemporary or historical person. There are many comedians in such shows as *Saturday Night Live* who do excellent impressions of well-known political figures or movie stars or other celebrities. They pick on one or two salient features or characteristics and emphasize them much as a cartoonist might caricature them in a newspaper. The celebrated Al Hirschfeld was a past master at picking one or two physical features of an actor and drawing a sketch that was immediately recognizable with just one or two lines— quite a stunning achievement. Performing a role that is a full, organic characterization based on reality is as different from doing an imitation of a well-known person as Rembrandt's portraits are from Hirschfeld's line drawings.

There have been brilliant impressionists such as Frank Gorshin, who was much more of an actor than most comedians, especially when he played George Burns in a Broadway one-man show. Yet he and other impressionists belong in the category of standup comics, as opposed to actors. I enjoy them enormously. They observe the celebrity they wish to impersonate carefully, and then duplicate their facial expressions and speech patterns. And in order to make us laugh, they comment on their subject by exaggerating one or two characteristics in which the audience recognizes the real person. I remember when Frank Gorshin did his impression of Burt Lancaster talking to Kirk Douglas: he simply bared the upper part of his teeth for Lancaster and the lower part of his teeth for Douglas, and it was hilarious. I think a person is born with the desire and skill to do impressions like that, and I don't think it is something you can easily learn.

In the old days of the Hollywood studio systems, actors were given the opportunity to develop distinctive, individual personas over a period of years. Scripts were written for these stars, with those personas in mind. They were carefully and beautifully groomed, "packaged," and presented to the public. It was therefore easy for impersonators to imitate James Mason, Kirk Douglas, Burt Lancaster, Judy Garland, John Wayne, Cary Grant, Katherine Hepburn, Bette Davis, Joan Crawford, Humphrey Bogart, Edward G. Robinson, James Cagney, Jimmy Stewart, Henry Fonda, W. C. Fields, Mae West, and a host of others. Even the featured character actors who were part of the studios' stables developed personas. Nowadays, the means by which actors can develop a persona no longer exist. Since the entire studio system came crashing down and films are called "independent" features, it has become much more difficult to become the sort of actor of whom someone can do a recognizable impression. Many of today's film stars, such as Harrison Ford, Jodie Foster, Nicole Kidman, and others, do not have a really distinct persona and risk oversaturating the public if they appear in too many films in a short period of time. And they are apt to hear complaints by the fans and the critics that they are doing too much! But in the days of the Hollywood studio system, all of us eagerly looked forward to each new film starring James Cagney, Bette Davis, James Stewart, and the other stars. Today's oversaturation is also a result of the multitudes of entertainment and interview shows produced on television, not to mention the gossip pages in the tabloids, all of which present these famous faces to us every single day, until we grow tired of them.

Bette Davis, who was notorious for her outspoken battles with the studios, changed her mind about the studio system in her later years. When she saw the chaotic non-system of independent producers and distributors that had replaced it, she realized that the studio system was actually a great idea—that, quite aside from providing hundreds of actors with a great deal of work, it was the best way to make the best product. As evidence of that fact, the public still cannot get enough of the old films. Television channels that show classic movies are doing great business, and video and DVD collections sell like hotcakes. All the great stars remain in our collective consciousness in this way. And they are not going to bore us by appearing on the multitude of current gossip shows.

For famous personalities, living or dead, there is a great quantity of documentary evidence in the form of films, newscasts, biographies, autobiographies, memoirs, diaries, letters and journals, as well as photographs or paintings. There are descriptions of many historical figures that tell us how they behaved, and even what their voices were like. If you are going to play someone like Abraham Lincoln, you will have all the facts that have been documented about his background, including descriptions of exactly those things. There are even some accounts of how he delivered certain speeches. A journalist who was present at Lincoln's delivery of the Gettysburg Address and reported the speech tells us that he delivered the famous line "of the people, by the people, for the people" with an emphasis on the word "people." This gives the actor choices, because nobody is going to complain, since nobody knows how he actually sounded or how he really delivered that famous speech. (Maybe he would have disagreed with the journalist, and said, "I didn't say it like that.") You have to go to the Abraham Lincoln that is inside you, and make your choices organic.

When you play any historical character, you have to ap-

proach the character as you would one that is entirely fictitious. And, of course, you must build the character from the
inside out. The only thing that is different from pure fiction is
the background information that is supplied by history. But
you will want to be very careful not to rely on just the surface things you might see in such sources as news interviews
and documentary films. You will want to incorporate all the
sounds, gestures, mannerisms, speech patterns, and so forth,
but always with the understanding that all of the behavior
is coming from a source in the character's background and
psyche. You will want to discover what makes them talk and
walk the way they do. You will make choices of objectives,
value systems, and physical realities, all stemming from the
research you do into their background—personal facts that
you will make yours, whereas the impersonator or impres-
sionist really doesn't care about those things. It is up to you
to create the internal life of the character, because you are
personalizing, as opposed to impersonating.

Playing someone who once actually lived, as opposed to
a person derived purely from an author's imagination, can
give the actor an almost spiritual experience. I once had the
unusual privilege of coaching Harry Belafonte to play a character who was actually on the set. Harry received an Emmy
nomination for his performance as the famous football coach
Eddie Robinson from Grambling State College in Louisiana
in the television movie *Grambling's White Tiger* (1981). Coach
Robinson was actually there while the movie was being shot.
At that time, Grambling was known as the greatest football
farm for every position on the team except quarterback, because it was a black college in the days of segregation, and the
quarterback position was reserved for whites in professional
football. The movie was based on the true story of a white
student, played by Bruce Jenner, who integrated a black college in order to be trained by Robinson. The school was on a
spring break, but a lot of the students were there to take part
in the film. The shortest student was six feet six inches tall.

So there was Harry, and there was Eddie Robinson, a love-ly, spiritual man. We were certainly not planning to actually imitate him. After all, we had the script, and Robinson was not a recognizable figure to television audience, even though he was a well-known coach. But I wanted to get the essence of Eddie into Harry's character in addition to the information in the script. I wanted Harry to make specific and personal Rob-inson's value system, and to find out and incorporate what meant more to him than anything else, and also to observe his mannerisms. We needed to determine what his life drives truly were. We soon discovered that he was a very religious man, and he used that side of himself when he coached the players. Harry had to go all the way back to his childhood to get comfortable with the kind of religious feelings that Eddie had. It was a great boon having the role model right there.

On another occasion, I had the delight of reviewing dozens of interviews and taped concerts of Elvis Presley as a prepara-tion for coaching Michael St. Gerard, who was to play Elvis from ages nineteen to twenty-one for a nine-part television se-ries. We then created an entire character chart for the young and talented singer who would go on to become the King, live a remarkable life, and suffer a tragic end. We felt very close to him as together we searched for reasons why Elvis had been fated to rise and fall as he did. Of course, Michael was able to imitate his moves and guitar-playing, and he lip-synched the songs perfectly, but for the rest of the scenes, he lived the part!

In order to bring about the illusion of Elvis and other very well-known figures, the most important element for an ac-tor is an understanding of the character's point of view and philosophy, which are the reasons and justification for the character's behavior and self-image. The actor works in col-laboration with the author, of course, but at the same time must have a strong opinion about the famous person, and will want to incorporate it into the characterization. I remem-ber working with an actor who was rehearsing Julian Barry's play *Lenny*, which is about the comic Lenny Bruce. In this instance, the actor was himself a tremendous fan, and actually loved Lenny Bruce, yet he had to turn that love into self-loathing before he could become the driven comedian who ended up dead from a drug overdose. Feeling love, pity, or even distaste can be a part of an actor's inspiration, and the actor must never ignore his true feelings about the famous character when beginning to work. There will be times when the actor can turn his own feelings into how the character feels about himself. As another example, having to overcome the deep sense of pity any young actress will feel for Anne Frank can be an inspiration and help to create a personal understanding of Anne's courage.

You can suggest the character's persona and his or her way of being and behaving without doing a complete imitation. David Strathairn in *Good Night, and Good Luck* (2005) seemed to be Edward R. Murrow as many remember him. The actor captured his way of looking with intensity at the people he was interviewing, as well as the way he phrased his sentences and placed his voice, and of course he used that ever-present cigarette, but he did not attempt to do an actual imitation, even while giving a sensitive performance. He didn't go to the lengths that Philip Seymour Hoffman went to in his Academy-Award-winning performance in *Capote* (2005) that same year.

Hoffman as Capote had to play in many more diverse settings than Strathairn had to, and the movie took place over a longer period of time and in several locations. He did a brilliant job of incorporating all of Truman Capote's mannerisms, his facial expressions, and his peculiarly high-pitched voice, and at the same time he filled the character with such vulnerability and complex character traits, which only the actor himself could have chosen from his personal point of view. And he won a well-deserved Oscar. As a comparison, I would say that while David Strathairn admired Edward R. Murrow and was proud to portray him, Phillip Seymour Hoffman probably had mixed feelings about Truman Capote and allowed his own discomfort to become that of the character.

Robert Morse also played Capote in a Tony-Award-winning performance in Jay Presson Allen's 1990 Broadway one-person play *Tru*. But his beautifully observed performance was very different from Hoffman's, even though both actors tried to look and sound like Capote and capture his personality, and both were brilliant. For the film, Hoffman was extremely detailed, right down to the movement of his eyebrows and the way Capote curled his upper lip, whereas Morse on stage was broader in his behavior and less detailed. He was doing a solo performance in which he talked to the audience eight times a week. Both actors were completely appropriate to the medium in which they were performing; Hoffman chose to be absolutely specific and detailed for the camera, while Morse's behavior was entirely convincing in the theater.

In Alan J. Pakula's film *All The President's Men* (1976), Robert Redford played the investigative reporter Bob Woodward, and did a fine job giving him a personality that did not seem too far from his own, while his costar, Dustin Hoffman, played his partner Carl Bernstein as someone very different from his own persona: a nervous, chain-smoking hypochondriac on a mission. His characterization was just short of actual impersonation, I am sure. In general, Redford never seems to go too far afield from himself in his movie roles. Hoffman, on the other hand, relishes playing characters that are extremely different from himself. Even as a young man, he was a "character actor."

In close-ups on film, you can do a great deal more in some ways than you can on stage, because you have all the time and the many takes to make sure you are doing exactly what you want. But once the takes are over, your performance is finished. On stage, however, you had better find a character that you can sustain, and that will carry the play through the evening and the run. You don't want to think about where your arm went, or about how your face appeared. In film, you can think about exactly that sort of thing, and, depending on the relationship you have with the director, you can look at the take on the ever-present video monitor, and then do another one if you are not satisfied.

Complete Character Charts

Walter Cole (Teacher), known as "Teach" for short, in David Mamet's *American Buffalo*

The story of *American Buffalo* is quite simple: It unfolds in Don's Resale Shop, a junk shop in Chicago, sometime in the 1970s, on one Friday, like a classic drama that follows the unities of time and place. The first act takes place in the morning; the second starts at around 11:00 the same night. Three small-time crooks want to steal a valuable coin collection. The calm and fairly easygoing Don's gopher, Bob, is a dumb kid, and Teach is a wonderful, violent, showy character. The three of them discuss an essentially vicious, exploitative economic system—American capitalism—which is dog-eat-dog, as they see it, and is particularly awful as these three embody it on the rawest level.

Background

1. **Where was I born?** Chicago.
2. **What size family did I come from?** Only child.
3. **What was/is my father's occupation?** A janitor.
4. **Is my father living or dead?** Dead.
5. **What was/is my mother's occupation?** She worked at night, cleaning office buildings.
6. **Is my mother living or dead?** Dead.
7. **How far did my education go, and what is the highest degree I earned?** I went through grammar school and quit high school at sixteen.
8. **What occupation(s) have I had?** Construction; numbers runner; petty thief.
9. **What is my marital status?** Single.

10. Do I have any children? No.

11. If I have any hobbies, what are they? Movies.

All of these answers are made up, since they are not stated in the play.

Character Traits

Angry	Narcissistic
Resentful	Lonely
Hotheaded	Suspicious
Hostile	Paranoid
Misogynistic	Distrustful
Homophobic	Hyperactive
Irascible	Violent

Life Drives

(1) To be a leader; (2) to be treated with respect; (3) to have lots of money.

Emma in Harold Pinter's *Betrayal*

Pinter's story is told in an unusual way: backwards in time. In 1983, the play was made into a film starring Jeremy Irons (Jerry), Ben Kingsley (Robert), and Patricia Hodge (Emma). The film, of course, opens up the locations that are more limited on the stage, and adds characters we hear about in the stage piece without ever seeing them, but otherwise it is very much the play filmed; the screenplay is by Pinter himself.

In the first scene of this play about an extramarital affair that lasted for four years, we see the end result of the betrayals all the partners have inflicted on each other, and the big and small lies they have all told, as the former lovers Emma and Jerry meet and discuss the affair that is long over. We then go gradually back in time, from 1977 to 1968, until we reach the very beginning of the affair.

Jerry is married to Judith, whom we never meet—she is an inner object for the actors playing Jerry, Emma, and Robert, who will each use their own substitutions for her and for their respective children, who also never appear in the play, although Emma's children do appear briefly in the film.

Emma's husband, Robert, and Jerry are each other's oldest and best friends and associates in the publishing business. Robert is a publisher, and Jerry is a literary agent. There are scenes in which we see their relationship, which is at times quite simple, and at times convoluted, particularly once Robert has learned about the affair, which he chooses not to mention to Jerry. Robert's resentment and hurt are nevertheless apparent, although Jerry, slightly puzzled by Robert's ironic attitude, does not understand what is going on. In any case, he has been betraying Emma with a series of other women.

At the beginning of the play—long after the affair is over, and as Robert and Emma are about to be separated—Emma lies to Jerry when she tells him she has just told Robert about the affair the night before this first scene takes place: she has told him years before.

Background

1. **Where was I born?** London.
2. **What size family did I come from?** I have a brother and a sister.
3. **What was/is my father's occupation?** A teacher, retired.
4. **Is my father living or dead?** Living.
5. **What was/is my mother's occupation?** Housewife.
6. **Is my mother living or dead?** Living.
7. **How far did my education go, and what is the highest degree I earned?** I went through university.
8. **What occupation(s) have I had?** I run an art gallery.
9. **What is my marital status?** Married.
10. **Do I have any children?** I have a son and a daughter.
11. **If I have any hobbies, what are they?** Reading, music, sketching, tennis.

Character Traits

Social	Sentimental
Vulnerable	Loving
Sensitive	Romantic
Stylish	Patient
Responsible	Soft-spoken
Mature/Immature	Insecure

Life Drives

(1) To be successful; (2) to be independent.

Holden Caulfield in J. D. Salinger's *Catcher in the Rye*

J. D. Salinger's classic novel, *The Catcher in the Rye* (1951), and its hero, seventeen-year-old Holden Caulfield, have been icons for all disenchanted teenagers since World War Two. Mike Nichols' award-winning film of Charles Webb's novel, with a screenplay by Calder Willingham, *The Graduate* (1967), and Kenneth Lonergan's brilliant play *This Is Our Youth* (2000), are only two of the many plays and screenplays that owe their recognizable and profoundly seriocomic young characters to Salinger's Caulfield. With dialogue that can be taken straight from the book, it has become a rite of passage for all young men to portray Holden in their acting classes. Many years ago, the young Jeff Bridges did a Holden Caulfield monologue in my class at HB Studio.

Background

1. **Where was I born?** New York City.
2. **What size family did I come from?** I have two brothers (one deceased) and one younger sister.
3. **What was/is my father's occupation?** Lawyer.
4. **Is my father living or dead?** Living.
5. **What was/is my mother's occupation?** A housewife and mother.

6. Is my mother living or dead? Living.

7. How far did my education go, and what is the highest degree I earned? I went through grade school, and then to prep schools. I am in between my sophomore and senior years.

8. What occupation(s) have I had? None.

9. What is my marital status? Single.

10. Do I have any children? No.

11. If I have any hobbies, what are they? I enjoy writing and some sports.

Character Traits

Honest	Unhappy
Intelligent	Bored
A dreamer	Given to depression
A loner	Sensitive
Angry	I have a temper
Troubled	Rebellious
A virgin	Dependent/Independent
Searching	Sarcastic
Perceptive	Cynical
Defensive	Distrustful of myself and others

Life Drives

(1) To be on my own and to be content with life; (2) to have an identity that raises me above the crowd.

PART 3

The Steps Condensed When You Have No Time

My Experience in the Media

CHAPTER 15

The Ideal and the Practical: Working in Film and Television

||||||||||||||||||||||||||||||||||||||||||||||||||

This book has presented an ideal step-by-step approach to rehearsing, and we have essentially been discussing the time the actor should be given to develop a fully formed character. It is only after the actor feels what's happening internally over the course of rehearsals that he or she can put a label on behavior so that it can become a set of reflexes in performance. This is absolutely required in the theater, because it is the actor's work to build a performance that has to be sustained for an indefinite period of time. The stage is the playwright's and the actor's medium.

I remember when I began acting and coaching in feature films how struck I was by the fact that each day I could just throw away the pages of the scenes that had been shot! The performance was done, and I could forget about those pages—just fold them over or rip them out and discard them. But when I was doing a play, the entire manuscript stayed with me all during the rehearsal period, the run of the show, and afterward as well. On the other hand, a screenplay or a television script goes through constant changes anyway—white pages, blue pages, pink pages, and amber pages are handed out to distinguish the newest from the oldest versions of a scene. All screenplays are written in three separate stages: pre-production, production, and post-production, when the actors are no longer there.

Not having to sustain a character over a long period of time, and performing in short increments, is what enables the actor to condense the steps discussed in this book and still create a full and original, and not merely indicated or illustrated character, who will fulfill the vision of the director and/ or producer. And actors who have been trained to rehearse appropriately will be better able to condense and abbreviate these steps as necessary. If you have a background in script analysis of scenes from plays, you can much more easily add something to what might simply be suggested in the description or the dialogue of a two-dimensional television character. To be able to add the third dimension, you want these steps to become part of you, and the best way to do that is by working on scenes in class, until eventually the process of contracting the steps will be much easier. You don't want to go for the end result first. You want instead to create a habit of beginning at the beginning as the best means of getting to your final destination: the character.

To summarize: the eleven steps in part 2 begin with an exploration of the material in the first readings, and then move on to a discovery of the underlying conflict through the relationships with the other actors. They describe how to use the text to build the relationship and to define the circumstances, and then how to make decisions about what your character wants—what the character's objectives are. In the first rehearsal, you can discuss your objectives with each other, but after that any further change of objective is your secret. You also need to know quite early in the process precisely what place you are in, its proportions, and your personal relationship to it. And with the circumstances and place, you can choose the activity, which is what you might be doing physically, and which is secondary to the conflict in the material.

And for class scenes, part of the first rehearsal is also devoted to the prior relationship of the two characters, and how they came to this point. If they are strangers, like the two men who meet by chance in Hitchcock's *Strangers on a Train* (1951), for instance, or like the man who sits on a bench to read his newspaper in Central Park and is approached by a complete stranger in Edward Albee's *The Zoo Story*, there is no prior relationship between the characters, and each one is open to the speculation of the other—which is not to be discussed between the actors. Or the two people in the scene may be friends or lovers who have known each other for a longer or shorter time, or family members, for which I suggest my students use substitutions to begin with.

In the following rehearsals, the students put the scene on its feet and start working out the situation both physically and psychologically. Once they feel comfortable and free with the situation, and have absorbed the lines (as opposed to coldly memorizing them), they ought to begin to feel somewhat like the character by the fifth rehearsal. Working in this organic way, your character is actually the last piece of the puzzle, the last thing you come up with.

What is expected in performing for the television medium, unfortunately, is that you know the character first, which always creates the risk of ending up with a cliché. If you are a pimp or an addict or a prostitute or a student or an athlete, you are expected to behave in a certain way that is often blatantly written into the script. It is so unlike the organic process of acting, that, in fact, it is anti-acting. You are being asked to illustrate, or represent, rather than to become, a character. The producers in television, by allowing the actors no time to come up with their character, are asking for instant gratification, and not a sustained work of art. The actor no longer has the opportunity of working his or her way through the material, so that the character can be revealed, which is a more personal and not an intellectual experience. Even if you are a guest actor and will only be playing the character once, and the cliché is therefore more or less expected of you, you must avoid it at all costs anyway. As I have taught all my students who have successfully auditioned for television roles, the casting personnel may expect the cliché, but at the same time they are bored with it, and they will perk up when they see a good and original interpretation.

Becoming familiar with the actual physical setting or place where the scene happens is another very important part of the process of building a role. But, of course, if you are cast in a television program or movie, you are not going to see the place until you actually get there. The trained actor, who knows how important place is, will have to immediately start to look around, and find things he can anchor himself to. It is difficult sometimes to remember to do this, because you are concerned with the lines, and with what the director wants. You have to find space and time for yourself to get comfortable, but this is usually of no interest to the director or the other people on the set.

It would be wonderful to have a director who really understood the actor's process and could help it along, but even with that kind of director, you still have to be able to know how to work to set the process in motion.

The most beneficial way to approach an actual filming or taping session, once you have read the script, is to look first at your fellow actors, whom you have to play with in the scenes, and to begin to relate to them. A "particularization" can be made of the other actor(s) by freely wondering or speculating about them and who they are, what their background might be, and so forth. You may never have met them before the first day of taping or shooting, but if you don't do what I am suggesting, you will risk remaining in a world of your own, isolated from any real interaction. And, of course, in your preparation, you may already have substituted people you know, which will help open you up to the strangers before you. If you are playing a love scene, you may have to imagine your ideal lover, perhaps substituting someone from your past life. But, remember, you actually have to work with the other actor who has been cast to play opposite you, even if you don't really find her or him attractive, so you had better relate to that person and not to an image you personified when you were alone examining the material.

One important note: Just as you will be developing your own character via a personal process, you should let the other actors decide how to play their roles, and not say, as I have often heard, "I need such and such from that actor in order to play the scene." Let the other actors do their job, and let the director make the necessary adjustments.

Once you understand and absorb the logic that is inherent in the order of the steps, preferably by practicing it in scene study classes, you won't be frustrated with the fact that you don't have all the time you would like; you can still do the work. This order can be followed even in one evening, if that is all the time you have, with the understanding that, without the other actors to relate to, you will be relying more than you normally would on substitutions, and on emotional or affective memory. And you can save the final memorization of the lines and choices for behavior for the day of the shoot, when there will always be some time, at least between camera setups. There are other considerations that cannot be anticipated, such as slowdowns because of weather (if you are on an outdoor location), which will also give you time to study. As a matter of fact, on most production days, there can be at least twice as much "down" time—the time when you are not required to be in front of the camera—as actual time spent acting. And that is a conservative estimate. This is one reason why it bears repeating that the serious actor will always feel much more accomplishment, and instant gratification, because of a job well done on the stage than he can ever feel about his film work. By the time the finished film is seen by the public, the actors are very distant from it.

If you can be disciplined and confident enough to avoid making the lines your first priority, it will be easier to access them when you need them—that is, in front of the camera. In other words, as I stated earlier, cramming the lines and going for facile emotional results without having first explored the subtext will work against you, and the lines will vanish into thin air when you are confronted with the pressure of performing. At the very least, the experience will be highly unsatisfactory, just like an unappetizing meal.

There are some film directors who really do rehearse. Among them is the Swedish director Ingmar Bergman, with his distinctive style of filmmaking; he has also directed for the stage. And he had a wonderful company of actors to work with on stage and in films. Once he had a finished screenplay, he would rehearse for an entire month with the principal cast and then go off with his cinematographer, Sven Nyquist, scouting for locations and deciding on camera angles and a shot list. Throughout this time, he would stay in touch with his actors through letters, writing internal monologues for them to think, so that by the time the actors stepped in front of the camera, they were securely locked into their characters. You just have to see any one of his films to feel the richness of their performances and the fluid ensemble work.

Mike Leigh of England is another wonderful film director who spends months in pre-production with his cast doing improvisations and writing scenes—before even a single day of shooting has taken place. Brilliant acting ensembles are the result in such films as *Vera Drake* (2004) and *Secrets and Lies* (1996). He is known as the director "without a script," since everything he puts on screen is the result of collaboration with his actors, under his artistic control.

This is not to say that acting in American films today, where rehearsal is most often nonexistent, is entirely unrewarding. In any film, you are always doing what amounts to an improvisation, no matter how much you may have been given the privilege of rehearsing, because there are many other things to deal with, such as technical, mechanical, and location problems. You will start the process of building your character on the first day of shooting, regardless of what scene is being shot—it may be the first scene, or even the last scene of the movie. But as far as you, the actor, are concerned, your first day of shooting is actually also your first day as the character.

On your second day of shooting, you will be a little more familiar with your character. And this is your second day as the character, no matter where in the sequence of the story the scene occurs. Perhaps it will be a scene that happens before the one you shot on your first day, or perhaps it will be a scene that occurs much later in the script, or maybe even another part of the same scene. Also, the second day for your character may be scheduled a week after the first day's shooting. If you are on location, all the scenes that take place in that location, no matter where they occur in the script and no matter how out of sequence they are, need to be shot at the location, for obvious logistical reasons—all that lighting and camera equipment and the necessity of transporting it, for one thing.

With no rehearsals beforehand, and an erratic shooting schedule, you will be *accumulating* the character. So by the end, you may feel that you have achieved and properly played the character, having experienced the different aspects of your character in each scene. When you think about it, this is a bit like playing in some regional theaters, particularly summer stock. Considering the short period of rehearsal that is expected to bring to life a complete play or musical, you can only hope that your character will come together by your final performance. I know of actors, Sean Penn and Ben Kingsley being prime examples, who, when acting in a movie, stay "in character" as much as possible all day long, even off-camera. I am *not* suggesting this as absolutely necessary, but in any case you will constantly be reminded of "who you are" throughout the production day, as you are being tapped for wardrobe and freshening up makeup, etc. Depending on the length of your shooting days, you will probably feel as if you are living the character during all your off hours, at home or in the hotel.

Dustin Hoffman as Carl Bernstein in Alan Pakula's *All the President's Men* comes to mind whenever I want to point out a great example of an accumulated performance. Because of the story construction, this was a film that had to be shot very much out of sequence. All the exterior scenes in Washington, D.C. were filmed on location during the first half of the shooting schedule, while all the interior shots of the *Washington Post* offices were shot in the latter half of the shooting schedule in a studio in Los Angeles. In the final cut, the scenes were juxtaposed. Hoffman worked on the character in a very organic way in pre-production preparation, and he was able to scatter all of his character's nervous, chain-smoking mannerisms throughout the making of the movie, but in the final edit, his performance gave the viewers the impression that little by little he became more and more anxious and hyperactive as the tensions in the story increased.

Feature films traditionally require eight weeks of shooting. Television movies shoot in four weeks, and are cut in a relatively short amount of time in order to be ready to broadcast on schedule. And in order to keep the time and money spent at a minimum, two or three cameras are generally used on set, and the attention paid to each shot is less than that for a theatrical film. Nighttime television dramas usually require six days of filming. Sitcoms rehearse for four or five days and tape in front of a live audience on the fifth or sixth day. And, finally, miniseries can vary anywhere from six weeks of shooting to the better part of a year or more, depending on how many broadcast hours are planned and on how much travel time is needed between locations.

I have had experience as an acting coach—I am occasionally listed in the credits as the Dialogue Coach—on all of the above. My personal goal is to assist the director in achieving the performance(s) he or she wants, regardless of who hired me—the producers, the network, the director, or the star. My ability to work with actors each day to prepare for their scenes took some of the burden off the usually overworked and sometimes overwrought director, and was certainly a help to a first-time director, although the less experienced the director was, the more fearful he or she was, and the more difficult it became to form a collaboration. A movie director has to be secure, leaving the various departments to do their job; experienced directors have learned to keep their ego out of the day-to-day work.

Today, many people don't realize that using an acting or dialogue coach was common in the early Hollywood system. The coach was present in the studio and the actors were assigned to work with him or her either a day or so in advance, or on the very day the scene they were doing was being filmed. I know that this system was particularly useful in making the great movie musicals, where the greater part of the production time was taken up by the musical numbers, meticulously rehearsed in a brilliant coordination of performers and camera (sadly a lost art today), and the singers and/or dancers would work on the dialogue scenes with a coach. Wonderful young performers, such as Judy Garland, Mickey Rooney, Fred Astaire, Jane Powell, Frank Sinatra, Gene Kelly, and others were coached for all their dialogue scenes.

Since that time things have changed. As controlling as the studio bosses were, they believed in nurturing their talent pool and took great care that the product would show them off in their best light. Now, in the world of independent productions, there is a lack of sensitivity to the needs of actors, so much so that on occasion I was forced to stand up to the unfounded prejudice that the acting coach was interfering with or undermining the director's authority. Since I considered my job to be to assist the director, I felt this was unfair, and indeed I was sometimes put to the test.

Another awful truth is that, during production, too often the actors—even above-the-title stars, at times—are treated no differently from the props that dress up the set. There is so much activity swirling around the movie set on any given day, and each department is only concerned with its own narrow responsibility, that the actors become merely objects that have to be dressed by wardrobe, made up by makeup, be line-perfect for the script department, and be on their marks for the electricians and the camera crew. Otherwise, they are in the way. And, compounding the awfulness, some of the movie stars turn around and treat everyone else horribly, throwing tantrums, making impossible demands, or walking off the set and insulting their fellow actors.

In 1985 I was coaching in England on a television miniseries called *Lace II*, a sequel to *Lace*, which had been a success the year before. One of the stars was a lovely young American actress, Phoebe Cates (Mrs. Kevin Kline today), who was so sweet and considerate that someone on the crew remarked that she deserved a Miss Congeniality award for her friendliness and good humor. In one scene, she was supposed to be pushed into a swimming pool, and she was insecure about the whole thing. She arrived on the set wearing a bikini underneath her bathrobe, and was almost immediately pursued by a stills photographer, who insisted that she remove the bathrobe so he could take publicity pictures, which she was reluctant to do until after the scene was shot. I went to the producer for her and asked him to call off his photographer and to wait until after the scene was done; then, I told him, Phoebe said she would be happy to dry off and pose for pictures. The producer unexpectedly went ballistic and said he was sick and tired of her behaving like the typical American movie star with her diva-like attitude. I was taken aback, because his comment was so far off the mark where Phoebe, who was still in her teens, was concerned, but I understood where he was coming from.

In England, the actors, crew, producers, and director all cooperate and treat each other with the utmost respect. Because the actors there are treated like that from the beginning and all the way through their careers, I have found that, in general, the English actors I have met and worked with were all ladies and gentlemen, and much easier to approach than their American counterparts. In their culture, famous actors and actresses are accepted as respected members of the community, and not doggedly pursued by the fans and the media, at least not to the extent that happens in the United States. In America, the stars generally have had to fight their way to the top, and have been treated disrespectfully and often insultingly every step of the way, which is why, when they do reach the top, some of them behave badly. There are many stories about stars walking off the set in a huff when they didn't get their way or when they disagreed with someone. They appear to have no consideration for anyone else. Such behavior is always shocking to English crews, who are not used to that kind of thing. But Phoebe was not at all like that. When I explained this to the producer, adding that she was only trying to concentrate before doing a scene that she found rather frightening, he calmed down, saw the light, and asked the stills photographer to wait until a more convenient time to take his pictures.

I was helping a new producer to cast his picture once, and I criticized his manner at the casting sessions. I have done the same with new directors, and I am forceful in my explanations to them as to how to get the best out of the actors that come up for casting, by being cordial and welcoming. The producer sat in on some of my classes. He asked me why I treated all the actors with kid gloves whenever I was correcting them, while I was always much rougher with him. To explain it, I told him that actors need the support, while producers create the atmosphere in which we all have to work.

How often have I heard the cynical remark, "The actor's job is to know his lines and show up on time"? As if that was all there was to it! The reality is that the serious actor wants to be prepared to his or her own satisfaction, as well as the director's, and stay committed to the performance. That is the only way the actor can acknowledge him- or herself as a true artist, and feel like an integral part of the production, and not just "the talent," as actors are called on sets. When I was a new coach, I knew a New York-based electrician who called producers "the peasants," the crew "gorillas," and actors "the puppets!"

In the old days of the big studios, some of our favorite black-and-white "B" movies—which are today looked upon as classics—were shot in two to four weeks, very often in sequence and in single long takes that afforded great freedom to the mostly highly skilled performers who came out of theater and vaudeville. The camera was often stationary, and the perfectly blocked and rehearsed scenes accommodated the story's action, which would take place in all four corners of the screen and include "depth of field"—which means remaining in focus both far and near. The relationships between the characters were much more realized, since they often appeared together, responding to each other, and not in separate takes, as is the more common style today. And the actors often appeared together in different films. Some of them might even be working on more than one film at a time, traveling from lot to lot or movie set to movie set. I recommend watching any Spencer Tracy movie, especially a comedy, such as *Father of the Bride* (1950), and seeing him leave the scene, go into another room (or off the set, probably), and return with something he has retrieved, to deliver the rest of his lines—all in one long take and with perfect continuity of activity and emotion. Long takes are the main dividing line between how films were shot then and how they are done now.

Also, in the screenplays of those days, more time was given to developing the relationships. Movies made today—at least in the United States—are intent on "cutting to the chase," not only in action films, with their minimalist scripts and little consideration for logic, but also in dramas and romantic comedies, always impatiently arriving at the climax. In the past, it was the director and the actors, most of them having worked in the theater, who, with their greater flexibility and confidence in sustaining a long scene, built the tension and suspense. Now that is more or less left to the post-production editors. It has become an unhappy fact that in today's world of "independent films" there is a wide rift between those who make the movie and those who appear in it.

Uta Hagen began working in film late in her career, having been a victim of the 1950s blacklist. In the late 1960s, she acted in a television drama for Playhouse 90, an anthology series, and in a short scene—called a "teaser," which was a preview for the following week—she had an opportunity to see herself as the character days before principal photography was to begin. She was shocked to learn that she was not required in any way to create the environment, which was the Old West, because the editor would be cutting to the exteriors of the actual location for her. She had to adjust to doing much less than she would have had to do on stage, or come across as grossly overacting.

Another time, when she was forced to spend many weeks in a small town in northern California, working in the movie *The Other* (1972), she wrote to me, "You have to be a moron to work in the movies!" In other words, she was painfully bored, and had to come to terms with the fact that there was a lot of leisure time during the movie-making process. If you are used to the stage and love to work, acting in films becomes an endurance test. Yet actors who go from the stage to the movies have a much easier time of it than movie actors who do stage work. The transition is especially difficult for those actors who go from television to the theater. Actors trained for the stage understand how to give their performance an arc: a beginning, middle, and end, something that can never be learned from only doing movies or television.

And I have too often observed that wonderful theater actors, who have made the shift to film successfully, can eventually develop a certain laziness when and if they come back to the stage. I saw a recent Broadway production of a Shakespeare play starring an exciting movie actor who had begun his career on the stage, and whom I had enjoyed and admired early on. But he appeared inert while on stage when he was not engaged in verbal interaction with the other characters. It felt as though he was standing on the sidelines waiting for the director to call "Action!" It hurts me to the quick to see potentially great American actors fade away onto the screen, and lose their edge. There are some American stars, however, who divide their time between the media, just as actors from the United Kingdom do, and keep their edge: Kevin Kline, Meryl Streep, and Al Pacino are among them.

Today's style of making feature films is to use "quick cuts," in which the editor cuts swiftly from one shot to another, from a close-up to the other actor's close-up to a medium shot and back and forth, and cutting in "insert" shots of clouds or light shining through the leaves of a tree onto a lawn. Traditionally, the post-production editor(s) have the responsibility for the actors' performances and the shape of the film, so one might be inclined to agree with movie producers that rehearsals are not necessary, and that they only cost time and money. Yet how else can an actor build a character, especially one that is not well written? The truth is that if the character is not fully drawn, it will require more rehearsal, or, at the very least, more discussion and analysis, in order to add the missing dimensions to the character! The current notion that rehearsals are unnecessary, unwieldy, too expensive, and obsolete may have started with the movies, but it was further cemented by the overwhelming advent of filmed television series.

Actors who are the principal players in a television series working together every week for ten months out of the year can and often do develop into a "family." But the guest player is not permitted the artist's opportunity to build a character through the relationships, either before or during production. And the writers of the series, whether dramatic or comic, are often inspired by the social interaction among the principal actors off the set to write what they have observed into the weekly episodes. After a long period of this sort of experience, the actor may find him- or herself unable to distinguish a friendly, social relationship from a working one. It is a working relationship that is needed to create a character.

Some actors in television are used to blurring the differences between their self-image and the scripted character they are playing. I suppose, in a way, this echoes the phenomenon of the old-fashioned big-screen persona, like that of John Wayne, Mae West, or Clint Eastwood, except for the fact that today's actors don't have the studio system to develop scripts for them. And in television and film, the scripts are frequently simplistic and single-minded: the action is the action, the chase is the chase and there is little subtlety or nuance involved. All of this digs a huge hole for American actors to fall into, diminishing their ability to ever play a character other than themselves.

My job in coaching an actor preparing for a film role starts with reading the script, of course, and continues with my going on the character's journey with the actor. We break down each scene, with or without dialogue, for its primary objective (see step three), which, at times, turns out to be a major challenge. Once I was coaching the leading actor in a chase film, who was being pursued throughout the entire script up to the explosive climax, picking up a gorgeous woman along the way. To define objectives for each scene, I was forced to resort to the thesaurus, to look up synonyms for being chased: escaping, fleeing, running away, avoiding capture, hiding, eluding, slipping away, breaking free, and so forth. It was important to remember that no matter where and when the principal couple stopped running, no matter what they were talking about, and despite the growing sexual attraction between them, the immediacy of their circumstances and objective, which was to find safety, could never be ignored, or the entire story would be let down, and the performances rendered illogical.

It was on one of my first jobs as a dialogue coach, while working in Mexico on the western *Buck and the Preacher* (1972), that I learned how each cut was done in a typical scene, from the master shot of the whole scene (if there was one), to the smaller cuts, doubles, singles, and close-ups. Each requires its own objective. Let us suppose, for instance, that the master shot had two people involved in a verbal conflict: one of the characters wants to convince the other character "to stay on with me and fight," while the latter wants "to break away and continue my life." However long the scene continues, with all sorts of moves and secondary physical life, these objectives will serve as throughlines for the actors, just as they might in a scene on the stage.

However, when the characters are separated in single shots, these are called points of view, or POVs. Each POV will have its own small objective, cut down to size from the larger scene objective. This is not too far afield from the beats of a scene in a play, except that in movie takes, the size of the take will vary greatly with each new setup, and its smaller objective will have to be defined accordingly. The reasoning behind this rule is that the actor requires the right amount of energy for the objective of any scene, large or small. If you are only doing a portion of a larger scene, you don't want to "over-shoot the mark."

In the example above, after two takes or more of the master shot, the camera moved in for the smaller, shorter cuts. Suddenly the characters were alone in their respective medium-sized shots. The objective for each had to change to accommodate the new, smaller scene. Depending on how much of the scene will play out from his POV, character #1 may merely want "to butter up" character #2; and for his shot, character #2 may only need "to toss off the argument."

When the camera comes in for a closer shot, the actor is often forced to "cheat" the physical life. Sometimes you have to stand or sit on boxes of different sizes, called "apple-boxes," and remain in what could be an uncomfortably immobile position during the filming. Sometimes you are is forced into an awkward position not facing the other characters with whom you're supposed to be talking. At other times, you may not even be able to see the other actor, but instead must talk to an "x" on a card or to a piece of tape on the camera near the lens opening, or to the cameraman's hand. The latter is very common in television series, where two or three monster cameras are obstructing the actor's view. And sometimes the actor is obliged to look at the "x" or the hand because the other actor in the scene has been dismissed or simply gone home, as some big stars do. In such a case, the actor in the close-up has to listen to the lines and sometimes just the cues spoken by the script person and respond truthfully to them.

In scenes where there are phone calls, there is often nobody on the other end, so the actor is talking to nobody. Of course, this is always true in a stage play. But in a play, the actor has rehearsed the scene in context over and over again. In a film, on the other hand, it behooves a sensitive director to provide somebody to supply the other half of the phone conversation. Often, as a coach, I have gotten the sound engineer to hook me into the prop phone so that I can give the actor on camera the other end of the conversation, whether it is scripted or improvised.

There can be no denying that the actor's psychological and emotional life is at risk when cheating for the camera, and when he or she is in an uncomfortable physical position. The actor must find ways to compensate. In another scene in *Buck and the Preacher*, the very fine actress Ruby Dee was taken by surprise when Sidney Poitier, playing her husband, came through the door alive, after she had been told he was dead. In the master shot, she took a moment for the reality to sink in, and then leapt into his arms, buried herself in his embrace, and began sobbing, in what was an intensely emotional scene. When the director, who was Sidney Poitier himself, wanted a close-up of her face, he asked her to modify her actions and try to stay clear of him in the embrace, so as to be in the light, and this, needless to say, felt very strange to her. In order for her to follow the direction, and at the same time not to lose her emotional intensity, I suggested that she use the justification that she had speculated about how he had been killed—shot in the head or the heart, or hanged by the neck. Then, when the camera rolled, and she ran toward him, I advised her to take a moment to look for the wound, in order to satisfy herself that it didn't exist, before collapsing into his arms. Ruby was able to hold on to all of her emotions, and the close-up could be successfully cut into the wider shot.

When it comes to the mechanics of standing on a box, hitting your mark, or looking at nothing, your imagination is stretched, and the challenge is to justify what you have to do in those circumstances with a newly defined objective that will carry you through what might otherwise feel unreal and/or physically uncomfortable. A thought might come to you due to the physical strangeness of looking off into space, such as "I'm feeling distant from you (the other character)" or "I can feel your absence, or your aloofness." Since you want always to be free to think on camera, this sort of thing may get you over the hurdle of your discomfort.

In the childhood game "Freeze," one child would swing another around and a third child would call out, "Freeze!" At that point, the child who has "frozen" in position, no matter how awkward, has to express what he or she was caught in the act of doing, such as flying a kite, fishing, or frying an egg. In the game, the physical position suggests the action. Similarly, when as an actor you are forced to assume a position for mechanical and technical reasons, you may have to think about what you would be doing there that is different from, or added to, what you were doing in the previous takes of the same scene. You don't want to let a moment go by that is without meaning for your character.

Finally, it is apparent to me that the mechanics of making film and television presents obstacles that no classroom can duplicate. When I was once asked by a publisher to write a book on "film acting," I balked and said there was no such thing. Acting is acting! The better the actor is at the pure craft of acting, the easier it is to work in the media. Under pressure, your survival instinct is bound to take over, and camera nerves disappear, the frustration level of waiting around diminishes, and you learn the ability to find your concentration while caught up in the maelstrom of the shooting day, whether in a studio or on location. It's all worth it, if you know what you are doing in that comparatively brief time in front of the camera.

CHAPTER 16

The Director and the Camera

IIIIIIIIIIIIIIIIIIIIIIIIIIIIIIIIIIIIIIIIIIIIIIIIIIII

Doing scenes without a director for years in class can cause problems for the student who is hired to play a part professionally for the first time. Having worked for so long without the benefit of direction, what is the student to do when he or she has to collaborate with a director? Or when he or she encounters the television director who barely speaks to the actors except to say, "Do it less!" or "Throw it away!" or "Do it the way you did it in the audition"? For either television or film, there are certain rules of thumb as to how an actor should approach takes. In this chapter you'll learn the specifics of how to apply the acting techniques we've talked about to acting on camera, including working with a director's sometimes challenging instructions.

Camera Takes and How to Deal with Them

Camera takes are of different sizes, depending on whether the take is the "master shot" of the entire scene, which some film directors still do, but which television directors often don't bother with (because a master shot would be a waste of time on the small screen); a "two-shot," which is a shot of two actors that may be full-length or at medium height; a "single," which is a shot of an individual that may, again, show the actor medium or full-length; and close-ups of the actor's faces. Film directors traditionally work with one camera, and save close-ups for emphasizing the important moments.

Some film directors—especially those who are or have been actors, such as Robert Redford or Mike Nichols—being more sensitive to actors' needs, will block a scene so it feels right for the actor, and then direct the cameraman to follow the action, which may or may not require the actors to make some small adjustments. And great directors like the late Robert Altman and Milos Forman will use multiple cameras following the actors as they move, so as to continue the flow of action, which will be edited later. But this is rare, and more often the camera takes precedence. Television directors will block out a scene before the actors even arrive on the set, and will place taped "marks" on the floor that the actor has to "hit."

Film was certainly an exciting art form in its younger days, when the camera was often stationary, and the master take of a long scene was done without interruption. Spencer Tracy in *Father's Little Dividend* (1951) takes his grandson in a baby carriage to the park, where he gradually gets involved in a children's ball game (in one take). Finally, he can't resist actually playing, and when the game is over he starts to leave the park, forgetting the baby carriage. All of a sudden he realizes what he has done and turns back to get the carriage, running back and forth, because he is not sure where he left it (all in one take). There are long takes of him running until he arrives home, opens the front door, and sees his daughter (Elizabeth Taylor) asking his wife (Joan Bennett) where the baby is. He quietly closes the door, and, becoming more panicked, hails a taxi to take him to the police station. Except for some montage scenes of the kids playing in the park, everything is done in long takes, so that Tracy can really and brilliantly play the character's growing anxiety and sense of urgency.

In early films, the single camera would move in time with the actors throughout the set and capture the entire scene. Three-shots, two-shots, single shots, and close-ups were all done fluidly without a break! You just know that plenty of rehearsal time was set aside for this. Today everything is done with lots of "smash" cuts like those in music videos, and almost never in one long take. Camera operators without the earlier experience would find it next to impossible to light for and shoot, under pressure, one long scene with complex moves. And the actor, no longer required to sustain a long scene, forfeits his craft. This is why a good actor who works in film exclusively nowadays can grow lazy.

It has always been very difficult for film actors (who may have begun their careers as stage actors) to make the transition to the theater. When they do plays, they often forget that on stage you have to be actively involved; during camera takes, they simply have to be there, and they get used to it. But on stage you have to be active all the time. Even if you are just sitting in a chair, you are always involved with the action.

At least in film, as opposed to television, the actor gets a chance to do a scene, or a portion of a scene, many times in the course of the day's shoot. The final television edit is generally made up of close-ups, and there is seldom any kind of sweeping "establishing" shot that would set the scene, except perhaps before the titles, unless you count using a steadicam as "sweeping." The steadicam is a handheld or strapped-on camera that can track one or two actors by having the camera operator walking alongside or backwards in front of them. It, too, is used primarily to save time on a television set, and not for artistic reasons. And there is a lot more talking in television than there is in film, and rarely does the final edit focus on the people listening.

Surrendering Your Performance

Now that I have described the different kinds of shots, here is my best advice on how to deal with them. After you learn exactly what is required in the take and you understand it in the context of the rest of the scene or screenplay, you should then approach each take, no matter what the size or length of the take, as if it were the entire screenplay. In other words, approach each take as if it had a beginning, middle, and end, just like a complete scene. Don't worry about what happened before the take, or what will happen afterwards. Be in the moment.

This may sound like a contradiction in terms, but the best preparation for the beginning of a take is to "ground" yourself in the place by focusing on an object, which might be the person you're talking to or a physical object, perhaps even the floor you're standing on or the chair you're sitting in. If you are entering into the take, make sure to settle yourself in the place you're entering from by focusing on something there, even though you are off-camera. For instance, I recall in one film having to enter a living room from a kitchen in an actual apartment we were filming in, so I gave myself a different chore to do "in character" in the kitchen before each take. As a result, I was relaxed and felt prepared each time the director called, "Action!"

What you should not attempt to do is to work up your emotions regarding what has happened before the take, and certainly you must avoid any anticipation of what is to come after it. Since a film or a television show is shot out of sequence, you cannot expect to be in the same emotional state you were in days before, nor would you know where you might be in days to come. If you have broken down the scene, with or without the director's help, and made it personal to you (see part 2 of this book), then you are probably exactly where you should be emotionally, without needing to calculate or measure your emotional state.

When the director calls "Action," behave as if it were the beginning of the scene. Wherever the director calls "Cut" is the end of that scene, even if it is not the beginning or end of the scene as written in the script. The actor must treat each day of his or her performance as not necessarily connected to any other day or time of shooting; and each take should feel complete, or else the actor will make things very difficult for the editor, who is then stuck with that take. The editor must have the freedom to use any take at any place in the movie.

There have been many cases where being inventive in post-production created an entirely different movie from the one originally envisioned. An example is Tony Richardson's film *Tom Jones* (1963), which in its first release followed the screenplay exactly. According to legend, Richardson recalled all the prints and re-cut the film, scrambling up the scenes and ingeniously adding the outtakes, before releasing it again. This was the version that won the Academy Award. And it was Richardson who shaped the actors' performances so that he could tell the story as he envisioned it.

In essence, you have to *surrender* your acting performance, just as you do for the stage, where you give yourself up to it each time you do the show. In film, by way of contrast, once the scene has been shot, you can literally forget it; it is now in the hands of the editor and the director, and your work is finished.

I was once coaching one of the leading actors on the set of a western being shot in Mexico. And I kept telling my client *not* to prepare for the scene he was about to do, a "tracking" shot—which is where the camera dolly (the carriage that holds the camera) is placed on tracks, and the camera attached to it rolls along with the actor as he or she walks and talks at the same time. It takes quite a while to set up tracking shots, and the lighting and other elements have to be right, especially in the case of an outdoor scene, as this one was. Indoors, the lighting can obviously be controlled, and if the studio is as soundproof as it should be, you won't have to stop for that plane flying overhead.

In this case, the actor I was coaching was astride a horse. When the director called "Action," he was to ride a little way on the horse, then jump off it and meet up with a boy with whom there would then be a dialogue scene.

It was difficult to time things just right, and this actor managed to make mistakes that ruined one take after another. I said to him, "Please do not think about what's coming up, or what went before. Just play this particular scene. No other scene was ever shot before it. And nothing will ever be done after it." Well, he nodded his head, but I don't think he absolutely agreed with me. And in the next takes, there were some more fumbles. I finally went over to him and said, "Please, instead of 'preparing,' when the director says 'Action,' I want you to be doing exactly what the horse is doing. Just imitate the horse. The horse was perfect in every take." It was true: the horse was in touch with the dust, the heat, and the flies buzzing around her, and she really had been perfect in every take! Out of frustration, he reluctantly agreed, and once he had cleared his mind of clutter and gotten in touch with his environment, the take and scene went smoothly.

This anecdote illustrates what I mean by being in the moment. After all, the horse wasn't thinking about what had happened or what was about to happen. She was just there, being a horse. I have observed many actors getting into trouble by trying to continue an emotion or an action from a previous day's shooting, or even a previous take, or by anticipating what will come up later, as they work toward the place they want to take their character.

The story may indeed be continuing in the way the actor has imagined it would, but the editor and director will decide how to tell the story, and they may change their minds about some aspect of it when they see the different takes. There is a "continuity" or "script" person on every set who is watching for anything that does not "match."

There is a difference between continuity and matching. "Continuity" refers to a continuum of actions and emotions. "Matching" refers to a physical task. For instance, for every take you want to have the cigarette burned down to where it was in the previous take, or the glass filled to the level it was at. If you made a move at a place where there might be a cut, you want to make the same move in the same place on the next take. You don't want someone to have been eating in one shot, and in the next to have the audience see a full plate—a blooper that has been known to occur. And as an actor, you want to have the coffee cup in the same hand in every take. A good script person knows that not everything needs to be matched, because he or she knows where there probably will or won't be a cut—that is, where the editor will use material from another take when putting the scene together. It is the job of the script person to inform the actor appropriately if his or her physical actions don't match.

And remember—most importantly—*emotionally, you cannot repeat a moment in acting.* So however tempted you may be, don't even try. A moment occurs only once. If the camera has captured it, that's great. If not, when you do another take, there will be another way that the moment happens, and it will be just as good as the one you loved. The same principle applies on stage as well.

On stage, you are moving the story along. On film, however, the editor will eventually move the story along. Your short sequences should contain a moment-to-moment truth in relationship to what surrounds you, and they should be driven by a small objective. As Jack Lemmon once said, "On stage, it's *doing*; on film, it's *being*." He should have known, because he was great on both stage and screen.

Thinking on Film

On the stage there is no time to think, because you are always in action. Any thought that comes to the actor on stage usually happens in retrospect, after he or she has already done something. You've completed the action, and you might spontaneously speculate on it, but even then you cannot dwell on it, or you will slow down the life on stage, and probably lose your concentration. On camera, however, thinking is a very viable activity (see step 6), and it helps you to *be there* when there isn't a lot of dialogue. In any case, you don't continue the thought process for very long, since the take will end in just a few minutes. And, sad to say, you can actually think anything on camera; what you think doesn't even have to be related to the character you are playing, as long as you are really thinking.

I discovered that fact while I was working on my first film as an on-set coach, *Angel Levine* (1970). The movie was adapted from a Bernard Malamud short story, produced by and starring Harry Belafonte as the angel, and costarring the great comic actor Zero Mostel. In an exterior scene that took place on the stoop of a New York City brownstone, Belafonte listened for a long time while Mostel spoke. Because he hadn't done a movie role in ten years, he wasn't very confident, and after one take in which he appeared to be blank, I said to him, "You really have to be thinking about what Zero is saying."

"I thought I was," he said. And that was the point: he wasn't thinking, he just thought he was.

"No, you really weren't. You have to speculate more on what he is saying, and allow yourself to think freely."

There were two or three takes before he did the one that really worked. And I said, "Now you did it!"

He smiled mischievously. "You know what I was thinking? I was thinking about that girl (an extra) walking down the street and how gorgeous her legs were."

"Great!" I said, "as long as you were thinking!"

I came to the conclusion then that, when acting for the camera, at times the actor needs only to be involved in something. It's the viewing audience that really fills in the blanks.

Along the same lines, I remember reading an anecdote about the famous last scene of *On the Waterfront* (1954), in which Marlon Brando, bruised and bloodied, walks up the ramp after having taken revenge by beating up Lee J. Cobb. The director, Elia Kazan, an actors' director and a known perfectionist, demanded take after take. Between each take, Brando's makeup had to be re-applied, until finally he grew furious. He did a take in that angry mood, and that was the one Kazan used in the final cut. Brando later said that in that final take he had been thinking, "If I have to get this fuckin' makeup put on one more time, I'm gonna kill the director!"

While working on a television miniseries, a period piece called *Harem* (1987)—much of it shot on location in Seville—I had an experience that pointed up for me the necessity of coming up with an adjustment in the brief moments after the setup is complete, and before the camera begins to roll. Nancy Travis was playing a young American woman who was being transported on a litter carried by four "eunuchs" across a beautiful piazza to the boudoir of a Turkish sultan, played by Omar Sharif. She had been kidnapped, bathed, powdered, and wrapped in veils, to be "inducted" by him into his harem as a concubine. (When I read the script, I knew that this was not a winner!) The sweeping crane shot was to end up in a close-up of her face, and these were to be the final moments of the first night's episode, meant to be suspenseful enough to bring back the viewers the next night. But to the dismay of the already beleaguered director, Ms. Travis appeared completely blank during the dry run—terrifyingly so. Getting a panicked cue from him, I rushed over to the beginning mark, and, before the litter was lifted, directed Ms. Travis to recite the Lord's Prayer over and over again in her mind for as long as the shot lasted. When she did this, the expression on her face subtly changed and convinced us that she was a vulnerable victim of bizarre circumstances and that she was frightened. The direction worked for the actress because it was active rather than descriptive, as in "appear frightened." And it gave her something to think about.

I want to emphasize again that thinking on camera—unlike thinking on stage—is a legitimate activity; but so is *not* thinking—as in the famous direction Rouben Mamoulian gave to Greta Garbo for the legendary last shot in *Queen Christina* (1933): "Think of nothing!" Making your mind a blank can be just as active as choosing something to think, when it is appropriate.

So, to sum up, thinking and *being there* are essentials when the actor is in front of a camera. And while television will give you fewer opportunities, because of the dialogue and the speed with which it is shot, you want to be involved every moment. But film roles will always include some silent scenes, and of course, you would want to be inspired during those takes to think like the character.

Working with Directors: Translating the Director's Language

I remember that in the old days of the famous Actors Studio many of the members disparaged directors, and harked back to a time long gone when there were no directors, only actor-managers. But, of course, that ended in most places in the nineteenth and early twentieth centuries! I saw a production in progress at the Actors Studio of a play by Israel Horowitz, which the cast rehearsed for an entire season, or perhaps even two. They were planning to move it to an off-Broadway theater. When I asked who the director was going to be, they scoffed at me. They said they were not going to have a director, who might ruin all their fine work. But in the media and in the theater outside this particular kind of Actors Studio situation, there are always directors!

Since I knew my intermediate and advanced acting students already worked with and were going to continue to work with directors, I wanted to be sure they viewed the collaboration as the perfectly natural next step in their training. In other words, the step-by-step progress they were learning in order to bring a non-directed scene to life was perfectly in line with their eventual obligation to cooperate with a director, and to adhere to the director's point of view. But a director will often use language the acting student is unfamiliar with. Therefore, as an introduction to working with directors, I coined the term *translation* to describe how to mesh the actor's inner work with the direction, and how to "translate" the director's language into a language the actor knows. Here are some examples of *translation*:

1. The simple direction to move. The director says, "Move there!" If the move feels improbable for the character at that moment, you do not argue or refuse to do it, because you are under the obligation to take direction and to do what the director wants. You perform the move and find a way to make it real, giving it an inner justification, such as, simply, "I need to cross the room to see something on the other side." In another instance, you may feel like moving toward another actor for a tense moment of confrontation, but the director says, "Sit in that chair now." Your justification might be, "I suddenly feel a bit tired, a bit drained, because I have been so involved in this emotional scene with my acting partner. Although I remain just as involved, I have to sit down, at least for a second." If neither move is logical, then the director may be sensitive enough to see that, and rescind the direction. On the other hand, disagreeing with the director only leads to trouble and to worse direction.

2. The director wants the actor to go faster. This is a very common direction by most insecure directors, who believe that racing through the dialogue and picking up the cues will keep the audience alert, when in reality nothing causes an audience to fall asleep as quickly as watching actors rushing through their performances. As good actors know, timing is based on living truthfully and fully through actions and dialogue from moment to moment, even in a comedy, where we all know that the timing of punch lines is important. Arriving at a performance that goes from unanticipated moment to unanticipated moment is the actor's goal. It is a strange but true phenomenon that time shrinks throughout rehearsal and performance.

I remember rehearsing the two-act, two-character play *Two for the Seesaw* in a summer theater in only nine days! In the first run-through my costar and I took almost four hours to get through the play with costume changes and all. The next run-through took three hours and forty minutes. The director, an extremely sensitive guy who trusted us to do the job, said, "I need you to cut at least an hour by tomorrow's rehearsal, but keep all the values you have achieved, and don't rush." Somehow by the next night—which was our opening night—we played the entire play in two hours and thirty-five minutes.

But, in order to translate "Faster!" when the director wants it at a point in rehearsal that is usually too early, you simply have to justify the direction by telling yourself that you have a time problem: You or the other person is about to leave the room, or is late for some appointment, or for some other urgent reason that is your secret.

3. The director wants the actor to speak louder. This is another very common direction by insecure directors, but, to give the devil his due, in the theater some actors need to get in the habit of speaking louder from the beginning of rehearsals. This particular direction is unnecessary in films and television. In any case, you can "endow" the other actor(s) with being hard of hearing. You will then automatically speak up, and not feel that you are being false.

4. The director wants the actor to be "smaller," quieter, or to do less—which is usually the case in film and television. The translation of this direction is a bit more complicated. In this case, you have to search through the circumstances and find where you might be overdoing what should be a simple action. An action appropriate to the material has to be carried out with the appropriate energy. If you can see where you are overdoing an action, you can adjust or redefine the immediate objective accordingly.

In some cases, however, such as in television police and courtroom drama, which has become so stylized over the years, what is considered an appropriate action is in fact laughable. A shopkeeper survives a near-death experience with an armed robber, yet he is expected to behave as though it were an everyday occurrence. Or a woman who has witnessed a murder in her hallway is asked to speak in a very matter-of-fact tone. Of course, in real life, a normal person would be in shock or hysterical. In a stage play, on the other hand, a robbery or murder is usually a high-pitched event, and all the previous scenes have led up to it. In television, it just happens. Often, a police drama will open with a corpse.

In order to justify the unnatural response usually required in a nighttime television drama, a logical solution is for the actor to communicate his lines in a confidential manner, as if wanting no one around to hear. The more normal hysterical reaction is thus controlled, but the actor will experience it as a truthful reaction that has to be damped down. This could be quite effective, and the audience would then see how terrified and upset the person really is underneath the attempt to remain in control.

Television drama is so unrealistic because the American audience has gotten used to crime and violence via television for almost five decades now, and the producers of these network series continue to provide it as a daily diet. I am saddened that actors on television have been compelled to compromise their real impulses, and no longer are allowed to portray the truth of a situation. There are ways to give the television producers what they want and still hold on to one's integrity.

5. A more complicated direction: the director wants the character to have more or less of a certain quality (mean, cowardly, tough, shy, etc.), while the actor involved in his or her own process is developing the character in an organic way, by uncovering the subtext and finding the character underneath. To justify such instant gratification for the director, you almost have to do cartwheels. Starting with the premise that you want to feel that you have succeeded in achieving a

three-dimensional, fully felt performance, I must warn you that obeying a note that brings you to results too soon will end up with your either playing a cliché or a caricature. You must find your way to achieving character traits demanded by the director from a personal source with which you are familiar. And you must be able to tap into that source almost instantly, in order to be within the time frame that is imposed on you, perhaps because the director is under pressure from the producers.

The direction "be more nervous or frightened" can be followed and the desired result achieved if you think about someone you find to be dangerous. If you are confronted with a character who is your enemy, you might immediately think of someone you dislike, or fear. If you are being mugged in a scene, even if you have never been mugged in real life, you might think immediately of some terribly upsetting experience, or of a time when you were deathly afraid.

You might translate the direction "be tougher" by reminding yourself that you can be tough when a situation demands it. You can then endow the situation or the other character(s) in the scene with a quality that makes you feel that way; perhaps they are "helpless" or "weak" or "childlike."

Since characters on nighttime television seem to fall into categories—for example, the pimp, the prosecutor, the cop, the perpetrator, the dumb blonde, the hunk, and the nerd—it appears that television directors want no more than the two-dimensionality such categories represent. Yet you want to avoid instant characterizations, and create real, original characters, while also moving the plot along.

6. A very common direction given to actors on television and in film, especially in soap opera, but sometimes also on stage, is to look out front, or toward the camera, for particular bits of dialogue, while the person you are speaking to is a few steps behind you. It feels very odd, as if you are talking to the air, because it is more natural to "look the other guy in the

eye and tell the truth," as the great movie actor James Cagney once described his acting technique. The purpose behind this direction is obvious on film because it saves the time of a new camera set-up, since both faces will be captured in a single shot. But when this occurs on stage, the insensitive director, who may be inexperienced or just an old-fashioned academic, is fearful of the actor's back. This type of director wrongly feels that the actor must be facing the audience at all times.

Although it always involves stretching your imagination a bit, there are various ways you can justify such a direction. You can look for a reason why you are "hiding" from the other person—perhaps you are telling a lie, for example. In one emotional scene I had to do while playing on a three-sided arena stage, which often called for some strange blocking because of sight lines, I chose to "see" in the distance the past event I was describing, which happened to be a holocaust scene, and also chose not to look my husband in the eye, in order to spare him pain.

Bear in mind, too, that you will create a fourth wall in your imagination during rehearsal (see page 128). If you are directed to face out, you can therefore find something to focus on in order to feel comfortable, as if you were looking out of a window and seeing the sky or the street, for example. On a film set, you can always find a focus point away from the camera lens, and imagine it to be something specific you are looking at. Of course, a sensitive director in the theater, or behind the camera, would attempt to block his actors physically in a fashion that would feel natural to both the actors and the audience.

These are just a few samples of how to deal with a director's limited vocabulary when it comes to relating to the actor. The most important element for the actor to remember is that you should never merely *obey* the insensitive or illogical direction, but rather find a way to justify it and find some truthful reason for it. A direction that is simply obeyed appears mechanical and awkward. The director, no matter how inexperienced, will observe that, and believe it to be the actor's fault! According to him, the actor did not follow the instruction, since he or she failed to justify it.

If you are working organically, you should be able to work with all types of directors. Flexibility is required, especially in the United States, which has had no particular tradition of theater, and therefore throws together theater and film artists with many varied backgrounds and trainings.

Learning an effective acting technique is a serious necessity for actors today, since you will find that, a great deal of the time, there will be very little guidance or support from the outside. You have to be able to judge your own work, and to guard it while cooperating with the director, the other actors, and the crew. As any professional knows, the following rules apply: be on time, know your lines, and be cooperative—that is, if you want to get along in this business.

In filmmaking accidents happen when the actors don't like the director, or the crew doesn't feel respected by the actors, or—most particularly—when the director doesn't seem to be in charge. I have seen accidents involving not only stunt people, which is something to be expected, but the crew as well. On one film, I witnessed a terrible incident during night shooting on the roof of an abandoned building in Hell's Kitchen, New York City. I was hired as a coach to assist the first-time director. By that time, in the early 1980s, I was beginning to recognize that when the person who is supposed to be in charge—the director—is not in charge, one of the results is carelessness among the crew. The director was a nice guy, but was obviously insecure, and one of the stars, a legendary actress who was behaving like a diva, was openly critical of the director's lack of experience. Inevitably the crew was bummed out, too. Then, a couple of weeks into shooting, I watched in horror as a young crew member jumping from roof to roof in the dark fell between the buildings from six stories up.

On another movie, in which I was playing a role, I witnessed an electrician fall from the catwalk. Here again, the director was too new and inexperienced to control what went on. And, adding to the strained atmosphere, the star of the film was behaving in an aloof and condescending manner. Freud said that there are no such things as real accidents. There is always some reason for them. In this kind of case, resentment that cannot be expressed directly can lead people to injure themselves, instead of the person they really want to hurt: the director who is incompetent and probably defensive and demanding at the same time.

Rehearsal is the last thing on a new, inexperienced director's mind. He or she has so much else to think about that there is no time for it, and actors are left to develop their parts on their own, without guidance. And, sadly, some actors don't really care about rehearsals either, and even become satisfied with "phoning in" their job. Recently I spoke to a television actor who was in the cast of probably the most successful television sitcom ever aired. He was asked to be in a current Broadway hit, and turned it down because he couldn't imagine "the agony" of playing the same situations and speaking the same lines eight times a week! Conversely, I heard a very fine theater and film actor who is currently playing a leading role in a hit television series say that he's only doing it for the money, to put his children through college. Of course, the financial reward for going through the "grind" of the TV series is and will always be more lucrative than the theater.

When a television or movie actor works in the theater, it is usually for a very limited run. Granted, they have other career commitments that pay more, but they also fear "the grind" of it. On the other hand, there are actors who relish rehearsal time and long runs, but they appear to be a dwindling minority in today's world of media blitz, publicity, high salaries, and fierce competition.

A student told me not long ago that he finds rehearsing "a drag" because he gets too familiar with the other characters' lines. I looked at him in amazement and congratulated him, because it was something I'd never heard before, and I thought I had heard it all! It is true that beginners and children will not know what to do with "too much" rehearsal or "too many" takes—can there be too much rehearsal or too many takes? An accomplished actor usually welcomes as much time as he or she can get.

The primary reason actors study a technique based on Stanislavsky's System and principles is so that they will be capable of doing performance after performance and camera take after camera take, remaining fresh, and always speaking the lines and doing the action as if it was for the very first time. Having a good acting technique means having the capability to use every minute of rehearsal, as well as every performance, to discover more about your character. If a performance becomes boring and mechanical, continuing to do it night after night becomes terribly painful for any actor. And when this happens, it indicates that there was something wrong in the actor's approach to the role to begin with, and/or that he or she is not committed to Stanislavsky's basic principle of "every time is the first time." If you are committed to that principle, every performance and every camera take should be a joy and a discovery.

CHAPTER 17

Auditions

||||||||||||||||||||||||||||||||||||||||||||||||

You may think that the subject of auditions should come at the beginning of this book. Auditions would seem to be beginnings, after all. But, in fact, it is the study of the art and craft of acting that is the beginning. Only after you have done that are you ready to audition.

In this country, I meet more and more aspiring actors whose goal is to be in television or the movies. They spend their first year, and lots of money, getting their photos taken and trying to get auditions. Instead of studying their craft, they attend "classes" given by casting directors and agents, mainly so that they can meet them. I've often told them that if they wanted to be in any of the other performing arts, they would certainly study their craft first. You don't try to get an audition for the New York Philharmonic violin section without learning to play the violin, and you have to study for years to become proficient, let alone professional in your playing. The mistaken impression many young people have is that acting is a lesser craft, and requires less skill, or perhaps none at all, just desire. It is certainly true that when acting is good, it looks effortless. But the reality is that the study of acting is never-ending hard work.

When I was student in Herbert Berghof and Uta Hagen's

classes, I looked around and saw many older, already successful actors in the class, among them Zero Mostel, Geraldine
Page, and Maureen Stapleton. And even today in New York
and Los Angeles many serious-minded actors who are already
well known on the stage and in the media make time for class,
in order to keep their instruments sharpened, and to stretch
and try out new roles.

If you don't already know acting technique, classroom
training in "how to give a good audition" can only give you
a false sense of confidence. Also, it is impossible to re-create
the environment of an audition in a classroom, and to get the
adrenaline flowing as it is when there is an actual job on the
line. Besides, the budding actors in these classes are given
opinions only and not technique, especially when "taught" by
casting directors or their assistants.

Auditions come in all shapes and sizes, which is one other
reason I am skeptical about audition classes. Certainly, when
I was a student there was no such thing as a class just for
audition preparation. And when the first one I'd ever heard
of was offered at the HB Studio, I jokingly asked the regis-
trar if the teacher was going to line up everybody outside the
classroom, and then walk up and down the line, chewing on
a cigar, and pick out a few students to "audition," just as stage
managers used to do at the stage doors of Broadway houses. I
was shocked to hear that the class was indeed going to be set
up that way—minus the cigar, of course!

There are quite a lot of differences, as has been made
clear throughout this book, in the circumstances of theater,
film, and television acting. It stands to reason then that there
should be as many differences when it comes to the auditioning experience. What is constant in all of them, however, is
your ability to present yourself as a thinking, feeling, working
actor, who is capable of bringing a character to life from just
reading the sides.

Another constant, and one that is often overlooked in auditions, is the necessity of listening. You have to listen to whom-

ever you are reading with, no matter how monotonously they're doing it or how inappropriate they might be. All of you who have gone through auditions have already experienced "readers" in casting rooms and offices who are the wrong gender and the wrong age, who are dull and wooden in their readings, and who may even keep their heads down and their eyes in the script throughout the audition. Yet you must be alert and listen attentively to every word the reader says, because so much of what you want to convey about your character exists in your responses, and you don't want to respond as if you were in a vacuum. John Barrymore once said, "I could play Romeo to a tree stump!" And I would add that we have all had to play to tree stumps at auditions. The key is to "embrace" the reader in all his or her peculiarities. Of course you will have to make a substitution while preparing for an audition, and, just as when you make substitutions from your own life when you are preparing a role or a scene, here, too, in the audition situation, you can be inwardly surprised at how oddly the reader is behaving (see page 66). Committing yourself to *listening* in auditions and relating to the reader will also calm your nerves and stop the voices in your head that are repeatedly asking you, "How am I doing?" Let me add that there are times, of course, when you get a perfectly good reader to relate to.

The dynamics of the first reading (see page 85) apply to auditions, except that you will have made substitutions for the relationships and choices for the inner objects and objective in a short time—all from a personal point of view, in order to create vulnerability when you read the scene(s). If you get the job, all of these choices are subject to change.

Young actors tend to pay too much attention to the descriptions given in the breakdowns of the parts being auditioned. What you should be relying on is your personal exploration. You can use the descriptions as clues, but being influenced to play given results can sabotage you. When you receive the audition sides or script, begin with the material first and then look at how the character is described.

I do not recommend memorizing the lines for your first audition for any part! I know this is a departure from what many people believe. If you memorize lines for your very first audition, or even before your first callback, you risk a lapse in concentration, and you will forget the dialogue; this can easily occur when you are under stress. Much more impressive to those doing the casting than a preconceived and memorized piece is the opportunity to observe how you pick those words up off the page and look into the eyes of the reader, just as you've learned to do in first readings. Except for television auditions (see below), your audition should be regarded as a "work in progress," unless it is a screen test or a work-through session with the director—which usually only happens after you have passed at least two auditions.

Actors ask me about what they should wear, and my advice is always to dress comfortably in what makes you feel attractive, and according to the general truth of the status, occupation, or period of the character, short of renting a costume. You also want to feel that you are appearing at your best, without over or under-dressing.

Play, film, and television auditions are as different as the writing styles and the mechanics of each medium. Yet the commitment to all three is the same: you must treat them all as if they were an interview for a job, which they are, and not a trial where you are going to be judged before an inquisition.

Here is a brief breakdown of how to prepare for the different types of auditions.

Plays

At a play audition the director and/or writer and the casting director do not require you to be a fully developed character; they are more interested in aspects of you that will fit the character. A play is rich in dialogue and subtext, objectives and actions, and you are expected to show the potential employers that you can deal with all that, and that you can develop and build a full character in rehearsals. Therefore, the casting personnel, the playwright, and the director (the latter two may not be there until callbacks) all want to see if you will fit the role, both physically and qualitatively, and that you can handle the emotion, the dialogue, and its style, if the language is stylized.

They wish to see the living, breathing you—your soul, if you will—in the situation in the scene. If you present them with a preconceived character—something you as an original artist want to avoid at all costs anyway—it may not be the "character" the director or writer had in mind; and you don't want their first impression to be that you are an actor who sees things differently than they do. With the time allotted for rehearsals, the director, writer and producers want to know that you are someone they can work well with, and mold, if you will; someone who has made a personal commitment to the story and your role in it.

After you have been called for an audition, by all means read the whole play if the play is already published; or, in the case of a new play, when it is made available through your agent or at the casting office. Then break the required scene(s) down as you would a scene for class. Find out the personal facts of the relationships and make a preliminary choice of your character's primary objective, filling it with parallel experiences from your own life and with your personal philosophy and vulnerability. Leave the results and the outer life alone—how it sounds, how the story moves, etc. Avoid second guessing, as well. Don't be concerned about what you suspect they are looking for, since nine times out of ten you will probably be wrong.

I was working with a student on an audition for the part of Eliza Doolittle in *My Fair Lady*, the musical based on George Bernard Shaw's *Pygmalion*. She was asked to do a number of scenes, including the pivotal and climactic one, after Eliza has "learned to be a lady." And I spent most of our coaching session discussing what Shaw had in mind. In the slipper-throwing scene, it is very hard for her to do battle with Professor Higgins's self-centered, confident logic and vast vocabulary, given the newness and limits of her education, and yet she knows what she wants to say. Will she find the words to say it? She becomes very frustrated in the scene. Her objective seems to be "to test herself to see if she could ever reach his level," rather than what might at first glance seem like the more obvious choice, "to get him to respect her." And when she is frustrated in her objective in the end, she falls apart, crying. To examine the subtext further, what was the "battle of the sexes" issue Shaw intended to portray in the argument Higgins has with Eliza? Is it that men can get along as single, independent individuals while women always need a man? It was very exciting to look at the conflict in this way and to personalize it.

When she came to me, the actress was at first only concerned with displaying Eliza's fiery temperament and her Cockney accent, just as I expected she would be. I helped her to explore instead the subtext in Shaw's work, which touched a chord in her, and brought about emotions that surprised even her. The actress might have needed to work on the accent, but her preparation for the audition had to go deeper than that. Let the subtext be your main concern and don't worry about the outer behavior when you are preparing for a play audition.

Depending on the space provided for the audition, you can feel free to move around in the imaginary "place" while focused on the reader, who will probably be sitting in a chair close to those who are casting. Sometimes your impulses will lead you to be very active, and sometimes you will feel better sitting and concentrating on the give and take with the reader. Just be wary of any "obligations" to do it one way or another, and follow your impulses.

Film

When you are auditioning for a film, most of the time you will be put on tape and be expected to sit or stand, facing the camera, and to look at the reader who is sitting or standing beside it. This prohibits movement.

In your preparation for the film audition, make personal choices for the relationships and the objective for each scene. Because the material is usually described in more visually active terms than in a play, and the dialogue is generally less wordy and contains minimal subtext, you are expected to fill in the blanks with more concrete consideration for the character traits than you would for a play audition, by focusing on a part of you that is closest to the character.

For instance, if you are auditioning for a gangster role, you will try to find the parts of yourself that might be hostile, and perhaps taciturn, and angry enough to behave as that type of character does. You will want to free the internal life of such a character and arrive at his point of view, even if it is personally repulsive to you. Then the words, or "woids," if the gangster is from New York, will take care of themselves. You are not "acting" the part, but rather putting yourself in the part. If you are auditioning for the part of a priest or a nun, you will have to begin by looking within yourself for the calmness, serenity, and desire to serve people and God in the way a priest or a nun does.

Personalizing in this way will bring you close to actually becoming the character without making any conscious effort to look or outwardly behave like the character. You should be concentrating all your efforts on working from an internal point of view. Let whatever occurs externally illustrate all the work that you have done, which will still feel like a work in progress.

What you don't want to do is walk into the casting situation with a preconceived character, any more than you would in a play audition. For a film, the director wants to know that he will be able to collaborate with you, and that you will be able to give him the results he wants. As previously noted, usually a film has less dialogue than a play, and it is the character's very being, not just the character's actions, that tells the story on camera.

Also, you may have to use a lot more imagination in the audition than you would for a play. For instance, in the scene, your character may be in a car that's moving or one that crashes, or nearly crashes, but you don't want to "indicate" fear or fall off your chair. You can experience the fear in your imagination, and if you imperceptibly hold tight to your seat with your bottom and/or your free hand, you will feel as if it you were in the situation, and as if it were happening to you. This will register on the videotape. Similarly, if there is a kiss or a slap or a punch or even a bullet shot from a gun, you don't want to pantomime the event, and risk feeling ridiculous, but you can pause for a moment in the reading to imagine it, and let your response to it happen. This will make you feel as if the kiss or slap had really been delivered. It is always more important for you to believe it than to concern yourself with whether or not they believe it.

Although I have not seen the script of *Brokeback Mountain*, I think of scenes in the film with the two male leads, and especially of Ennis Del Mar, the character played so poignantly by the Australian actor Heath Ledger. If an actor were auditioning for that role, whose background and culture is that of the American West, he would not necessarily know how the Taiwanese director, Ang Lee, saw the character. Ennis is obviously a man of few words, as I'm sure his dialogue in the script shows. He was brought up to be a cowboy, has not had much formal education, and is not worldly or sophisticated in any way. In preparing the audition, the actor would also want to look thoroughly into what makes the character so inarticulate and withdrawn, aside from his cultural background. The character is meditative and almost painfully private. If you were auditioning for the role, you would have to find all that in yourself. What stops you from expressing yourself verbally, or from speaking too much? In what situation(s) do you find yourself tongue-tied? When have you been hesitant to express how you felt? The character is afraid to make his feelings known, and that characteristic exists in him even before he is aware of his homosexuality.

You have to look for substitutions immediately for the relationships and events that might have brought about these characteristics. An audition for a film should consist of going after the objectives that hold the scene(s) together, and the emotional center you have found for the character—what you believe makes that person tick.

Television

A television audition is quite unlike a play or film audition: for television, the casting agents and the director, producers, and writer want to see the character you come up with already fully realized! Since there will be *no* time spent during pre-production or on the shooting day in building the relationships or the character, you have to show them the behavior pretty much as you would do it on the shooting or taping day. Even though there are more words in a television script than a screenplay, they are probably less interesting, more expositional, and they certainly do not suggest a lot of subtext. Often, there are more detailed character descriptions as well.

Since television producers are only concerned about your being ready when the time comes, you will be expected to turn out a performance even for the audition itself. How often have I heard on the set, "Do it the way you did it in the audition"? Still, you want to try to avoid clichés or preconceptions. So anything you can do to create the yin and the yang of a stripper or a crook or a cop or a housewife, and to add dimension to the character, would be advantageous.

The television audition is the most harrowing of all, because the casting process and the material itself often have an assembly-line atmosphere. You will first face the casting director in an interview prior to the audition, and, if you pass that, then you will usually find yourself seated before a row of four or five interested people (producers, writer, and director), with a video camera directed at you, and under pressure to show them exactly what you're going to do with the part. Your job is to remain relaxed, to listen to the reader's entire dialogue, not just the cues, and to forget all those eyes staring at you. This is a difficult task until you get the hang of it.

I have heard of many frustrating experiences in television auditions. And I remember a particularly disturbing one of my own during an audition for *Law & Order*. Although I felt prepared for the scene, the casting assistant who was reading with me fumbled and mispronounced so many words that the scene made no sense. Yet the executives who were present did not seem to be aware of this, or to care, so I forced myself to carry on, but I imagine I had a very puzzled look on my face, which could not have been at all appropriate, even though it was honest.

For television auditions, study the material and make choices not only for the relationships, the place, and the objectives, but also for the character, as fully as possible. You will be expected to amaze the casting people with your own precise character choices as the cop, the criminal, the flustered parent, or the rebellious teenager, which you can do by making a character chart and using endowments and/or essences, and so forth (see step 10).

A long time ago, I balked at the assumption that for a television audition you needed to bring in a full character, including some creative touches, such as a limp or a lisp, in order to compete for the role. This is still a commonly held belief among West Coast actors. It worries me that the actor needs to become an originator and "write" his own character, instead of being an interpreter. It is a much better approach to break down the character (as per the character chart) and find his or her uniqueness in that way.

If you were auditioning for the part of a cowboy in a television show, as opposed to a movie like *Brokeback Mountain*, the casting people would want to hear the drawl and see the character's physical attitudes. Some of that would be written into the character description in the script, usually in a very simplistic way, and the dialogue would be much more expositional. Although the writer(s) of a teleplay think they have described the character beautifully, you as the actor have to decode it and make sense of what is at best a stereotype, and then arrive at the audition much like the character they think they've described, but without doing an awful cliché.

As with all auditions, you want to have fun and enjoy the opportunity to do a mini-performance. To summarize, when you audition for a play or a film, you are "in rehearsal"; for a television audition, you are already "in performance," even though you are not in the actual physical surroundings or working with the other actors.

Prepared Monologues

Although you will probably be doing scenes from the play when you are auditioning for a theatrical production, sometimes you are asked to do a monologue, particularly for some regional theaters or repertory companies, or for admission to a university drama program. Monologues are also often required in your search for representation by a talent agency or manager, particularly on the East Coast.

It is difficult to choose a monologue that is right for you, I know. You might ask your teacher or acting coach to suggest one, but, in any case, be aware of the following rules: first, you only need a minute and a half of material. It is a common mistake to do long monologues; auditors can recognize who you are in less time, and by sticking to a minute and a half, you will have the room to do at least two (sometimes three) contrasting ones. And, second, pick something that is meaningful to you, or gives you something to say. In order to hold onto monologues that you can use over a long period of time, you want to feel that the monologue contains something you really want to express. Ideally, the monologue should be from a play, which always has more meat than a screenplay.

A true monologue is a speech given when the character

is alone on stage talking to the audience (narrative), to her- or himself (soliloquy), to an imaginary creature that only the character can see, or to someone on the telephone. Since carrying around a prop phone would be clumsy, and since contemporary soliloquies are rare, actors for decades now have had to choose speeches that are actually part of a scene with one or more people.

If you are called on to do a monologue, you should read the entire play just as you would if you were preparing to do the scene, so that you can put the speech in its context. You should go through all the steps as well. You have to imagine that the other person is there, and choose a substitution for him or her.

Do not direct yourself. In order to avoid listening to yourself while you are working on the monologue, work in silence most of the time. The only exception to this is when the monologue is a true soliloquy: if you are supposed to be alone, then it is all right to work aloud with the text.

You should learn the words sooner than you would if you were preparing a scene, since they are really all you have. I advise my students to write or type out the words in a monologue in short sequential beats many times, and while reviewing in their minds the relationship, inner objects, and circumstances.

In a way, you are in rehearsal in your head, learning the words as you would for a play, attaching them to their meanings in the subtext. You can then test yourself on the words while you are alone, by mumbling them to yourself, much like a singer humming a tune, while you go about some routine task such as cleaning up, doing dishes, folding laundry, making breakfast or lunch, or getting ready to go out. By directing your physical energy toward something that does not require your full attention, instead of directing it at the monologue itself, you can ensure your subjectivity, because you are not watching or listening to yourself, which inevitably leads to editing and directing yourself. Remember, what you think you look like or sound like should not be on your mind, and is probably a false impression anyway.

Once you have done all this, try the monologue out in class or with a coach. And be patient. You don't want to rush through choosing and preparing a monologue to perform within a matter of days, but rather within a matter of weeks or even months. Although you shouldn't have to be prepared with monologues throughout your career, I have known cases in which a good monologue that was well worked on remained part of an actor's repertoire for a very long time, to be taken out and dusted off whenever needed. There is a common belief that you must keep changing your monologues in order "to keep them fresh," but this is a gross misconception. Serious artists want to do their best, and their best can only be attained over a period of time, so that the work becomes a living, breathing part of them, much like the work of a musician or a dancer.

You need to have only three prepared monologues: two that are contemporary (comedy and serious); and one classical monologue, perhaps from Shakespeare. In choosing something that is right for you, do not try to find a monologue or a speech that displays your entire range of emotions, because there are no such monologues anyway. Don't worry either about choosing something that has never been done before and is virtually unknown or obscure; it doesn't matter if the speech is well known or not, as long as you do it well.

The three most common misconceptions are:

1. An actor needs a whole host of monologues to pick and choose from. My response to that has always been that the acting student will be so busy selecting and practicing audition pieces that he or she will have no time to work on anything else, such as an actual part.
2. An actor must display a whole gamut of emotions. I warn you to be aware of the intimacy of the audition space, if you don't want to end up "with egg on your face." You don't want to tear a pas-

sion to tatters in an intimate space, so that the casting people have to put their fingers in their ears, or to be so intimate on a large stage that the casting people sitting in the theater cannot hear you.

3. The actor should find some unfamiliar piece of writing, such as something you wrote or a piece that was written for you by a friend. This usually diverts the casting people's attention and curiosity away from you, and toward the piece itself.

In your audition, physical moves should be minimal. You never know just how much space you will have to play in. If you are doing two contemporary monologues, I suggest sitting for one and standing for the other, if possible. You will want to map out the place beforehand in your mind so that you can endow the studio or room you are auditioning in with one or two of its qualities and properties, perhaps even with what is underfoot—imagining a Persian carpet, or a marble or parquet or dirt floor.

If you use published monologue books in order to get a quick overview of available material, once you have chosen a monologue, get a copy of the play, and read it. For those actors who mistakenly believe the monologue has to show off a variety of emotions, when the truth is that you merely want to show only that you are a good actor, let me reiterate that it doesn't matter whether the speech contains a big emotional event or a quiet reflection. But shouting or cursing often puts the observers off, and you don't want to do that.

Another suggestion: Before bringing a monologue into a class or to a private coach, you can try it out with someone who will not be critical. Having that other pair of ears listening to you paradoxically gives you the freedom to continue to be subjective. Someone else is listening to you, so you don't have to listen to yourself. And, lastly, you will have to pick a spot in an empty chair or on the wall in front of you to focus on if you are talking to another character, who only exists in your imagination.

It is indeed unfair for an actor to have to create the entire surroundings and the relationship by him- or herself, even for a minute and a half, but that has now become traditional. It is rare that you can look into the eyes of the auditor to deliver your rehearsed speech, but that can sometimes happen with a director, or if you are allowed to bring in a partner, or if one is provided.

When you are to begin your speech, be sure that you have first taken a moment of preparation, during which you should review the preceding circumstances and the place you are supposed to be in, focus on the imaginary person, and, finally, hear a "cue" in your imagination. This cue might be a question, or the line that comes before the speech, or even a gesture. Experiment with the immediately preceding moment to find the "cue" that will inspire you the most.

If you are doing two monologues back to back, be sure you really end one before preparing to begin the other. When I say "end," I mean that you should feel as though you have made an "exit," which you can do by simply turning away. With your back to the observers, "enter" the new space, turn back to them; and be sure to focus on the imaginary relationship, and to prepare the preceding moment by reviewing the circumstances, then by hearing or seeing the "cue."

You don't want to feel as though you are presenting yourself in any direct way to the observers, like meat on a platter. As with any performance, you want to have a fourth wall. Your goal when delivering a prepared monologue is to share a piece of the life of the character with those watching. Hopefully, you will move them to laughter or to tears, or at the very least bring them an understanding of the character you are playing.

A PARTING WORD

If you have gotten nothing else from this book, you should have gotten the idea that the only way you can deal with working conditions and the time and money constraints in the media today, as well as in the theater, is to prepare yourself as thoroughly as possible for everything you will have to cope with by studying and absorbing and really learning the art and the craft of acting—which must become an integral part of you. That is the only satisfactory and satisfying way to handle and keep abreast of the many challenging circumstances in which you will find yourself. They may be difficult, or they may be easy. You may be working with wonderful directors who really know what they are doing, or you may be working with people you consider unhelpful at best and incompetent at worst. But if you know how to act, if you have become a skillful professional actor in command of the necessary techniques and tools, you will be able to deal with anything.

To paraphrase Abraham Lincoln, you can fool all of the audience some of the time, and you can fool some of the audience all of the time, but if you do a genuine and true performance, you don't have to fool anybody! Secure and confident in the knowledge of your craft and your art, you will go home at the end of the day with a feeling of accomplishment, and with the idea that you have achieved something worthwhile and done your job well. You will know that you have made a contribution that is appreciated. Finally, I wish you all the very best in your chosen career, and all the success you want and hope for.

GLOSSARY OF ACTING TERMS

acting: Doing something truthfully for a purpose (Herbert Berghof's definition).

action: What the actor *does* at a particular moment.

activity: A physical task that is part of the secondary life of the character. It takes place while the character's primary life proceeds.

affective memory: The memory of emotions and feelings (emotional memory) based on an event from the past.

"as if": The projection of an imaginary quality or physical property onto a person, place, object, or event in the present moment. See also *endowment*.

attitude: A state of mind or feeling about something. Also, the position taken toward something, based on that feeling or state of mind.

beat: A piece or a bit of a scene measured by a small *objective*.

character chart: A three-part breakdown of a character's (1) biographical background; (2) character traits; and (3) life drives.

character traits: Distinguishing features of the character. They are often the character's vulnerabilities.

circumstances: The facts regarding the time and place of a scene, divided into three parts: (1) previous circumstances; (2) present circumstances; and (3) future circumstances.

endowment: A partial and imaginary investment of physical or psychological properties in a person, place, object, or event.

fourth wall: The imaginary wall between the actors and the audience. It helps create privacy. The term comes from the proscenium stage set, which ordinarily has three walls, the fourth one being the imaginary one through which the audience watches the play.

give and take: The back-and-forth reading of the lines; talking and listening; sending and receiving.

immediacy: The quality of something that is happening right now in the present. The answer to the question, "Why now?" See also *urgency*.

impulse: An impelling force; an urge, particularly the urge to move.

inner object: Any thing, person, place, or event referred to in the dialogue but not present in the scene or the play; a memory related to any of those things.

instinct: The innate aspect of behavior that is unlearned; an overwhelming motivation or impulse. See also *impulse*.

leader/follower: In a two-character scene, one leads and the other follows; it is the leader whose objective causes the scene to exist.

life drive: A character's overall objective; the main thrust and motivating factor of the character's general desires.

Method, the: A commonly used phrase from the 1950s referring to the Stanislavsky System. See also *Stanislavsky System*.

moment-to-moment: Remaining in the present; unpremeditated and unanticipated life on stage. See also *immediacy*.

object: A thing, person, or memory required by the actor to complete the objective. An object can be animate, inanimate (see *prop*), or intangible (see *inner object*).

objective: What the character wants; the character's goal; motivation, intention, aim, desire, wish, need, throughline.

obstacle: What is in the character's way; properties opposing the character's objective, which may be in the relationship, the place, the objects, or internal.

organic: Spontaneous, unanticipated.

particularization: The process of itemizing and making personal the details of a relationship or object; a growing familiarity with the particulars of any relationship.

personalization: Making the character's circumstances personal, individual, specific, and real to the actor. See also *endowment*; *substitution*.

place: Where one is located in space, which is imaginary in the theater, and can be an actual location in film.

preparation: A mental review of previous circumstances prior to entering or beginning a scene; steps taken to insure relaxation before an entrance.

presentational: According to Stanislavsky, being the character; the opposite of *representational*, which involves indicating or illustrating the character.

prior relationship: The relationship between the characters and how it proceeded before the play begins.

privacy: The feeling of being alone and unobserved by anyone outside the character's life. See also *fourth wall*.

prop: Stage property; a physical object the actor uses in order to complete an activity.

relationship: The nature of the character's connection to other characters, inner and external objects and to place.

relaxation: A relief of tension; looseness and flexibility; in acting, the appropriate amount of energy required to carry out the actions to complete one's goal.

representational: An illustrative approach to character. See also *presentational*.

score: A list of the order of events (beat objectives) in a given scene.

sense memory: The memory of sight, sound, taste, touch, or physical feelings such as an ache or pain connected to an event from the past.

speculation: Meditation or reflection on a given object.

Stanislavsky System: A way of working on building a character that involves observation and experimentation with the idea of becoming the character through personalization. *System* is a more appropriate term than *Method*.

substitution: The use by the actor of events, objects, people, or places from his or her own life, analogous to those things as experienced by the character; a conscious replacement of the fictitious objects in the play with remembered objects from the actor's own experience.

subtext: The underlying meaning of the text.

throughline: The primary or scene objective; the character's underlying desire throughout the scene; what the character wishes to achieve.

urgency: The state of compelling and impelling significance. In acting, the quality underlying the moment-to-moment life of a scene. See also *immediacy*.

BIBLIOGRAPHY

Adler, Stella. *The Technique of Acting.* Foreword by Marlon Brando. New York: Bantam Books, 1988.

Benedetti, Jean. *Stanislavski and the Actor.* London: Methuen Drama, 1998.

Bernhardt, Sarah. *The Art of the Theatre.* Translated by H. J. Stenning. New York: The Dial Press, 1925.

Blumenfeld, Robert. *Tools and Techniques for Character Interpretation: A Handbook of Psychology for Actors, Writers, and Directors.* Foreword by Alice Spivak. New York: Limelight, 2006.

Caine, Michael. *Acting in Film: An Actor's Take on Movie Making.* New York: Applause Theatre Books, 1990.

Chekhov, Michael. *To the Actor on the Technique of Acting.* Preface by Yul Brynner. New York: Harper & Row, 1953.

Garfield, David. *The Actors Studio: A Player's Place.* Preface by Ellen Burstyn. New York: Macmillan Collier Books, 1984.

Gorchakov, Nikolai. *Stanislavsky Directs.* Translated by Miriam Goldina. Foreword by Norris Houghton. Reprint. New York: Limelight Editions, 1991.

Hagen, Uta. *A Challenge for the Actor.* New York: Charles Scribner's Sons, 1991.

Hagen, Uta, with Haskell Frankel. *Respect for Acting.* New York: Macmillan, 1973.

Lumet, Sidney. *Making Films.* New York: Alfred A. Knopf, 1995.

Meisner, Sanford, and Dennis Longwell. *On Acting.* New York: Random House, 1987.

Moore, Sonia. *Training an Actor: The Stanislavsky System in Class.* New York: Penguin Books, 1979.

Sartre, Jean-Paul. *Being and Nothingness: An Essay on Phenomenological Ontology.* Translated by Hazel E. Barnes. New York: Philosophical Library, 1956.

Stanislavsky, Constantin. *An Actor Prepares.* Translated by Elizabeth Reynolds Hapgood. Introduction by John Gielgud. New York: Theatre Arts Books (23rd printing), 1936; 1969.

——. *Building a Character.* Translated by Elizabeth Reynolds Hapgood. Introduction by Joshua Logan. New York: Theatre Arts Books, 1949.

——. *Creating a Role.* Translated by Elizabeth Reynolds Hapgood. Foreword by Robert Lewis. New York: Theatre Arts Books, 1961.

——. *My Life in Art.* Translated by J. J. Robbins. New York: The World Publishing Co. Meridian Books, 1966.

——. *Stanislavsky Produces Othello.* Translated from the Russian by Dr. Helen Nowak. London: Godfrey Bles, 1948.

Strasberg, Lee. *A Dream of Passion.* New York: Penguin Plume Books, 1987.

INDEX OF PEOPLE

INDEX OF FILMS
AND TELEVISION PROGRAMS

INDEX OF PLAYS

ABOUT THE AUTHOR
AND COLLABORATOR

Alice Spivak began her career at an early age, joining Actors' Equity in 1956, Screen Actors Guild in 1959, and AFTRA in the early '60s. Having trained at the HB Studio with Herbert Berghof and Uta Hagen, she was made a teacher there in 1962, and taught on their faculty for fifteen years. Since that time, she has been a popular freelance acting teacher and acting coach, teaching advanced classes in New York City and coaching on numerous feature films, Broadway shows, regional shows, TV miniseries, pilots, etc., receiving technical credits on a few. She also taught film directing workshops and was given the Indie Award by the Association of Video and Filmmakers in 1977. In 1981, she was on the faculty of New York University's graduate program in film, teaching the course "Directing Actors." In 2003-4, she again taught this course, in Columbia University's graduate program. She is cowriter and director of a short film comedy, *Working for Peanuts*. She recently completed a screenplay, *No Right Turn*. As an actress, she has worked on Broadway, off Broadway, and in regional theater, receiving the Joseph Jefferson Award in Chicago in 1975 for Neil Simon's *Plaza Suite*. On television, audiences have seen her in *Law & Order, Sex and The City, Law & Order: Criminal Intent*, among others, and as Naomi, the court officer, on Sidney Lumet's *100 Centre Street*. Two of her favorite roles were Jenny in *Privilege*, written and directed by Yvonne Rainer, and Louise, an American tourist, in *An Electric Moon*, written by Arundhati Roy, directed by Pradip Krishen, shot entirely on location in India. She currently conducts advanced scene study workshops three times a year in New York City.

Robert Blumenfeld is the author of *Accents: A Manual for Actors* (Limelight, Revised and Expanded Edition, 2002); *Acting with the Voice: The Art of Recording Books* (Limelight, 2004); and *Tools and Techniques for Character Interpretation: A Handbook of Psychology for Actors, Writers, and Directors* (Limelight, 2006). He lives and works as an actor, dialect coach, and writer in New York City. Mr. Blumenfeld studied acting with Alice Spivak, and, more briefly, with Uta Hagen. As an actor, he has worked in numerous regional and New York theaters, and done many television and radio commercials. He created the roles of the Marquis of Queensberry and two prosecuting attorneys in Moisés Kaufman's Off-Broadway hit play *Gross Indecency: The Three Trials of Oscar Wilde*. He also worked as the dialect coach for that production and for Broadway's *Saturday Night Fever* and *The Scarlet Pimpernel* (third version and national tour). Mr. Blumenfeld has recorded more than three hundred Talking Books for the American Foundation for the Blind. He received the 1997 Canadian National Institute for the Blind's Torgi Award for the Talking Book of the Year in the Fiction category, for his recording of Pat Conroy's *Beach Music*; and the 1999 Alexander Scourby Talking Book Narrator of the Year Award in the Fiction category. He holds a B.A. in French from Rutgers University and an M.A. from Columbia University in French Language and Literature.